_PRICEWATERHOUSE_COOPERS

Illustrative IFRS corporate consolidated financial statements for 2010 year ends

Global Accounting Consulting Services
PricewaterhouseCoopers LLP

145 London Road
Kingston-upon-Thames
Surrey
KT2 6SR
Tel: +44 (0) 870 777 2906
Fax: +44 (0) 870 247 1184
E-mail: info@cch.co.uk
Website: www.cch.co.uk

ISBN 978-1-84798-337-4

Printed in Great Britain.

British Library Cataloguing-in-Publication Data.
A catalogue record for this book is available from the British Library.

Introduction

This publication provides an illustrative set of consolidated financial statements, prepared in accordance with International Financial Reporting Standards (IFRS) for a fictional manufacturing, wholesale and retail group (IFRS GAAP plc).

IFRS GAAP plc is an existing preparer of IFRS consolidated financial statements; IFRS 1, 'First-time adoption of International Financial Reporting Standards', is not applicable.

This publication is based on the requirements of IFRS standards and interpretations for financial years beginning on or after 1 January 2010.

PricewaterhouseCoopers' commentary has been provided, in grey boxes, to explain the detail behind the presentation of a number of challenging areas. These commentary boxes relate to the presentation in: the income statement, statement of comprehensive income, balance sheet, statement of changes in equity and statement of cash flows, the summary of significant accounting policies, and financial risk management.

> Areas in which presentation has changed significantly since 2009 have been highlighted in blue.

Readers should refer to PricewaterhouseCoopers' industry illustrative financial statements for industry-specific transactions and presentation. See inside front cover of this publication for details.

We have attempted to create a realistic set of financial statements for a corporate entity. Certain types of transaction have been excluded, as they are not relevant to the group's operations. The example disclosures for some of these additional items have been included in appendices III and IV.

The forthcoming IFRS requirements are outlined in Appendix VII.

The example disclosures should not be considered the only acceptable form of presentation. The form and content of each reporting entity's financial statements are the responsibility of the entity's management. Alternative presentations to those proposed in this publication may be equally acceptable if they comply with the specific disclosure requirements prescribed in IFRS.

These illustrative financial statements are not a substitute for reading the standards and interpretations themselves or for professional judgement as to fairness of presentation. They do not cover all possible disclosures that IFRS requires. Further specific information may be required in order to ensure fair presentation under IFRS. We recommend that readers refer to the 2010 version of GAAPChecker (our automated checklist), as well as our publication *IFRS disclosure checklist 2010*.

Abbreviations

IFRS1p37	=	International Financial Reporting Standard [number], paragraph number.
7p22	=	International Accounting Standards [number], paragraph number.
SIC-15p5	=	Standing Interpretations Committee [number], paragraph number.
DV	=	Disclose Voluntary. Disclosure is encouraged but not required and, therefore, represents best practice.

Contents

Consolidated income statement – by function of expense 1
Consolidated statement of comprehensive income 2
Consolidated balance sheet 10
Consolidated statement of changes in equity 14
Consolidated statement of cash flows 18
Notes to the consolidated financial statements: 22
1   General information 22
2   Summary of significant accounting policies: 22
    2.1   Basis of preparation 22
    2.2   Consolidation 26
    2.3   Segment reporting 29
    2.4   Foreign currency translation 29
    2.5   Property, plant and equipment 30
    2.6   Intangible assets 31
    2.7   Impairment of non-financial assets 32
    2.8   Non-current assets (or disposal groups) held-for-sale 32
    2.9   Financial assets 33
    2.10 Offsetting financial instruments 34
    2.11 Impairment of financial assets 34
    2.12 Derivative financial instruments and hedging activities 35
    2.13 Inventories 37
    2.14 Trade receivables 37
    2.15 Cash and cash equivalents 37
    2.16 Share capital 38
    2.17 Trade payables 38
    2.18 Borrowings 38
    2.19 Compound financial instruments 38
    2.20 Current and deferred income tax 39
    2.21 Employee benefits 40
    2.22 Share-based payments 41
    2.23 Provisions 42
    2.24 Revenue recognition 42
    2.25 Leases 44
    2.26 Dividend distribution 44
3   Financial risk management 48
    3.1   Financial risk factors 48
    3.2   Capital risk management 52
    3.3   Fair value estimation 53
4   Critical accounting estimates and judgements 62
    4.1   Critical accounting estimates and assumptions 62
    4.2   Critical judgements in applying entity's accounting policies 64
5   Segment information 65
6   Property, plant and equipment 70
7   Intangible assets 72
8   Investments in associates 74
9a Financial instruments by category 75
9b Credit quality of financial assets 77
10 Available-for-sale financial assets 78
11 Derivative financial instruments 79

Contents

12	Trade and other receivables	80
13	Inventories	82
14	Financial assets at fair value through profit or loss	82
15	Cash and cash equivalents	83
16	Non-current assets held for sale and discontinued operations	83
17	Share capital and premium	87
18	Share-based payment	87
19	Retained earnings	89
20	Other reserves	90
21	Trade and other payables	91
22	Borrowings	92
23	Deferred income tax	95
24	Retirement benefit obligations	96
25	Provisions for other liabilities and charges	102
26	Other (losses)/gains – net	103
27	Other income	104
28	Loss on expropriated land	104
29	Expenses by nature	104
30	Employee benefit expense	104
31	Finance income and costs	105
32	Income tax expense	105
33	Net foreign exchange gains/(losses)	108
34	Earnings per share	108
35	Dividends per share	109
36	Cash generated from operations	109
37	Contingencies	110
38	Commitments	110
39	Business combinations	111
40	Related-party transactions	114
41	Events after the balance sheet date	117
	Auditors' report	119

Appendices

Appendix I	Operating and financial review	121
Appendix II	Alternative presentation of primary statements	124
Appendix III	Policies and disclosures for areas not relevant to IFRS GAAP plc	136
Appendix IV	Critical accounting estimates and judgements not relevant to IFRS GAAP plc	148
Appendix V	IFRS 9	149
Appendix VI	First-time adoption of IFRS	179
Appendix VII	Forthcoming requirements	196

(All amounts in C thousands unless otherwise stated)

Consolidated income statement – by function of expense

		Note	Year ended 31 December 2010	2009
1p81(b), 84 1p10(b), 12 1p113, 1p38				
	Continuing operations			
1p82(a)	Revenue	5	**211,034**	112,360
1p99, 103	Cost of sales		**(77,366)**	(46,682)
	Gross profit		**133,668**	65,678
1p99, 103	Distribution costs		**(52,140)**	(21,213)
1p99, 103	Administrative expenses		**(28,778)**	(10,426)
1p99, 103	Other income	27	**2750**	1,259
1p85	Other (losses)/gains – net	26	**(90)**	63
1p85	Loss on expropriated land	28	**(1,117)**	–
1p85	**Operating profit[1]**		**54,293**	35,361
1p85	Finance income	31	**1,730**	1,609
1p82(b)	Finance costs	31	**(8,173)**	(12,197)
1p85	Finance costs – net	31	**(6,443)**	(10,588)
1p82(c)	Share of (loss)/profit of associates	8(b)	**(174)**	145
1p85 1p82(d),	**Profit before income tax**		**47,676**	24,918
12p77	Income tax expense	32	**(14,611)**	(8,670)
1p85	**Profit for the year from continuing operations**		**33,065**	16,248
IFRS5p33(a)	**Discontinued operations**			
	Profit for the year from discontinued operations	16	**100**	120
1p82(f)	**Profit for the year**		**33,165**	16,368
	Profit attributable to:			
1p83(a)(ii)	Owners of the parent		**30,617**	15,512
1p83(a)(i)	Non-controlling interest		**2,548**	856
			33,165	16,368

		Note	2010	2009
	Earnings per share from continuing and discontinued operations attributable to the equity holders of the company during the year (expressed in C per share)			
	Basic earnings per share			
33p66	From continuing operations	34	**1.31**	0.75
33p68	From discontinued operations[2]		**0.01**	0.01
			1.32	0.76
	Diluted earnings per share			
33p66	From continuing operations	34	**1.19**	0.71
33p68	From discontinued operations		**0.01**	0.01
			1.20	0.72

The notes on pages 1 to 118 are an integral part of these consolidated financial statements.

[1] IAS 1 does not prescribe the disclosure of operating profit on the face of the income statement. However, entities are not prohibited from disclosing this or a similar line item.
[2] EPS for discontinued operations may be given in the notes to the accounts instead in the income statement.

(All amounts in C thousands unless otherwise stated)

Consolidated statement of comprehensive income

		Note	Group Year ended 31 December 2010	2009
	Profit for the year		**33,165**	16,368
	Other comprehensive income:			
16p77(f)	Gains on revaluation of land and buildings	20	–	759
IFRS7p20 (a)(ii)	Available-for-sale financial assets	20	**362**	62
	Share of other comprehensive income of associates	20	**(86)**	91
19p93A	Actuarial loss on post employment benefit obligations	24	–	(494)
1p106(b), IFRS7p23(c)	Impact of change in Euravian tax rate on deferred tax[1]	23	**(10)**	–
1p106(b)	Cash flow hedges	20	**64**	(3)
1p106(b)	Net investment hedge	20	**(45)**	40
IFRS3p59	Currency translation differences	20	**2,318**	(261)
	Increase in fair values of proportionate holding of ABC Group	20	**850**	–
	Other comprehensive income for the year, net of tax		**3,453**	194
	Total comprehensive income for the year		**36,618**	16,562
	Attributable to:			
1p83(b)(ii)	– Owners of the parent		**33,818**	15,746
1p83(b)(i)	– Non-controlling interest		**2,800**	816
	Total comprehensive income for the year		**36,618**	16,562

Items in the statement above are disclosed net of tax. The income tax relating to each component of other comprehensive income is disclosed in note 32.

The notes on pages 1 to 118 are an integral part of these consolidated financial statements.

Commentary – income statement and statement of comprehensive income

The commentary that follows explains some of the key requirements in IAS 1, 'Presentation of financial statements', and other requirements that impact the income statement/statement of comprehensive income.

1p81 1 Entities have a choice of presenting all items of income and expense recognised in a period either:

(a) in a single statement of comprehensive income; or

(b) in two statements (as adopted by IFRS GAAP plc) comprising:
(i) a separate income statement, which displays components of profit or loss; and
(ii) a statement of comprehensive income, which begins with profit or loss and displays components of other comprehensive income.

The main difference between these two options is that in option (a), profit for the year is shown as a sub-total rather than the 'bottom line', and the statement continues down to total comprehensive income for the year.

[1] The impact of change in Euravian tax rate is shown for illustrative purposes.

(All amounts in C thousands unless otherwise stated)

2   The relationship between the old and new formats is illustrated in the following diagram:

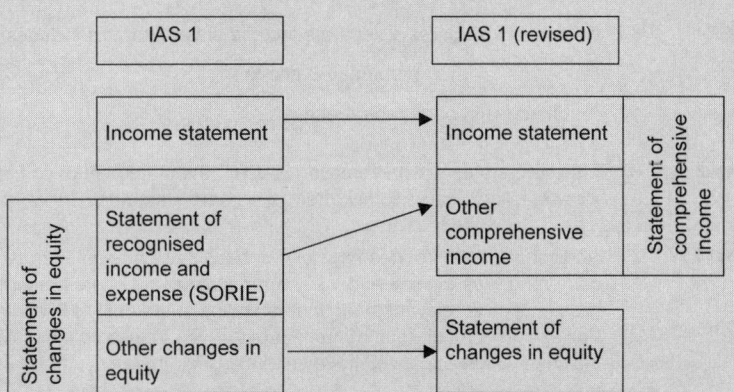

1p82   3   A single statement of comprehensive income includes, as a minimum, the following line items:

(a)   Revenue.

(b)   Finance costs.

(c)   Share of the profit or loss of associates and joint ventures accounted for using the equity method.

(d)   Tax expense.

(e)   A single amount comprising the total of:
  (i)   the post-tax profit or loss of discontinued operations; and
  (ii) the post-tax gain or loss recognised on the measurement to fair value less costs to sell or on the disposal of the assets or disposal group(s) constituting the discontinued operation.

(f)   Profit or loss.

(g)   Each component of other comprehensive income classified by nature.

(h)   Share of the other comprehensive income of associates and joint ventures accounted for using the equity method.

(i)   Total comprehensive income.

1p83   4   The following items are disclosed as allocations for the period:

(a)   Profit or loss attributable to:
  (i)   non-controlling interests; and
  (ii) owners.

(b)   Total comprehensive income for the period attributable to:
  (i)   non-controlling interests; and
  (ii) owners.

IFRS5
p33(d)   (c)   From 1 July 2009, the amount of income attributable to owners of the parent from:

<table>
<tr><td></td><td></td><td colspan="2">(i)   continued operations; and</td></tr>
<tr><td></td><td></td><td colspan="2">(ii) discontinued operations.</td></tr>
</table>

1p84   5   If the entity prepares a separate income statement, this includes:

       (a) Items (a)-(f) in paragraph 3 above.

       (b) Item (a) in paragraph 4 above.

1p12   6   If the two-statement presentation is used, the statement of comprehensive income follows immediately after the income statement.

1p85   7   Additional line items, headings and subtotals are presented in the statement of comprehensive income and the income statement (where presented) when such presentation is relevant to an understanding of the entity's financial performance. For example, a sub-total of gross profit (revenue less cost of sales) may be included where expenses have been classified by function.

Framework p31 CESR/05-178b   8   Additional sub-headings should be used with care. The 'Framework for the preparation and presentation of financial statements' states that, to be useful, information must be reliable; that is, free from material error and bias. The apparent flexibility in IAS 1 can therefore only be used to enhance users' understanding of the GAAP-compliant numbers. It cannot be used to detract from the GAAP numbers. The Committee of European Securities Regulators (CESR)'s recommendation on disclosure of alternative performance measures provides useful guidance on the use of sub-totals and alternative performance measures:

       (a) GAAP numbers should be given at least equal prominence to non-GAAP numbers.

       (b) Additional line items, sub-totals and columns may be used, but only if they do not detract from the GAAP numbers by introducing bias or by overcrowding the income statement.

       (c) Each additional line item or column should contain all the revenue or expenses that relate to the particular line item or column inserted.

       (d) Each additional line item or column should contain only revenue or expense that is revenue or expense of the entity itself.

       (e) Items may be segregated (for example, by use of columns or sub-totals) where they are different in nature or function from other items in the income statement.

       (f) An entity should not mix natural and functional classifications of expenses where these categories of expenses overlap.

       (g) Terms used for additional line items and sub-totals should be defined if they are not terms recognised in IFRS.

       (h) Additional line items, columns and sub-totals should only be presented when they are used internally to manage the business.

       (i) Various presentations will be acceptable individually, but consideration should be given to the aggregate effect of these presentations, so that the overall message of the income statement is not distorted or confused.

       (j) The presentation method should generally be consistent from year to year.

(All amounts in C thousands unless otherwise stated)

9   EBIT (earnings before interest and tax) may be an appropriate sub-heading to show in the income statement. This line item usually distinguishes between the pre-tax profits arising from operating activities and those arising from financing activities.

10   In contrast, a sub-total for EBITDA (earnings before interest, tax, depreciation and amortisation) can only be included as a sub-total where the entity presents its expenses by nature and provided the sub-total does not detract from the GAAP numbers either by implying that EBITDA is the 'real' profit or by overcrowding the income statement so that the reader cannot determine easily the entity's GAAP performance. Where an entity presents its expenses by function, it will not be possible to show depreciation and amortisation as separate line items in arriving at operating profit, because depreciation and amortisation are types of expense, not functions of the business. In this case, EBITDA can only be disclosed by way of footnote, in the notes or in the review of operation.

Material items of income and expense

1p97   11   When items of income and expense are material, their nature and amount is disclosed separately either in the income statement or in the notes. In the case of IFRS GAAP plc these disclosures are made on the face of the income statement and in note 29a.

1p85, 97   12   IAS 1 does not provide a specific name for the types of items that should be separately disclosed. Where an entity discloses a separate category of 'exceptional', 'significant' or 'unusual' items either in the income statement or in the notes, the accounting policy note should include a definition of the chosen term. The presentation and definition of these items should be applied consistently from year to year. However, it is not appropriate to show an operating profit line which excludes these items.

13   Where an entity classifies its expenses by nature, it must take care to ensure that each class of expense includes all items related to that class. Material restructuring cost may, for example, include redundancy payments (employee benefit cost), inventory write-downs (changes in inventory) and impairments in property, plant and equipment. It is not be acceptable to show restructuring costs as a separate line item in an analysis of expenses by nature where there is an overlap with other line items.

14   Entities that classify their expenses by function include the material items within the function to which they relate. In this case, material items can be disclosed as footnotes or in the notes to the financial statements.

Operating profit

1BC56   15   An entity may elect to include a sub-total for its result from operating activities. This is permitted, but care should be taken that the amount disclosed is representative of activities that would normally be considered to be 'operating'. Items that are clearly of an operating nature (for example, inventory write-downs, restructuring and relocation expenses) are not excluded simply because they occur infrequently or are unusual in amount. Nor can expenses be excluded

(All amounts in C thousands unless otherwise stated)

on the grounds that they do not involve cash flows (for example, depreciation or amortisation). As a general rule, operating profit is the subtotal after 'other expenses' – that is, excluding finance costs and the share of profits of equity-accounted investments – although in some circumstances it may be appropriate for the share of profits of equity-accounted investments to be included in operating profit (see paragraph 17 below).

Re-ordering of line items

1p86   16   The line items and descriptions of those items are re-ordered where this is necessary to explain the elements of performance. However, entities are required to make a 'fair presentation' and should not make any changes unless there is a good reason to do so.

17   For example, the share of profit of associates is normally shown after finance cost. However, where the group conducts a significant amount of its business through associates (or joint ventures), it may be more appropriate to show finance costs after the share of profit of associates. Management may even insert a sub-total 'profit before finance costs if the business conducted through associates is a strategically significant component of the group's business activity'. However, an inclusion of the share of profit of associates in operating profit is only appropriate if the associates (or joint ventures) are regarded as a primary vehicle for the conduct of the group's operations.

18   Finance revenue cannot be netted against finance costs; it is included in 'other revenue/other income' or shown separately in the income statement. Where finance income is an incidental benefit, it is acceptable to present finance revenue immediately before finance costs and include a sub-total of 'net finance costs' in the income statement. Where earning interest income is one of the entity's main line of business, it is presented as 'revenue'.

Discontinued operations

1p82(e)   19   As stated in paragraph 3(e) above, entities disclose a single amount in the
IFRS5   statement of comprehensive income (or separate income statement), comprising
p33(a)(b)   the total of (i) the post-tax profit or loss of discontinued operations, and (ii) the post-tax gain or loss recognised on the measurement to fair value less costs to sell or on the disposal of the assets or disposal group(s) constituting the discontinued operation. Paragraph 33 of IFRS 5, 'Non-current assets held for sale and discontinued operations', also requires an analysis of this single amount. This analysis may be presented in the notes or in the statement of comprehensive income (separate income statement). If it is presented in the income statement, it should be presented in a section identified as relating to discontinued operations – that is, separate from continuing operations. The analysis is not required for disposal groups that are newly acquired subsidiaries that meet the criteria to be classified as held for sale on acquisition (see IFRS 5 para 11).

Earnings per share

33p66   20   IAS 33, 'Earnings per share', requires an entity to present in the statement of comprehensive income basic and diluted earnings per share (EPS) for profit or loss from continuing operations attributable to the ordinary equity holders of the parent entity and for total profit or loss attributable to the ordinary equity holders of the parent entity for each class of ordinary shares. Basic and diluted EPS is disclosed with equal prominence for all periods presented.

33p67A   21   If an entity presents a separate income statement, basic and diluted earnings per share are presented at the end of that statement.

33p67   22   If diluted EPS is reported for at least one period, it should be reported for all periods presented, even if it equals basic EPS. If basic and diluted EPS are equal, dual presentation can be accomplished in one line in the statement of comprehensive income.

33p68   23   An entity that reports a discontinued operation discloses the basic and diluted amounts per share for the discontinued operation either in the statement of comprehensive income or in the notes to the financial statements.

33p69, 41, 43   24   Basic and diluted EPS is disclosed even if the amounts are negative (that is, a loss per share). However, potential ordinary shares are only dilutive if their conversion would increase the loss per share. If the loss decreases, the shares are anti-dilutive.

33p4   25   When an entity presents both consolidated financial statements and separate financial statements prepared in accordance with IAS 27, 'Consolidated and separate financial statements', the disclosures required by IAS 33 are presented only on the basis of the consolidated information. An entity that chooses to disclose EPS based on its separate financial statements presents such EPS information only in its separate statement of comprehensive income.

Components of other comprehensive income

1p7   26   Components of other comprehensive income (OCI) are items of income and expense (including reclassification adjustments) that are not recognised in profit or loss as required or permitted by other IFRSs. They include: changes in the revaluation surplus relating to property, plant and equipment or intangible assets; actuarial gains and losses on defined benefit plans; gains and losses arising from translating the financial statements of a foreign operation; gains and losses on re-measuring available-for-sale financial assets; and the effective portion of gains and losses on hedging instruments in a cash flow hedge.

1p91
1p90   27   Entities may present components of other comprehensive income either net of related tax effect or before related tax effects. IFRS GAAP plc has chosen to present the items net of tax. In this case the amount of income tax relating to each component of OCI, including reclassification adjustments, is disclosed in the notes.

Reclassification adjustments

1p92, 94   28   An entity discloses separately any reclassification adjustments relating to components of other comprehensive income either in the statement of comprehensive income or in the notes. IFRS GAAP plc provides this information in note 20, 'Other reserves'.

1p7, 95 29 Reclassification adjustments are amounts reclassified to profit or loss in the current period that were recognised in other comprehensive income in the current or previous periods. They arise, for example, on disposal of a foreign operation, on derecognition of an available-for-sale financial asset and when a hedged forecast transaction affects profit or loss.

1p107 30 The amount of dividends recognised as distributions to owners during the period and the related amount per share are presented either in the statement of changes in equity or in the notes. Following the revisions made to IAS 1, dividends cannot be displayed in the statement of comprehensive income or income statement.

Consistency

1p45 31 The presentation and classification of items in the financial statements is retained from one period to the next unless:

(a) it is apparent, following a significant change in the nature of the entity's operations or a review of its financial statements that another presentation or classification would be more appropriate, addressing the criteria for the selection and application of accounting policies in IAS 8, 'Accounting policies, changes in accounting estimates and errors'; or

(b) IFRS requires a change in presentation.

Materiality and aggregation

1p29 32 Each material class of similar items is presented separately in the financial statements. Items of a dissimilar nature or function are presented separately unless they are immaterial.

Offsetting

1p32 33 Assets and liabilities, and income and expenses, are not offset unless required or permitted by an IFRS. Examples of income and expenses that are required or permitted to be offset are as follows:

1p34(a) (a) Gains and losses on the disposal of non-current assets, including investments and operating assets, are reported by deducting from the proceeds on disposal the carrying amount of the asset and related selling expenses.

1p34(b) (b) Expenditure related to a provision that is recognised in accordance with IAS 37, 'Provisions, contingent liabilities and contingent assets', and reimbursed under a contractual arrangement with a third party (for example, a supplier's warranty agreement) may be netted against the related reimbursement.

(All amounts in C thousands unless otherwise stated)

1p35   (c) Gains and losses arising from a group of similar transactions are reported on a net basis (for example, foreign exchange gains and losses or gains and losses arising on financial instruments held for trading). However, such gains and losses are reported separately if they are material.

Summary

34 The requirements surrounding components of OCI can be summarised as follows:

Item	Reference	Requirement in standard	Presentation in IFRS GAAP plc
Each component of other comprehensive income recognised during the period, classified by nature	IAS1 p82(g)	Statement of comprehensive income	Statement of comprehensive income
Reclassification adjustments during the period relating to components of other comprehensive income	IAS1 p92	Statement of comprehensive income or notes	Note 20
Tax relating to each component of other comprehensive income, including reclassification adjustments	IAS1 p90	Statement of comprehensive income or notes	Note 32
Reconciliation for each component of equity, showing separately: – Profit/loss – Each item of other comprehensive income – Transactions with owners	IAS1 p106(d)	Statement of changes in equity and notes (reconciliation showing separately each item of other comprehensive income)	Statement of changes in equity and note 20

(All amounts in C thousands unless otherwise stated)

Consolidated balance sheet

		Note	As at 31 December 2010	2009
1p54,				
1p113,				
1p38	**Assets**			
1p60	**Non-current assets**			
1p54(a)	Property, plant and equipment	6	**155,341**	100,233
1p54(c)	Intangible assets	7	**26,272**	20,700
1p54(e)	Investments in associates	8	**13,373**	13,244
1p54(o)	Deferred income tax assets	23	**3,520**	3,321
1p54(d),				
IFRS7p8(d)	Available-for-sale financial assets	10	**17,420**	14,910
1p54(d),				
IFRS7p8(a)	Derivative financial instruments	11	**395**	245
1p54(h),				
IFRS7p8(c)	Trade and other receivables	12	**2,322**	1,352
			218,643	154,005
1p60, 1p66	**Current assets**			
1p54(g)	Inventories	13	**24,700**	18,182
1p54(h),				
IFRS7p8(c)	Trade and other receivables	12	**19,765**	18,330
1p54(d),				
IFRS7p8(d)	Available-for-sale financial assets	10	**1,950**	–
1p54(d),				
IFRS7p8(a)	Derivative financial instruments	11	**1,069**	951
1p54(d),				
IFRS7p8(a)	Financial assets at fair value through profit or loss	14	**11,820**	7,972
1p54(i),				
IFRS7p8	Cash and cash equivalents (excluding bank overdrafts)	15	**17,928**	34,062
			77,232	79,497
IFRS5p38	Assets of disposal group classified as held for sale	16	**3,333**	–
			80,565	79,497
	Total assets		**299,208**	233,502
	Equity and liabilities			
1p54(r)	**Equity attributable to owners of the parent**			
1p78(e)	Ordinary shares	17	**25,300**	21,000
1p78(e)	Share premium	17	**17,144**	10,494
1p78(e)	Other reserves	20	**14,699**	7,005
1p78(e)	Retained earnings	19	**67,442**	48,681
			124,585	87,180
1p54(q)	**Non-controlling interests**		**7,188**	1,766
	Total equity		**131,773**	88,946

(All amounts in C thousands unless otherwise stated)

		Note	As at 31 December 2010	2009
	Liabilities			
1p60	**Non-current liabilities**			
1p54(m), IFRS7p8(f)	Borrowings	22	**115,121**	96,346
1p54(m), IFRS7p8(e)	Derivative financial instruments	11	**135**	129
1p54(o), 1p56	Deferred income tax liabilities	23	**12,370**	9,053
1p54(l), 1p78(d)	Retirement benefit obligations	24	**4,635**	2,233
1p54(l), 1p78(d)	Provisions for other liabilities and charges	25	**1,320**	274
			133,581	108,035
1p60, 1p69	**Current liabilities**			
1p54(k), IFRS7p8(f)	Trade and other payables	21	**16,670**	12,478
1p54(n)	Current income tax liabilities		**2,566**	2,771
1p54(m), IFRS7p8(f)	Borrowings	22	**11,716**	18,258
1p54(m), IFRS7p8(e)	Derivative financial instruments	11	**460**	618
1p54(l)	Provisions for other liabilities and charges	25	**2,222**	2,396
			33,634	36,521
IFRS5p38	Liabilities of disposal group classified as held-for-sale	16	**220**	–
			33,854	36,521
	Total liabilities		**167,435**	144,556
	Total equity and liabilities		**299,208**	233,502

10p17   The notes on pages 1 to 118 are an integral part of these consolidated financial statements.

The financial statements on pages 1 to 118 were authorised for issue by the board of directors on 24 February 2011 and were signed on its behalf.

CD Suede
Chief Executive

G Wallace
Finance Director

(All amounts in C thousands unless otherwise stated)

Commentary – balance sheet

The commentary that follows explains some of the key requirements in IAS 1, 'Presentation of financial statements', that impact the balance sheet/statement of financial position.

1p10   1   IAS 1 refers to the balance sheet as the 'statement of financial position'. This new title is not mandatory, so IFRS GAAP plc has elected to retain the better-known title of 'balance sheet'.

1p54, 55   2   Paragraph 54 of IAS 1 sets out the line items that are, as a minimum, required to be presented in the balance sheet. Additional line items, headings and subtotals are presented in the balance sheet when such presentation is relevant to an understanding of the entity's financial position.

1p77, 78   3   An entity discloses, either in the balance sheet or in the notes, further sub-classifications of the line items presented, classified in a manner appropriate to the entity's operations. The detail provided in sub-classifications depends on the IFRS requirements and on the size, nature and function of the amounts involved.

Current/non-current distinction

1p60   4   An entity presents current and non-current assets, and current and non-current liabilities, as separate classifications in its balance sheet except when a presentation based on liquidity provides information that is reliable and is more relevant. When that exception applies, all assets and liabilities are presented broadly in order of liquidity.

1p61   5   Whichever method of presentation is adopted, an entity discloses for each asset and liability line item that combines amounts expected to be recovered or settled (a) no more than 12 months after the reporting period; and (b) more than 12 months after the reporting period, the amount expected to be recovered or settled after more than 12 months.

1p66-70   6   Current assets include assets (such as inventories and trade receivables) that are sold, consumed or realised as part of the normal operating cycle even when they are not expected to be realised within 12 months after the reporting period. Some current liabilities, such as trade payables and some accruals for employee and other operating costs, are part of the working capital used in the entity's normal operating cycle. Such operating items are classified as current liabilities even if they are due to be settled more than 12 months after the reporting period.

1p68   7   The operating cycle of an entity is the time between the acquisition of assets for processing and their realisation in the form of cash or cash equivalents. When the entity's normal operating cycle is not clearly identifiable, its duration is assumed to be 12 months.

(All amounts in C thousands unless otherwise stated)

Consistency

1p45 8 The presentation and classification of items in the financial statements is retained from one period to the next unless:

(a) it is apparent, following a significant change in the nature of the entity's operations or a review of its financial statements, that another presentation or classification would be more appropriate according to the criteria for selecting and applying accounting policies in IAS 8, 'Accounting policies, changes in accounting estimates and errors'; or

(b) an IFRS requires a change in presentation.

Materiality and aggregation

1p29 9 Each material class of similar items is presented separately in the financial statements. Items of a dissimilar nature or function are presented separately unless they are immaterial.

Current and deferred tax assets and liabilities

1p54, 56 10 Current and deferred tax assets and liabilities are presented separately from each other and from other assets and liabilities. When a distinction is made between current and non-current assets and liabilities in the balance sheet, deferred tax assets and liabilities are presented as non-current.

Offsetting

1p32 11 An entity does not offset assets and liabilities unless required or permitted to by an IFRS. Measuring assets net of valuation allowances – for example, obsolescence allowances on inventories and doubtful debt allowances on receivables – is not offsetting.

Three balance sheets required in certain circumstances

1p39 12 If an entity has applied an accounting policy retrospectively, restated items retrospectively or reclassified items in its financial statements, it provides a third balance sheet as at the beginning of the earliest comparative period presented. However, where the retrospective change in policy or the restatement has no effect on this earliest statement of financial position, we believe that it would be sufficient for the entity merely to disclose that fact.

(All amounts in C thousands unless otherwise stated)

Consolidated statement of changes in equity

1p106,108,109		Note	Share capital	Share premium	Other reserves	Retained earnings	Total	Non-controlling interest	Total equity
			Attributable to owners of the parent						
	Balance at 1 January 2009		20,000	10,424	6,364	48,470	85,258	1,500	86,758
	Comprehensive income								
1p106 (d)(i)	Profit or loss		–	–	–	15,512	15,512	856	16,368
1p106 (d)(ii)	**Other comprehensive income**								
16p77(f) 1p82(g)	Gain on the revaluation of land and buildings	20	–	–	759	–	759	–	759
16p41	Depreciation transfer on land and buildings, net of tax	19	–	–	(87)	87	–	–	–
1p82(g), IFRS7 p20(a)(ii)	– Available-for-sale financial assets	20	–	–	62	–	62	–	62
1p82(h)	Share of other comprehensive income/(loss) of associates	20	–	–	91	–	91	–	91
19p93A(b)	Actuarial loss on post employment benefit obligations		–	–	–	(494)	(494)	–	(494)
1p82(g), IFRS 7p23(c)	Cash flow hedges, net of tax	20	–	–	(3)	–	(3)	–	(3)
1p82(g), 39p102(a)	Net investment hedge	20	–	–	40	–	40	–	40
1p82(g), 21p52(b)	Currency translation differences	20	–	–	(221)	–	(221)	(40)	(261)
	Total other comprehensive income		–	–	641	(407)	234	(40)	194
1p106(a)	**Total comprehensive income**		–	–	641	15,105	15,746	816	16,562
	Transactions with owners								
	Employees share option scheme:								
IFRS2p50	– Value of employee services	19	–	–	–	822	822	–	822

(All amounts in C thousands unless otherwise stated)

	Note	Share capital	Share premium	Other reserves	Retained earnings	Total	Non-controlling interest	Total equity
		\multicolumn{5}{Attributable to owners of the parent}			
IFRS2p50 – Proceeds from shares issued	17	1,000	70	–	–	1,070	–	1,070
– Tax credit relating to share option scheme	19	–	–	–	20	20	–	20
1p106 (d)(iii) Dividends relating to 2008	35	–	–	–	(15,736)	(15,736)	(550)	(16,286)
1p106 (d)(iii) **Transaction with owners**		**1,000**	**70**	**–**	**(14,894)**	**(13,824)**	**(550)**	**(14,374)**
Balance at 1 January 2010		**21,000**	**10,494**	**7,005**	**48,681**	**87,180**	**1,766**	**88,946**
Comprehensive income								
1p106 (d)(i) Profit or loss		–	–	–	30,617	30,617	2,548	33,165
1p106 (d)(ii) **Other comprehensive income**		–	–	–	–	–	–	–
1p82(g) Gain on the revaluation of land and buildings		–	–	–	–	–	–	–
16p41 Depreciation transfer on land and buildings, net of tax	19	–	–	(100)	100	–	–	–
1p82(g), IFRS7 p20(a)(ii) - Available-for-sale financial assets	20	–	–	362	–	362	–	362
Share of other comprehensive income/(loss) of associates		–	–	(86)	–	(86)	–	(86)
1p82(g), IFRS 7p23(c) Cash flow hedges, net of tax	20	–	–	64	–	64	–	64
1p82(g), 39p102(a) Net investment hedge	20	–	–	(45)	–	(45)	–	(45)
1p82(g), 21p52(b) Currency translation differences	20	–	–	2,066	–	2,066	252	2,318
12p81 (a),(b) Impact of the change in the Euravian tax rate on deferred tax	23	–	–	–	(10)	(10)	–	(10)
Total other comprehensive income		–	–	2,261	90	3,201	252	2,603
1106(a) **Total comprehensive income for the period**		**–**	**–**	**2,261**	**30,707**	**32,968**	**2,800**	**35,768**

(All amounts in C thousands unless otherwise stated)

			Attributable to owners of the parent						
		Note	Share capital	Share premium	Other reserves	Retained earnings	Total	Non-controlling interest	Total equity
IFRS2p50	Transactions with owners - Value of employee services	19	–	–	–	690	690	–	690
IFRS2p50	- Proceeds from shares issued	17	750	200	–	–	950	–	950
	- Tax credit relating to share option scheme	19	–	–	–	30	30	–	30
1p106 (d)(iii)	Issue of ordinary shares related to business combination	17	3,550	6,450	–	–	10,000	–	10,000
1p106 (d)(iii)	Purchase of treasury shares	19	–	–	–	(2,564)	(2,564)	–	(2,564)
	Convertible bond – equity component, net of tax	20	–	–	5,433	–	5,433	–	5,433
1p106 (d)(iii)	Dividends relating to 2008	35	–	–	–	(10,102)	(10,102)	(1,920)	(12,022)
1p106 (d)(iii)	Total contributions by and distributions to owners		4,300	6,650	5,433	(11,946)	4,437	(1,920)	2,517
	Changes in ownership interests in subsidiaries that do not result in a loss of control								
1p106 (d)(iii)	Non-controlling interest arising on business combination	39	–	–	–	–	–	4,542	4,542
1p106 (d)(iii)	**Total transactions with owners**		**4,300**	**6,650**	**5,433**	**(11,946)**	**4,437**	**2,622**	**7,059**
	Balance at 31 December 2010		**25,300**	**17,144**	**14,699**	**67,442**	**124,585**	**7,188**	**131,773**

The notes on pages 1 to 118 are an integral part of these consolidated financial statements.

A statement of changes in equity for the group is required by IAS 1. It has not been included in this set of illustrative financial statements.

(All amounts in C thousands unless otherwise stated)

Commentary – statement of changes in equity

The commentary that follows explains some of the key requirements in IAS 1, 'Presentation of financial statements', and other aspects that impact the statement of changes in equity.

Non-controlling interest

1p106 1 Information to be included in the statement of changes in equity includes:

(a) Total comprehensive income for the period, showing separately the total amounts attributable to owners of the parent and to non-controlling interest.

(b) For each component of equity, the effects of retrospective application or retrospective restatement recognised in accordance with IAS 8.

(c) For each component of equity, a reconciliation between the carrying amount at the beginning and the end of the period, separately disclosing changes resulting from:
(i)   profit or loss;
(ii) each item of other comprehensive income; and
(iii) transactions with owners in their capacity as owners, showing separately contributions by and distributions to owners and changes in ownership interests in subsidiaries that do not result in loss of control.

2 The IASB has published an amendment to IAS 1, which is applicable from 1 January 2011. The standard was amended to state explicitly that an entity presents the components of changes in equity either in the statement of changes in equity or in the notes to the financial statements. Unless otherwise specified, the proposed effective date for the amendments is for annual periods beginning on or after 1 January 2011, although entities are permitted to adopt them earlier.

IFRS GAAP plc has included the items in the statement of changes in equity.

1p107 3 The amount of dividends recognised as distributions to owners during the period and the related amount per share are now disclosed either in the statement of changes in equity or in the notes and can no longer be presented in the income statement. IFRS GAAP plc presents this information in note 35.

(All amounts in C thousands unless otherwise stated)

Consolidated statement of cash flows

7p10, 18(b),
1p38

1p113

		Note	Year ended 31 December 2010	2009
	Cash flows from operating activities			
	Cash generated from operations	36	**56,234**	41,776
7p31	Interest paid		**(7,835)**	(14,773)
7p35	Income tax paid		**(14,317)**	(10,526)
	Net cash generated from operating activities		**34,082**	16,477
7p21, 7p10	**Cash flows from investing activities**			
7p39	Acquisition of subsidiary, net of cash acquired	39	**(3,950)**	–
7p16(a)	Purchases of property, plant and equipment (PPE)	6	**(9,755)**	(6,042)
7p16(b)	Proceeds from sale of PPE	36	**6,354**	2,979
7p16(a)	Purchases of intangible assets	7	**(3,050)**	(700)
7p16(c)	Purchases of available-for-sale financial assets	10	**(2,781)**	(1,126)
7p16(e)	Loans granted to associates	40	**(1,000)**	(50)
7p16(f)	Loan repayments received from associates	40	**14**	64
7p16(e)	Loans granted to subsidiary undertakings		**–**	–
7p16(f)	Loan repayments received from subsidiary undertakings		**–**	–
7p31	Interest received		**1,254**	1,193
7p31	Dividends received		**1,180**	1,120
	Net cash used in investing activities		**(11,734)**	(2,562)
7p21, 7p10	**Cash flows from financing activities**			
7p17(a)	Proceeds from issuance of ordinary shares	17	**950**	1,070
7p17(b)	Purchase of treasury shares	19	**(2,564)**	–
7p17(c)	Proceeds from issuance of convertible bonds	22b	**50,000**	–
7p17(c)	Proceeds from issuance of redeemable preference shares	22c	**–**	30,000
7p17(c)	Proceeds from borrowings		**8,500**	18,000
7p17(d)	Repayments of borrowings		**(78,117)**	(34,674)
7p17(c)	Proceeds from loan from subsidiary undertaking		**–**	–
7p31	Dividends paid to company's shareholders	35	**(10,102)**	(15,736)
7p31	Dividends paid to holders of redeemable preferences shares		**(1,950)**	(1,950)
7p31	Dividends paid to non-controlling interests		**(1,920)**	(550)
	Net cash used in financing activities		**(35,203)**	(3,840)
	Net (decrease)/increase in cash and cash equivalents		**(12,855)**	10,075
	Cash, cash equivalents and bank overdrafts at beginning of year	15	**27,598**	17,587
	Exchange gains/(losses) on cash and cash equivalents		**535**	(64)
	Cash and cash equivalents at end of year	15	**15,278**	27,598

The notes on pages 1 to 118 are an integral part of these consolidated financial statements.

(All amounts in C thousands unless otherwise stated)

Commentary – Statement of cash flows

The commentary that follows explains some of the key requirements in IAS 7, 'Statements of cash flows'.

Reporting cash flows

Cash flows from operating activities

7p18   1   Cash flows from operating activities are reported using either:

    (a) the direct method, whereby major classes of gross cash receipts and gross cash payments are disclosed; or

    (b) the indirect method, whereby profit or loss is adjusted for the effects of transactions of a non-cash nature, any deferrals or accruals of past or future operating cash receipts or payments, and items of income or expense associated with investing or financing cash flows.

7p20   2   IFRS GAAP plc continues to use the indirect method. For an illustration of a statement of cash flows presented using the direct method, refer to appendix II.

Cash flows from investing and financing activities

7p21   4   Major classes of gross cash receipts and gross cash payments arising from investing and financing activities are reported separately, except to the extent that cash flows described in paragraphs 22 and 24 of IAS 7 are reported on a net basis.

Sale of property, plant and equipment held for rental to others

7p14   5   Cash flows from the sale of property, plant and equipment are normally presented as cash flows from investing activities. However, cash payments to manufacture or acquire assets that will be held for rental to others and subsequently for sale are cash flows from operating activities. The cash receipts from rents and subsequent sales of such assets are also therefore cash flows from operating activities.

Reporting on a net basis

7p22, 23   7   Cash flows arising from the following operating, investing or financing activities may be reported on a net basis:

    (a) cash receipts and payments on behalf of customers when the cash flows reflect the activities of the customer rather than those of the entity (for example, rents collected on behalf of, and paid over to, the owners of properties); and

    (b) cash receipts and payments for items in which the turnover is quick, the amounts are large, and the maturities are short (for example, advances made for, and repayment of, principal amounts relating to credit card customers).

7p24 8 Cash flows arising from each of the following activities of a financial institution may be reported on a net basis:

  (a) Cash receipts and payments for the acceptance and repayment of deposits with a fixed maturity date.

  (b) The placement of deposits with, and withdrawal of deposits from, other financial institutions.

  (c) Cash advances and loans made to customers and the repayment of those advances and loans.

Interest and dividends

7p31 9 Cash flows from interest and dividends received and paid are each disclosed separately. Each is classified in a consistent manner from period to period as either operating, investing or financing activities.

7p33 10 Interest paid and interest and dividends received are usually classified as operating cash flows for a financial institution. However, there is no consensus on the classification of these cash flows for other entities. Interest paid and interest and dividends received may be classified as operating cash flows because they enter into the determination of net profit or loss. Alternatively, interest paid and interest and dividends received may be classified as financing cash flows and investing cash flows respectively, because they are costs of obtaining financial resources or returns on investments.

7p34 11 Dividends paid may be classified as 'financing cash flows' because they are a cost of obtaining financial resources. Alternatively, they may be classified as operating cash flows to assist users to determine the ability of an entity to pay dividends out of operating cash flows.

Income taxes

7p35 12 Cash flows arising from income taxes are separately disclosed and classified as cash flows from operating activities unless they can be specifically identified with financing and investing activities.

Effects of exchange rate changes

7p28 13 Unrealised gains and losses arising from changes in foreign currency exchange rates are not cash flows. However, the effect of exchange rate changes on cash and cash equivalents held or due in a foreign currency are reported in the statement of cash flows in order to reconcile cash and cash equivalents at the beginning and the end of the period. This amount is presented separately from cash flows from operating, investing and financing activities. It also includes the differences, if any, had those cash flows been reported at period-end exchange rates.

(All amounts in C thousands unless otherwise stated)

Additional recommended disclosures

7p50   14   Additional information may be relevant to users in understanding the financial position and liquidity of an entity. Disclosure of this information, together with a commentary by management, is encouraged and may include:

7p50(a)   (a)   The amount of undrawn borrowing facilities that may be available for future operating activities and to settle capital commitments, indicating any restrictions on the use of these facilities.

7p50(c)   (b)   The aggregate amount of cash flows that represent increases in operating capacity separately from those cash flows that are required to maintain operating capacity.

7p50(d)   (c)   The amount of the cash flows arising from the operating, investing and financing activities of each reportable segment (see IFRS 8, 'Operating segments').

(All amounts in C thousands unless otherwise stated)

Notes to the consolidated financial statements

1 General information

1p138
(b)(c)
1p51(a)(b)
IFRS GAAP plc ('the company') and its subsidiaries (together, 'the group') manufacture distribute and sell shoes through a network of independent retailers. The group has manufacturing plants around the world and sells mainly in countries within the UK, the US and Europe. During the year, the group acquired control of 'ABC Group', a shoe and leather goods retailer operating in the US and most western European countries.

2 Summary of significant accounting policies

1p112(a)
1p117(b)
1p119
The principal accounting policies applied in the preparation of these consolidated financial statements are set out below. These policies have been consistently applied to all the years presented, unless otherwise stated.

2.1 Basis of preparation

1p116
1p117(a)
The consolidated financial statements of IFRS GAAP plc have been prepared in accordance with International Financial Reporting Standards and IFRIC interpretations. The consolidated financial statements have been prepared under the historical cost convention, as modified by the revaluation of land and buildings, available-for-sale financial assets, and financial assets and financial liabilities (including derivative instruments) at fair value through profit or loss.

The preparation of financial statements in conformity with IFRS requires the use of certain critical accounting estimates. It also requires management to exercise its judgement in the process of applying the group's accounting policies. The areas involving a higher degree of judgement or complexity, or areas where assumptions and estimates are significant to the consolidated financial statements are disclosed in note 4.

2.1.1 Going concern

As a result of the funding activities undertaken and the increased focus on working capital, despite significant additional debt arising from the acquisitions made in the last three years, the group has improved both its short-term and medium-term liquidity position. Interest is more than six times covered by operating profit and comfortably within the targets set by the Board. The group's forecasts and projections, taking account of reasonably possible changes in trading performance, show that the group should be able to operate within the level of its current financing.

After making enquiries, the directors have a reasonable expectation that the group has adequate resources to continue in operational existence for the foreseeable future. The group therefore continues to adopt the going concern basis in preparing its consolidated financial statements.

2.1.2 Changes in accounting policy and disclosures

(a) New and amended standards adopted by the group

The following new standards and amendments to standards are mandatory for the first time for the financial year beginning 1 January 2010.

(All amounts in C thousands unless otherwise stated)

8p28 ■ IFRS 3 (revised), 'Business combinations', and consequential amendments to IAS 27, 'Consolidated and separate financial statements', IAS 28, 'Investments in associates', and IAS 31, 'Interests in joint ventures', are effective prospectively to business combinations for which the acquisition date is on or after the beginning of the first annual reporting period beginning on or after 1 July 2009.

The revised standard continues to apply the acquisition method to business combinations but with some significant changes compared with IFRS 3. For example, all payments to purchase a business are recorded at fair value at the acquisition date, with contingent payments classified as debt subsequently re-measured through the statement of comprehensive income. There is a choice on an acquisition-by-acquisition basis to measure the non-controlling interest in the acquiree either at fair value or at the non-controlling interest's proportionate share of the acquiree's net assets. All acquisition-related costs are expensed.

The revised standard was applied to the acquisition of the controlling interest in ABC Group on 1 March 2010. This acquisition has occurred in stages. The revised standard requires goodwill to be determined only at the acquisition date rather than at the previous stages. The determination of goodwill includes the previously held equity interest to be adjusted to fair value, with any gain or loss recorded in the income statement. Contingent consideration of C1,000 has been recognised at fair value at 1 March 2010. The contingent consideration would not have previously been recorded at the date of acquisition, as the payment to the former owners of ABC Group was not probable. Acquisition-related costs of C200 have been recognised in the consolidated income statement, which previously would have been included in the consideration for the business combination. An indemnification asset of C1,000 has been recognised by the group at an amount equivalent to the fair value of the indemnified liability. The indemnification asset is deducted from consideration transferred for the business combination. This possible compensation from the selling shareholders of ABC Group would not have previously been recognised as an indemnification asset of the acquirer and would have been adjusted against goodwill once received from the vendor. Subsequent measurement of the indemnification asset and contingent liability will have no net impact on future earnings, unless the indemnification asset becomes impaired. The group has chosen to recognise the non-controlling interest at fair value of C6,451 for this acquisition rather than the proportionate share of net assets of ABC Group of C4,542, which is also allowed. Previously there was no choice, and the non-controlling interest would have been recognised at the proportionate share (30%) of the net assets of ABC Group of C4,542. See note 39 for further details of the business combination that occurred in 2010.

IAS 27 (revised) requires the effects of all transactions with non-controlling interests to be recorded in equity if there is no change in control and these transactions will no longer result in goodwill or gains and losses. The standard also specifies the accounting when control is lost. Any remaining interest in the entity is re-measured to fair value, and a gain or loss is recognised in profit or loss. IAS 27 (revised) has had no impact on the current period, as none of the non-controlling interests have a deficit balance; there have been no transactions whereby an interest in an entity is retained after the loss of control of that entity, and there have been no transactions with non-controlling interests.

(All amounts in C thousands unless otherwise stated)

(b) New and amended standards, and interpretations mandatory for the first time for the financial year beginning 1 January 2010 but not currently relevant to the group (although they may affect the accounting for future transactions and events)[1]

8p30   The following standards and amendments to existing standards have been published and are mandatory for the group's accounting periods beginning on or after 1 January 2010 or later periods, but the group has not early adopted them.

- IFRIC 17, 'Distribution of non-cash assets to owners' (effective on or after 1 July 2009). The interpretation was published in November 2008. This interpretation provides guidance on accounting for arrangements whereby an entity distributes non-cash assets to shareholders either as a distribution of reserves or as dividends. IFRS 5 has also been amended to require that assets are classified as held for distribution only when they are available for distribution in their present condition and the distribution is highly probable.

- IFRIC 18, 'Transfers of assets from customers', effective for transfer of assets received on or after 1 July 2009. This interpretation clarifies the requirements of IFRSs for agreements in which an entity receives from a customer an item of property, plant and equipment that the entity must then use either to connect the customer to a network or to provide the customer with ongoing access to a supply of goods or services (such as a supply of electricity, gas or water). In some cases, the entity receives cash from a customer that must be used only to acquire or construct the item of property, plant, and equipment in order to connect the customer to a network or provide the customer with ongoing access to a supply of goods or services (or to do both).

- IFRIC 9, 'Reassessment of embedded derivatives and IAS 39, Financial instruments: Recognition and measurement', effective 1 July 2009. This amendment to IFRIC 9 requires an entity to assess whether an embedded derivative should be separated from a host contract when the entity reclassifies a hybrid financial asset out of the 'fair value through profit or loss' category. This assessment is to be made based on circumstances that existed on the later of the date the entity first became a party to the contract and the date of any contract amendments that significantly change the cash flows of the contract. If the entity is unable to make this assessment, the hybrid instrument must remains classified as at fair value through profit or loss in its entirety.

- IFRIC 16, 'Hedges of a net investment in a foreign operation' effective 1 July 2009. This amendment states that, in a hedge of a net investment in a foreign operation, qualifying hedging instruments may be held by any entity or entities within the group, including the foreign operation itself, as long as the designation, documentation and effectiveness requirements of IAS 39 that relate to a net investment hedge are satisfied. In particular, the group should clearly document its hedging strategy because of the possibility of different designations at different levels of the group. IAS 38 (amendment), 'Intangible assets', effective 1 January 2010. The amendment clarifies guidance in measuring the fair value of an intangible asset acquired in a business combination and permits the grouping of intangible assets as a single asset if each asset has similar useful economic lives.

---

[1] A detailed list of standards and interpretations in issue at 1 June 2010 that are effective for annual reporting periods beginning after 1 January 2010 is provided in Appendix VII.

(All amounts in C thousands unless otherwise stated)

- IAS 1 (amendment), 'Presentation of financial statements'. The amendment clarifies that the potential settlement of a liability by the issue of equity is not relevant to its classification as current or non current. By amending the definition of current liability, the amendment permits a liability to be classified as non-current (provided that the entity has an unconditional right to defer settlement by transfer of cash or other assets for at least 12 months after the accounting period) notwithstanding the fact that the entity could be required by the counterparty to settle in shares at any time.

- IAS 36 (amendment), 'Impairment of assets', effective 1 January 2010. The amendment clarifies that the largest cash-generating unit (or group of units) to which goodwill should be allocated for the purposes of impairment testing is an operating segment, as defined by paragraph 5 of IFRS 8, ' Operating segments' (that is, before the aggregation of segments with similar economic characteristics).

- IFRS 2 (amendments), 'Group cash-settled share-based payment transactions', effective form 1 January 2010. In addition to incorporating IFRIC 8, 'Scope of IFRS 2', and IFRIC 11, 'IFRS 2 – Group and treasury share transactions', the amendments expand on the guidance in IFRIC 11 to address the classification of group arrangements that were not covered by that interpretation.

- IFRS 5 (amendment), 'Non-current assets held for sale and discontinued operations'. The amendment clarificaties that IFRS 5 specifies the disclosures required in respect of non-current assets (or disposal groups) classified as held for sale or discontinued operations. It also clarifies that the general requirement of IAS 1 still apply, in particular paragraph 15 (to achieve a fair presentation) and paragraph 125 (sources of estimation uncertainty) of IAS 1.

(c) New standards, amendments and interpretations issued but not effective for the financial year beginning 1 January 2010 and not early adopted

The group's and parent entity's assessment of the impact of these new standards and interpretations is set out below.

- IFRS 9, 'Financial instruments', issued in November 2009. This standard is the first step in the process to replace IAS 39, 'Financial instruments: recognition and measurement'. IFRS 9 introduces new requirements for classifying and measuring financial assets and is likely to affect the group's accounting for its financial assets. The standard is not applicable until 1 January 2013 but is available for early adoption. However, the standard has not yet been endorsed by the EU.

  The group is yet to assess IFRS 9's full impact. However, initial indications are that it may affect the group's accounting for its debt available-for-sale financial assets, as IFRS 9 only permits the recognition of fair value gains and losses in other comprehensive income if they relate to equity investments that are not held for trading. Fair value gains and losses on available-for-sale debt investments, for example, will therefore have to be recognised directly in profit or loss. In the current reporting period, the group recognised C5,000 of such gains in other comprehensive income.

- Revised IAS 24 (revised), 'Related party disclosures', issued in November 2009. It supersedes IAS 24, 'Related party disclosures', issued in 2003. IAS 24 (revised) is mandatory for periods beginning on or after 1 January 2011. Earlier application, in whole or in part, is permitted. However, the standard has not yet been endorsed by the EU.

(All amounts in C thousands unless otherwise stated)

The revised standard clarifies and simplifies the definition of a related party and removes the requirement for government-related entities to disclose details of all transactions with the government and other government-related entities. The group will apply the revised standard from 1 January 2011. When the revised standard is applied, the group and the parent will need to disclose any transactions between its subsidiaries and its associates. The group is currently putting systems in place to capture the necessary information. It is, therefore, not possible at this stage to disclose the impact, if any, of the revised standard on the related party disclosures.

■ 'Classification of rights issues' (amendment to IAS 32), issued in October 2009. The amendment applies to annual periods beginning on or after 1 February 2010. Earlier application is permitted. The amendment addresses the accounting for rights issues that are denominated in a currency other than the functional currency of the issuer. Provided certain conditions are met, such rights issues are now classified as equity regardless of the currency in which the exercise price is denominated. Previously, these issues had to be accounted for as derivative liabilities. The amendment applies retrospectively in accordance with IAS 8 'Accounting policies, changes in accounting estimates and errors'. The group will apply the amended standard from 1 January 2011.

■ IFRIC 19, 'Extinguishing financial liabilities with equity instruments', effective 1 July 2010. The interpretation clarifies the accounting by an entity when the terms of a financial liability are renegotiated and result in the entity issuing equity instruments to a creditor of the entity to extinguish all or part of the financial liability (debt for equity swap). It requires a gain or loss to be recognised in profit or loss, which is measured as the difference between the carrying amount of the financial liability and the fair value of the equity instruments issued. If the fair value of the equity instruments issued cannot be reliably measured, the equity instruments should be measured to reflect the fair value of the financial liability extinguished. The group will apply the interpretation from 1 January 2011, subject to endorsement by the EU. It is not expected to have any impact on the group or the parent entity's financial statements.

■ 'Prepayments of a minimum funding requirement' (amendments to IFRIC 14). The amendments correct an unintended consequence of IFRIC 14, 'IAS 19 – The limit on a defined benefit asset, minimum funding requirements and their interaction'. Without the amendments, entities are not permitted to recognise as an asset some voluntary prepayments for minimum funding contributions. This was not intended when IFRIC 14 was issued, and the amendments correct this. The amendments are effective for annual periods beginning 1 January 2011. Earlier application is permitted. The amendments should be applied retrospectively to the earliest comparative period presented. The group will apply these amendments for the financial reporting period commencing on 1 January 2011.

1p119   **2.2 Consolidation**

27p12   *(a) Subsidiaries*

27p14
27p30   Subsidiaries are all entities (including special purpose entities) over which the group has the power to govern the financial and operating policies generally accompanying a shareholding of more than one half of the voting rights. The existence and effect of potential voting rights that are currently exercisable or convertible are considered

when assessing whether the group controls another entity. Subsidiaries are fully consolidated from the date on which control is transferred to the group. They are de-consolidated from the date that control ceases.

IFRS3p5
IFRS3p37
IFRS3p39
IFRS3p53
IFRS3p18
IFRS3p19
The group uses the acquisition method of accounting to account for business combinations. The consideration transferred for the acquisition of a subsidiary is the fair values of the assets transferred, the liabilities incurred and the equity interests issued by the group. The consideration transferred includes the fair value of any asset or liability resulting from a contingent consideration arrangement. Acquisition-related costs are expensed as incurred. Identifiable assets acquired and liabilities and contingent liabilities assumed in a business combination are measured initially at their fair values at the acquisition date. On an acquisition-by-acquisition basis, the group recognises any non-controlling interest in the acquiree either at fair value or at the non-controlling interest's proportionate share of the acquiree's net assets.

Investments in subsidiaries are accounted for at cost less impairment. Cost is adjusted to reflect changes in consideration arising from contingent consideration amendments. Cost also includes direct attributable costs of investment.

IFRS3p32
IFRS3p34
The excess of the consideration transferred, the amount of any non-controlling interest in the acquiree and the acquisition-date fair value of any previous equity interest in the acquiree over the fair value of the group's share of the identifiable net assets acquired is recorded as goodwill. If this is less than the fair value of the net assets of the subsidiary acquired in the case of a bargain purchase, the difference is recognised directly in the statement of comprehensive income (note 2.6).

27p24
27p28
Inter-company transactions, balances and unrealised gains on transactions between group companies are eliminated. Unrealised losses are also eliminated. Accounting policies of subsidiaries have been changed where necessary to ensure consistency with the policies adopted by the group.

(b) Transactions and non-controlling interests

27p30,31
The group treats transactions with non-controlling interests as transactions with equity owners of the group. For purchases from non-controlling interests, the difference between any consideration paid and the relevant share acquired of the carrying value of net assets of the subsidiary is recorded in equity. Gains or losses on disposals to non-controlling interests are also recorded in equity.

27p34,35,
28p18
When the group ceases to have control or significant influence, any retained interest in the entity is remeasured to its fair value, with the change in carrying amount recognised in profit or loss. The fair value is the initial carrying amount for the purposes of subsequently accounting for the retained interest as an associate, joint venture or financial asset. In addition, any amounts previously recognised in other comprehensive income in respect of that entity are accounted for as if the group had directly disposed of the related assets or liabilities. This may mean that amounts previously recognised in other comprehensive income are reclassified to profit or loss.

28p19A
If the ownership interest in an associate is reduced but significant influence is retained, only a proportionate share of the amounts previously recognised in other comprehensive income are reclassified to profit or loss where appropriate.

1p119 *(c) Associates*

28p13
28p11
Associates are all entities over which the group has significant influence but not control, generally accompanying a shareholding of between 20% and 50% of the voting rights. Investments in associates are accounted for using the equity method of accounting and are initially recognised at cost. The group's investment in associates includes goodwill identified on acquisition, net of any accumulated impairment loss.

28p29
28p30
The group's share of its associates' post-acquisition profits or losses is recognised in the income statement, and its share of post-acquisition movements in other comprehensive income is recognised in other comprehensive income. The cumulative post-acquisition movements are adjusted against the carrying amount of the investment. When the group's share of losses in an associate equals or exceeds its interest in the associate, including any other unsecured receivables, the group does not recognise further losses, unless it has incurred obligations or made payments on behalf of the associate.

28p22
28p26
Unrealised gains on transactions between the group and its associates are eliminated to the extent of the group's interest in the associates. Unrealised losses are also eliminated unless the transaction provides evidence of an impairment of the asset transferred. Accounting policies of associates have been changed where necessary to ensure consistency with the policies adopted by the group.

Dilution gains and losses arising in investments in associates are recognised in the income statement.

Changes in accounting policy

8p28
The group has changed its accounting policy for transactions with non-controlling interests and the accounting for loss of control or significant influence from 1 January 2010 when revised IAS 27, 'Consolidated and separate financial statements', became effective. The revision to IAS 27 contained consequential amendments to IAS 28, 'Investments in associates', and IAS 31, 'Interests in joint ventures'.

Previously transactions with non-controlling interests were treated as transactions with parties external to the group. Disposals therefore resulted in gains or losses in profit or loss and purchases resulted in the recognition of goodwill. On disposal or partial disposal, a proportionate interest in reserves attributable to the subsidiary was reclassified to profit or loss or directly to retained earnings.

Previously, when the group ceased to have control or significant influence over an entity, the carrying amount of the investment at the date control or significant influence became its cost for the purposes of subsequently accounting for the retained interests as associates, jointly controlled entity or financial assets.

The group has applied the new policy prospectively to transactions occurring on or after 1 January 2010. As a consequence, no adjustments were necessary to any of the amounts previously recognised in the financial statements.

(All amounts in C thousands unless otherwise stated)

1p119   2.3 Segment reporting

IFRS8p5(b) Operating segments are reported in a manner consistent with the internal reporting provided to the chief operating decision-maker. The chief operating decision-maker, who is responsible for allocating resources and assessing performance of the operating segments, has been identified as the steering committee that makes strategic decisions.

1p119   2.4 Foreign currency translation

1p119   *(a) Functional and presentation currency*

21p17
21p9, 18
1p51(d)
Items included in the financial statements of each of the group's entities are measured using the currency of the primary economic environment in which the entity operates ('the functional currency'). The consolidated financial statements are presented in 'currency' (C), which is the group's presentation currency.

1p119   *(b) Transactions and balances*

21p21, 28
21p32
39p95(a)
39p102(a)
Foreign currency transactions are translated into the functional currency using the exchange rates prevailing at the dates of the transactions or valuation where items are re-measured. Foreign exchange gains and losses resulting from the settlement of such transactions and from the translation at year-end exchange rates of monetary assets and liabilities denominated in foreign currencies are recognised in the income statement, except when deferred in other comprehensive income as qualifying cash flow hedges and qualifying net investment hedges.

Foreign exchange gains and losses that relate to borrowings and cash and cash equivalents are presented in the income statement within 'finance income or cost'. All other foreign exchange gains and losses are presented in the income statement within 'other (losses)/gains – net'.

39AG83 Changes in the fair value of monetary securities denominated in foreign currency classified as available for sale are analysed between translation differences resulting from changes in the amortised cost of the security and other changes in the carrying amount of the security. Translation differences related to changes in amortised cost are recognised in profit or loss, and other changes in carrying amount are recognised in other comprehensive income.

21p30 Translation differences on non-monetary financial assets and liabilities such as equities held at fair value through profit or loss are recognised in profit or loss as part of the fair value gain or loss. Translation differences on non-monetary financial assets, such as equities classified as available for sale, are included in other comprehensive income.

1p119   *(c) Group companies*

21p39 The results and financial position of all the group entities (none of which has the currency of a hyper-inflationary economy) that have a functional currency different from the presentation currency are translated into the presentation currency as follows:

21p39(a) (a) assets and liabilities for each balance sheet presented are translated at the closing rate at the date of that balance sheet;

(All amounts in C thousands unless otherwise stated)

21p39(b)
21p39
(b) income and expenses for each income statement are translated at average exchange rates (unless this average is not a reasonable approximation of the cumulative effect of the rates prevailing on the transaction dates, in which case income and expenses are translated at the rate on the dates of the transactions); and

1p79(b)
(c) all resulting exchange differences are recognised in other comprehensive income.

1p79(b)
21p39(c)
1p79(b)
39p102
On consolidation, exchange differences arising from the translation of the net investment in foreign operations, and of borrowings and other currency instruments designated as hedges of such investments, are taken to other comprehensive income . When a foreign operation is partially disposed of or sold, exchange differences that were recorded in equity are recognised in the income statement as part of the gain or loss on sale.

21p47
Goodwill and fair value adjustments arising on the acquisition of a foreign entity are treated as assets and liabilities of the foreign entity and translated at the closing rate.

1p119
2.5 Property, plant and equipment

16p73(a)
16p35(b)
16p15
16p17
39p98(b)
Land and buildings comprise mainly factories, retail outlets and offices. Land and buildings are shown at fair value, based on annual valuations by external independent valuers, less subsequent depreciation for buildings. Any accumulated depreciation at the date of revaluation is eliminated against the gross carrying amount of the asset, and the net amount is restated to the revalued amount of the asset. All other property, plant and equipment is stated at historical cost less depreciation. Historical cost includes expenditure that is directly attributable to the acquisition of the items. Cost may also include transfers from equity of any gains/losses on qualifying cash flow hedges of foreign currency purchases of property, plant and equipment.

16p12
Subsequent costs are included in the asset's carrying amount or recognised as a separate asset, as appropriate, only when it is probable that future economic benefits associated with the item will flow to the group and the cost of the item can be measured reliably. The carrying amount of the replaced part is derecognised. All other repairs and maintenance are charged to the income statement during the financial period in which they are incurred.

16p39,
1p79(b)
1p79(b)
16p40
16p41
Increases in the carrying amount arising on revaluation of land and buildings are credited to other comprehensive income and shown as other reserves in shareholders' equity. Decreases that offset previous increases of the same asset are charged in other comprehensive income and debited against other reserves directly in equity; all other decreases are charged to the income statement. Each year the difference between depreciation based on the revalued carrying amount of the asset charged to the income statement, and depreciation based on the asset's original cost is transferred from 'other reserves' to 'retained earnings'.

16p73(b),
50
16p73(c)
Land is not depreciated. Depreciation on other assets is calculated using the straight-line method to allocate their cost or revalued amounts to their residual values over their estimated useful lives, as follows:

- Buildings   25-40 years
- Machinery   10-15 years
- Vehicles   3-5 years
- Furniture, fittings and equipment   3-8 years

(All amounts in C thousands unless otherwise stated)

16p51   The assets' residual values and useful lives are reviewed, and adjusted if appropriate, at the end of each reporting period.

36p59   An asset's carrying amount is written down immediately to its recoverable amount if the asset's carrying amount is greater than its estimated recoverable amount (note 2.7).

16p68, 71   Gains and losses on disposals are determined by comparing the proceeds with the carrying amount and are recognised within 'Other (losses)/gains – net' in the income statement.

16p41,
1p79(b)   When revalued assets are sold, the amounts included in other reserves are transferred to retained earnings.

1p119   **2.6 Intangible assets**

1p119   *(a) Goodwill*

IFRS3p51
38p108(a)
IFRS3p54
36p124   Goodwill represents the excess of the cost of an acquisition over the fair value of the group's share of the net identifiable assets of the acquired subsidiary at the date of acquisition. Goodwill on acquisitions of subsidiaries is included in 'intangible assets'. Goodwill is tested annually for impairment and carried at cost less accumulated impairment losses. Impairment losses on goodwill are not reversed. Gains and losses on the disposal of an entity include the carrying amount of goodwill relating to the entity sold.

36p80   Goodwill is allocated to cash-generating units for the purpose of impairment testing. The allocation is made to those cash-generating units or groups of cash-generating units that are expected to benefit from the business combination in which the goodwill arose, identified according to operating segment.

1p119   *(b) Trademarks and licences*

38p74
38p97
38p118
(a)(b)   Separately acquired trademarks and licences are shown at historical cost. Trademarks and licences acquired in a business combination are recognised at fair value at the acquisition date. Trademarks and licences have a finite useful life and are carried at cost less accumulated amortisation. Amortisation is calculated using the straight-line method to allocate the cost of trademarks and licences over their estimated useful lives of 15 to 20 years.

38p4
38p118
(a)(b)   Acquired computer software licences are capitalised on the basis of the costs incurred to acquire and bring to use the specific software. These costs are amortised over their estimated useful lives of three to five years.

(c) Contractual customer relationships

Contractual customer relationships acquired in a business combination are recognised at fair value at the acquisition date. The contractual customer relations have a finite useful life and are carried at cost less accumulated amortisation. Amortisation is calculated using the straight-line method over the expected life of the customer relationship.

(All amounts in C thousands unless otherwise stated)

1p119   *(d) Computer software*

38p57   Costs associated with maintaining computer software programmes are recognised as an expense as incurred. Development costs that are directly attributable to the design and testing of identifiable and unique software products controlled by the group are recognised as intangible assets when the following criteria are met:

- it is technically feasible to complete the software product so that it will be available for use;

- management intends to complete the software product and use or sell it;

- there is an ability to use or sell the software product;

- it can be demonstrated how the software product will generate probable future economic benefits;

- adequate technical, financial and other resources to complete the development and to use or sell the software product are available; and

- the expenditure attributable to the software product during its development can be reliably measured.

38p66   Directly attributable costs that are capitalised as part of the software product include the software development employee costs and an appropriate portion of relevant overheads.

38p68, 71   Other development expenditures that do not meet these criteria are recognised as an expense as incurred. Development costs previously recognised as an expense are not recognised as an asset in a subsequent period.

38p97
38p118
(a)(b)   Computer software development costs recognised as assets are amortised over their estimated useful lives, which does not exceed three years.

1p119   **2.7 Impairment of non-financial assets**

36p9
36p10   Assets that have an indefinite useful life – for example, goodwill or intangible assets not ready to use – are not subject to amortisation and are tested annually for impairment. Assets that are subject to amortisation are reviewed for impairment whenever events or changes in circumstances indicate that the carrying amount may not be recoverable. An impairment loss is recognised for the amount by which the asset's carrying amount exceeds its recoverable amount. The recoverable amount is the higher of an asset's fair value less costs to sell and value in use. For the purposes of assessing impairment, assets are grouped at the lowest levels for which there are separately identifiable cash flows (cash-generating units). Non-financial assets other than goodwill that suffered an impairment are reviewed for possible reversal of the impairment at each reporting date.

1p119   **2.8 Non-current assets (or disposal groups) held for sale**

IFRS5p6,
15   Non-current assets (or disposal groups) are classified as assets held for sale when their carrying amount is to be recovered principally through a sale transaction and a sale is considered highly probable. They are stated at the lower of carrying amount and fair value less costs to sell if their carrying amount is to be recovered principally through a sale transaction rather than through continuing use and a sale is considered highly probable.

(All amounts in C thousands unless otherwise stated)

1p119   **2.9 Financial assets**

2.9.1 Classification

IFRS7p21
39p9
The group classifies its financial assets in the following categories: at fair value through profit or loss, loans and receivables, and available for sale. The classification depends on the purpose for which the financial assets were acquired. Management determines the classification of its financial assets at initial recognition.

(a) Financial assets at fair value through profit or loss

39p9
Financial assets at fair value through profit or loss are financial assets held for trading. A financial asset is classified in this category if acquired principally for the purpose of selling in the short term. Derivatives are also categorised as held for trading unless they are designated as hedges. Assets in this category are classified as current assets if expected to be settled within 12 months; otherwise, they are classified as non-current.

(b) Loans and receivables

39p9
1p66, 68
Loans and receivables are non-derivative financial assets with fixed or determinable payments that are not quoted in an active market. They are included in current assets, except for maturities greater than 12 months after the end of the reporting period. These are classified as non-current assets. The group's loans and receivables comprise 'trade and other receivables' and 'cash and cash equivalents' in the balance sheet (notes 2.12 and 2.13).

(c) Available-for-sale financial assets

39p9
1p66, 68
IFRS7
AppxB5(b)
Available-for-sale financial assets are non-derivatives that are either designated in this category or not classified in any of the other categories. They are included in non-current assets unless the investment matures or management intends to dispose of it within 12 months of the end of the reporting period.

2.9.2 Recognition and measurement

39p38
IFRS7
AppxBp5
39p43
39p16
39p46
Regular purchases and sales of financial assets are recognised on the trade-date – the date on which the group commits to purchase or sell the asset. Investments are initially recognised at fair value plus transaction costs for all financial assets not carried at fair value through profit or loss. Financial assets carried at fair value through profit or loss are initially recognised at fair value, and transaction costs are expensed in the income statement. Financial assets are derecognised when the rights to receive cash flows from the investments have expired or have been transferred and the group has transferred substantially all risks and rewards of ownership. Available-for-sale financial assets and financial assets at fair value through profit or loss are subsequently carried at fair value. Loans and receivables are subsequently carried at amortised cost using the effective interest method.

39p55(a)
IFRS7Appx
Bp5(e)
Gains or losses arising from changes in the fair value of the 'financial assets at fair value through profit or loss' category are presented in the income statement within 'other (losses)/gains – net' in the period in which they arise. Dividend income from financial assets at fair value through profit or loss is recognised in the income statement as part of other income when the group's right to receive payments is established.

(All amounts in C thousands unless otherwise stated)

39p55(b)
IFRS7
AppxB
p5(e)
39AG83
1p79(b)
Changes in the fair value of monetary and non-monetary securities classified as available for sale are recognised in other comprehensive income.

39p67
When securities classified as available for sale are sold or impaired, the accumulated fair value adjustments recognised in equity are included in the income statement as 'gains and losses from investment securities'.

Interest on available-for-sale securities calculated using the effective interest method is recognised in the income statement as part of other income. Dividends on available-for-sale equity instruments are recognised in the income statement as part of other income when the group's right to receive payments is established.

2.10 Offsetting financial instruments

32p42
Financial assets and liabilities are offset and the net amount reported in the balance sheet when there is a legally enforceable right to offset the recognised amounts and there is an intention to settle on a net basis or realise the asset and settle the liability simultaneously.

2.11 Impairment of financial assets

(a) Assets carried at amortised cost

39p58
39p59
The group assesses at the end of each reporting period whether there is objective evidence that a financial asset or group of financial assets is impaired. A financial asset or a group of financial assets is impaired and impairment losses are incurred only if there is objective evidence of impairment as a result of one or more events that occurred after the initial recognition of the asset (a 'loss event') and that loss event (or events) has an impact on the estimated future cash flows of the financial asset or group of financial assets that can be reliably estimated.

IFRS7
AppxB5(f)
The criteria that the group uses to determine that there is objective evidence of an impairment loss include:

- significant financial difficulty of the issuer or obligor;

- a breach of contract, such as a default or delinquency in interest or principal payments;

- the group, for economic or legal reasons relating to the borrower's financial difficulty, granting to the borrower a concession that the lender would not otherwise consider;

- it becomes probable that the borrower will enter bankruptcy or other financial reorganisation;

- the disappearance of an active market for that financial asset because of financial difficulties; or

- observable data indicating that there is a measurable decrease in the estimated future cash flows from a portfolio of financial assets since the initial recognition of those assets, although the decrease cannot yet be identified with the individual financial assets in the portfolio, including:

(All amounts in C thousands unless otherwise stated)

> (i) adverse changes in the payment status of borrowers in the portfolio; and
>
> (ii) national or local economic conditions that correlate with defaults on the assets in the portfolio.

39p64 The group first assesses whether objective evidence of impairment exists.

IFRS7p16 For loans and receivables category, the amount of the loss is measured as the difference
39AG84 between the asset's carrying amount and the present value of estimated future cash flows (excluding future credit losses that have not been incurred) discounted at the financial asset's original effective interest rate. The carrying amount of the asset is reduced and the amount of the loss is recognised in the consolidated income statement. If a loan or held-to-maturity investment has a variable interest rate, the discount rate for measuring any impairment loss is the current effective interest rate determined under the contract. As a practical expedient, the group may measure impairment on the basis of an instrument's fair value using an observable market price.

IFRS7 If, in a subsequent period, the amount of the impairment loss decreases and the decrease
AppxB5(d) can be related objectively to an event occurring after the impairment was recognised
39p65 (such as an improvement in the debtor's credit rating), the reversal of the previously recognised impairment loss is recognised in the consolidated income statement.

(b) Assets classified as available for sale

39p67
39p68
39p69 The group assesses at the end of each reporting period whether there is objective evidence that a financial asset or a group of financial assets is impaired. For debt securities, the group uses the criteria refer to (a) above. In the case of equity investments
39p70 classified as available for sale, a significant or prolonged decline in the fair value of the security below its cost is also evidence that the assets are impaired. If any such evidence exists for available-for-sale financial assets, the cumulative loss – measured as the difference between the acquisition cost and the current fair value, less any impairment loss on that financial asset previously recognised in profit or loss – is removed from equity and recognised in the separate consolidated income statement. Impairment losses recognised in the separate consolidated income statement on equity instruments are not reversed through the separate consolidated income statement. If, in a subsequent period, the fair value of a debt instrument classified as available for sale increases and the increase can be objectively related to an event occurring after the impairment loss was recognised in profit or loss, the impairment loss is reversed through the separate consolidated income statement.

Impairment testing of trade receivables is described in note 2.14.

1p119 **2.12 Derivative financial instruments and hedging activities**

IFRS7p21 Derivatives are initially recognised at fair value on the date a derivative contract is entered
IFRS7p22 into and are subsequently re-measured at their fair value. The method of recognising the resulting gain or loss depends on whether the derivative is designated as a hedging instrument, and if so, the nature of the item being hedged. The group designates certain derivatives as either:

(a) hedges of the fair value of recognised assets or liabilities or a firm commitment (fair value hedge);

(All amounts in C thousands unless otherwise stated)

    (b) hedges of a particular risk associated with a recognised asset or liability or a highly probable forecast transaction (cash flow hedge); or

    (c) hedges of a net investment in a foreign operation (net investment hedge).

39p88 The group documents at the inception of the transaction the relationship between hedging instruments and hedged items, as well as its risk management objectives and strategy for undertaking various hedging transactions. The group also documents its assessment, both at hedge inception and on an ongoing basis, of whether the derivatives that are used in hedging transactions are highly effective in offsetting changes in fair values or cash flows of hedged items.

IFRS7p23, 24 The fair values of various derivative instruments used for hedging purposes are disclosed in note 11. Movements on the hedging reserve in other comprehensive income are shown in note 20. The full fair value of a hedging derivative is classified as a non-current asset or liability when the remaining hedged item is more than 12 months, and as a current asset or liability when the remaining maturity of the hedged item is less than 12 months. Trading derivatives are classified as a current asset or liability.

39p89 *(a) Fair value hedge*

Changes in the fair value of derivatives that are designated and qualify as fair value hedges are recorded in the income statement, together with any changes in the fair value of the hedged asset or liability that are attributable to the hedged risk. The group only applies fair value hedge accounting for hedging fixed interest risk on borrowings. The gain or loss relating to the effective portion of interest rate swaps hedging fixed rate borrowings is recognised in the income statement within 'finance costs'. The gain or loss relating to the ineffective portion is recognised in the income statement within 'other gains/(losses) – net'. Changes in the fair value of the hedge fixed rate borrowings attributable to interest rate risk are recognised in the income statement within 'finance costs'.

39p92 If the hedge no longer meets the criteria for hedge accounting, the adjustment to the carrying amount of a hedged item for which the effective interest method is used is amortised to profit or loss over the period to maturity.

39p95 *(b) Cash flow hedge*

1p79(b) The effective portion of changes in the fair value of derivatives that are designated and qualify as cash flow hedges is recognised in other comprehensive income. The gain or loss relating to the ineffective portion is recognised immediately in the income statement within 'other gains/(losses) – net'.

39p99, 100 Amounts accumulated in equity are reclassified to profit or loss in the periods when the hedged item affects profit or loss (for example, when the forecast sale that is hedged **39p98(b)** takes place). The gain or loss relating to the effective portion of interest rate swaps hedging variable rate borrowings is recognised in the income statement within 'revenue'. However, when the forecast transaction that is hedged results in the recognition of a non-financial asset (for example, inventory or fixed assets), the gains and losses previously deferred in equity are transferred from equity and included in the initial measurement of the cost of the asset. The deferred amounts are ultimately recognised in cost of goods sold in the case of inventory or in depreciation in the case of fixed assets.

39p101 When a hedging instrument expires or is sold, or when a hedge no longer meets the criteria for hedge accounting, any cumulative gain or loss existing in equity at that time

(All amounts in C thousands unless otherwise stated)

remains in equity and is recognised when the forecast transaction is ultimately recognised in the income statement. When a forecast transaction is no longer expected to occur, the cumulative gain or loss that was reported in equity is immediately transferred to the income statement within 'other gains/(losses) – net'.

**39p102
(a)(b)**

(c) Net investment hedge

Hedges of net investments in foreign operations are accounted for similarly to cash flow hedges.

1p79(b)

Any gain or loss on the hedging instrument relating to the effective portion of the hedge is recognised in other comprehensive income. The gain or loss relating to the ineffective portion is recognised immediately in the income statement within 'other gains/(losses) – net'.

Gains and losses accumulated in equity are included in the income statement when the foreign operation is partially disposed of or sold.

1p119

2.13 Inventories

**2p36(a), 9
2p10, 25
23p6, 7
2p28, 30
39p98(b)**

Inventories are stated at the lower of cost and net realisable value. Cost is determined using the first-in, first-out (FIFO) method. The cost of finished goods and work in progress comprises design costs, raw materials, direct labour, other direct costs and related production overheads (based on normal operating capacity). It excludes borrowing costs. Net realisable value is the estimated selling price in the ordinary course of business, less applicable variable selling expenses. Costs of inventories include the transfer from equity of any gains/losses on qualifying cash flow hedges purchases of raw materials[1]

1p119

2.14 Trade receivables

IFRS7p21

Trade receivables are amounts due from customers for merchandise sold or services performed in the ordinary course of business. If collection is expected in one year or less (or in the normal operating cycle of the business if longer), they are classified as current assets. If not, they are presented as non-current assets.

**39p43
39p46(a)
39p59
IFRS7
AppxBp5(f)
IFRS7
AppxB
p5(d)**

Trade receivables are recognised initially at fair value and subsequently measured at amortised cost using the effective interest method, less provision for impairment.

1p119

2.15 Cash and cash equivalents

**IFRS7p21
7p45**

In the consolidated statement of cash flows, cash and cash equivalents includes cash in hand, deposits held at call with banks, other short-term highly liquid investments with original maturities of three months or less and bank overdrafts. In the consolidated balance sheet, bank overdrafts are shown within borrowings in current liabilities.

---

[1] Management may choose to keep these gains in equity until the acquired asset affects profit or loss. At this time, management should re-classify the gains to profit or loss.

(All amounts in C thousands unless otherwise stated)

1p119   2.16 Share capital

IFRS7p21
32p18(a) Ordinary shares are classified as equity. Mandatorily redeemable preference shares are classified as liabilities (note 2.16).

32p37 Incremental costs directly attributable to the issue of new ordinary shares or options are shown in equity as a deduction, net of tax, from the proceeds.

32p33 Where any group company purchases the company's equity share capital (treasury shares), the consideration paid, including any directly attributable incremental costs (net of income taxes) is deducted from equity attributable to the company's equity holders until the shares are cancelled or reissued. Where such ordinary shares are subsequently reissued, any consideration received, net of any directly attributable incremental transaction costs and the related income tax effects, is included in equity attributable to the company's equity holders.

1p119   2.17 Trade payables

Trade payables are obligations to pay for goods or services that have been acquired in the ordinary course of business from suppliers. Accounts payable are classified as current liabilities if payment is due within one year or less (or in the normal operating cycle of the business if longer). If not, they are presented as non-current liabilities.

IFRS7p21
39p43 Trade payables are recognised initially at fair value and subsequently measured at amortised cost using the effective interest method.

1p119   2.18 Borrowings

IFRS7p21
39p43
39p47 Borrowings are recognised initially at fair value, net of transaction costs incurred. Borrowings are subsequently carried at amortised cost; any difference between the proceeds (net of transaction costs) and the redemption value is recognised in the income statement over the period of the borrowings using the effective interest method.

Fees paid on the establishment of loan facilities are recognised as transaction costs of the loan to the extent that it is probable that some or all of the facility will be drawn down. In this case, the fee is deferred until the draw-down occurs. To the extent there is no evidence that it is probable that some or all of the facility will be drawn down, the fee is capitalised as a pre-payment for liquidity services and amortised over the period of the facility to which it relates.

32p18(a)
32p35 Preference shares, which are mandatorily redeemable on a specific date, are classified as liabilities. The dividends on these preference shares are recognised in the income statement as interest expense.

2.19 Compound financial instruments

32p28 Compound financial instruments issued by the group comprise convertible notes that can be converted to share capital at the option of the holder, and the number of shares to be issued does not vary with changes in their fair value.

32AG31 The liability component of a compound financial instrument is recognised initially at the fair value of a similar liability that does not have an equity conversion option. The equity component is recognised initially at the difference between the fair value of the compound

(All amounts in C thousands unless otherwise stated)

financial instrument as a whole and the fair value of the liability component. Any directly attributable transaction costs are allocated to the liability and equity components in proportion to their initial carrying amounts.

32p36 Subsequent to initial recognition, the liability component of a compound financial instrument is measured at amortised cost using the effective interest method. The equity component of a compound financial instrument is not re-measured subsequent to initial recognition except on conversion or expiry.

1p69, 71 Borrowings are classified as current liabilities unless the group has an unconditional right to defer settlement of the liability for at least 12 months after the end of the reporting period.

1p119 **2.20 Current and deferred income tax**

12p58
12p61A The tax expense for the period comprises current and deferred tax. Tax is recognised in the income statement, except to the extent that it relates to items recognised in other comprehensive income or directly in equity. In this case, the tax is also recognised in other comprehensive income or directly in equity, respectively.

12p12
12p46 The current income tax charge is calculated on the basis of the tax laws enacted or substantively enacted at the balance sheet date in the countries where the company and its subsidiaries operate and generate taxable income. Management periodically evaluates positions taken in tax returns with respect to situations in which applicable tax regulation is subject to interpretation. It establishes provisions where appropriate on the basis of amounts expected to be paid to the tax authorities.

12p24
12p15
12p47 Deferred income tax is recognised, using the liability method, on temporary differences arising between the tax bases of assets and liabilities and their carrying amounts in the consolidated financial statements. However, deferred tax liabilities are not recognised if they arise from the initial recognition of goodwill; deferred income tax is not accounted for if it arises from initial recognition of an asset or liability in a transaction other than a business combination that at the time of the transaction affects neither accounting nor taxable profit or loss. Deferred income tax is determined using tax rates (and laws) that have been enacted or substantially enacted by the balance sheet date and are expected to apply when the related deferred income tax asset is realised or the deferred income tax liability is settled.

12p24, 34 Deferred income tax assets are recognised only to the extent that it is probable that future taxable profit will be available against which the temporary differences can be utilised.

12p39, 44 Deferred income tax is provided on temporary differences arising on investments in subsidiaries and associates, except for deferred income tax liability where the timing of the reversal of the temporary difference is controlled by the group and it is probable that the temporary difference will not reverse in the foreseeable future.

12p74 Deferred income tax assets and liabilities are offset when there is a legally enforceable right to offset current tax assets against current tax liabilities and when the deferred income taxes assets and liabilities relate to income taxes levied by the same taxation authority on either the same taxable entity or different taxable entities where there is an intention to settle the balances on a net basis.

(All amounts in C thousands unless otherwise stated)

1p119 **2.21 Employee benefits**

(a) Pension obligations

19p27
19p25
19p7
19p120A(b)
Group companies operate various pension schemes. The schemes are generally funded through payments to insurance companies or trustee-administered funds, determined by periodic actuarial calculations. The group has both defined benefit and defined contribution plans. A defined contribution plan is a pension plan under which the group pays fixed contributions into a separate entity. The group has no legal or constructive obligations to pay further contributions if the fund does not hold sufficient assets to pay all employees the benefits relating to employee service in the current and prior periods. A defined benefit plan is a pension plan that is not a defined contribution plan. Typically defined benefit plans define an amount of pension benefit that an employee will receive on retirement, usually dependent on one or more factors such as age, years of service and compensation.

19p79
19p80
19p64
The liability recognised in the balance sheet in respect of defined benefit pension plans is the present value of the defined benefit obligation at the end of the reporting period less the fair value of plan assets, together with adjustments for unrecognised past-service costs. The defined benefit obligation is calculated annually by independent actuaries using the projected unit credit method. The present value of the defined benefit obligation is determined by discounting the estimated future cash outflows using interest rates of high-quality corporate bonds that are denominated in the currency in which the benefits will be paid, and that have terms to maturity approximating to the terms of the related pension obligation. In countries where there is no deep market in such bonds, the market rates on government bonds are used.

19p93-93D
19p120A(a)
Actuarial gains and losses arising from experience adjustments and changes in actuarial assumptions are charged or credited to equity in other comprehensive income in the period in which they arise.

19p96
Past-service costs are recognised immediately in income, unless the changes to the pension plan are conditional on the employees remaining in service for a specified period of time (the vesting period). In this case, the past-service costs are amortised on a straight-line basis over the vesting period.

19p44
For defined contribution plans, the group pays contributions to publicly or privately administered pension insurance plans on a mandatory, contractual or voluntary basis. The group has no further payment obligations once the contributions have been paid. The contributions are recognised as employee benefit expense when they are due. Prepaid contributions are recognised as an asset to the extent that a cash refund or a reduction in the future payments is available.

(b) Other post-employment obligations

19p120A
(a-b)
Some group companies provide post-retirement healthcare benefits to their retirees. The entitlement to these benefits is usually conditional on the employee remaining in service up to retirement age and the completion of a minimum service period. The expected costs of these benefits are accrued over the period of employment using the same accounting methodology as used for defined benefit pension plans. Actuarial gains and losses arising from experience adjustments and changes in actuarial assumptions are charged or credited to equity in other comprehensive income in the period in which they arise. These obligations are valued annually by independent qualified actuaries.

(All amounts in C thousands unless otherwise stated)

(c) Termination benefits

19p133
19p134
19p139
19p140

Termination benefits are payable when employment is terminated by the group before the normal retirement date, or whenever an employee accepts voluntary redundancy in exchange for these benefits. The group recognises termination benefits when it is demonstrably committed to a termination when the entity has a detailed formal plan to terminate the employment of current employees without possibility of withdrawal. In the case of an offer made to encourage voluntary redundancy, the termination benefits are measured based on the number of employees expected to accept the offer. Benefits falling due more than 12 months after the end of the reporting period are discounted to their present value.

(d) Profit-sharing and bonus plans

19p17

The group recognises a liability and an expense for bonuses and profit-sharing, based on a formula that takes into consideration the profit attributable to the company's shareholders after certain adjustments. The group recognises a provision where contractually obliged or where there is a past practice that has created a constructive obligation.

1p119   **2.22 Share-based payments**

IFRS2
p15(b)
IFRS2p19

The group operates a number of equity-settled, share-based compensation plans, under which the entity receives services from employees as consideration for equity instruments (options) of the group. The fair value of the employee services received in exchange for the grant of the options is recognised as an expense. The total amount to be expensed is determined by reference to the fair value of the options granted:

IFRS2p21 ■ including any market performance conditions (for example, an entity's share price);

IFRS2p20 ■ excluding the impact of any service and non-market performance vesting conditions (for example, profitability, sales growth targets and remaining an employee of the entity over a specified time period); and

IFRS2p21A ■ including the impact of any non-vesting conditions (for example, the requirement for employees to save).

IFRS2p15
IFRS2p20

Non-market vesting conditions are included in assumptions about the number of options that are expected to vest. The total expense is recognised over the vesting period, which is the period over which all of the specified vesting conditions are to be satisfied. At the end of each reporting period, the entity revises its estimates of the number of options that are expected to vest based on the non-marke vesting conditions. It recognises the impact of the revision to original estimates, if any, in the income statement, with a corresponding adjustment to equity.

When the options are exercised, the company issues new shares. The proceeds received net of any directly attributable transaction costs are credited to share capital (nominal value) and share premium when the options are exercised.

The grant by the company of options over its equity instruments to the employees of subsidiary undertakings in the group is treated as a capital contribution. The fair value of employee services received, measured by reference to the grant date fair value, is recognised over the vesting period as an increase to investment in subsidiary undertakings, with a corresponding credit to equity.

(All amounts in C thousands unless otherwise stated)

> The social security contributions payable in connection with the grant of the share options is considered an integral part of the grant itself, and the charge will be treated as a cash-settled transaction.

1p119 **2.23 Provisions**

37p14
37p72
37p63

Provisions for environmental restoration, restructuring costs and legal claims are recognised when: the group has a present legal or constructive obligation as a result of past events; it is probable that an outflow of resources will be required to settle the obligation; and the amount has been reliably estimated. Restructuring provisions comprise lease termination penalties and employee termination payments. Provisions are not recognised for future operating losses.

37p24

Where there are a number of similar obligations, the likelihood that an outflow will be required in settlement is determined by considering the class of obligations as a whole. A provision is recognised even if the likelihood of an outflow with respect to any one item included in the same class of obligations may be small.

37p45

Provisions are measured at the present value of the expenditures expected to be required to settle the obligation using a pre-tax rate that reflects current market assessments of the time value of money and the risks specific to the obligation. The increase in the provision due to passage of time is recognised as interest expense.

1p119 **2.24 Revenue recognition**

18p35(a)

Revenue comprises the fair value of the consideration received or receivable for the sale of goods and services in the ordinary course of the group's activities. Revenue is shown net of value-added tax, returns, rebates and discounts and after eliminating sales within the group.

The group recognises revenue when the amount of revenue can be reliably measured, it is probable that future economic benefits will flow to the entity and when specific criteria have been met for each of the group's activities as described below. The group bases its estimates on historical results, taking into consideration the type of customer, the type of transaction and the specifics of each arrangement.

18p14 *(a) Sales of goods – wholesale*

The group manufactures and sells a range of footwear products in the wholesale market. Sales of goods are recognised when a group entity has delivered products to the wholesaler, the wholesaler has full discretion over the channel and price to sell the products, and there is no unfulfilled obligation that could affect the wholesaler's acceptance of the products. Delivery does not occur until the products have been shipped to the specified location, the risks of obsolescence and loss have been transferred to the wholesaler, and either the wholesaler has accepted the products in accordance with the sales contract, the acceptance provisions have lapsed or the group has objective evidence that all criteria for acceptance have been satisfied.

The footwear products are often sold with volume discounts; customers have a right to return faulty products in the wholesale market. Sales are recorded based on the price specified in the sales contracts, net of the estimated volume discounts and returns at the time of sale. Accumulated experience is used to estimate and provide for the discounts

(All amounts in C thousands unless otherwise stated)

and returns. The volume discounts are assessed based on anticipated annual purchases. No element of financing is deemed present as the sales are made with a credit term of 60 days, which is consistent with the market practice.

18p14   *(b) Sales of goods – retail*

The group operates a chain of retail outlets for selling shoes and other leather products. Sales of goods are recognised when a group entity sells a product to the customer. Retail sales are usually in cash or by credit card.

It is the group's policy to sell its products to the retail customer with a right to return within 28 days. Accumulated experience is used to estimate and provide for such returns at the time of sale. The group does not operate any loyalty programmes.

18p20   *(c) Sales of services*

The group sells design services and transportation services to other shoe manufacturers. These services are provided on a time and material basis or as a fixed-price contract, with contract terms generally ranging from less than one year to three years.

Revenue from time and material contracts, typically from delivering design services, is recognised under the percentage-of-completion method. Revenue is generally recognised at the contractual rates. For time contracts, the stage of completion is measured on the basis of labour hours delivered as a percentage of total hours to be delivered. For material contracts, the stage of completion is measured on the basis of direct expenses incurred as a percentage of the total expenses to be incurred.

Revenue from fixed-price contracts for delivering design services is also recognised under the percentage-of-completion method. Revenue is generally recognised based on the services performed to date as a percentage of the total services to be performed.

Revenue from fixed-price contracts for delivering transportation services is generally recognised in the period the services are provided, using a straight-line basis over the term of the contract.

If circumstances arise that may change the original estimates of revenues, costs or extent of progress toward completion, estimates are revised. These revisions may result in increases or decreases in estimated revenues or costs and are reflected in income in the period in which the circumstances that give rise to the revision become known by management.

18p30(a)   *(d) Interest income*

39p63   Interest income is recognised using the effective interest method. When a loan and receivable is impaired, the group reduces the carrying amount to its recoverable amount, being the estimated future cash flow discounted at the original effective interest rate of the instrument, and continues unwinding the discount as interest income. Interest income on impaired loan and receivables are recognised using the original effective interest rate.

18p30(b)   *(e) Royalty income*

Royalty income is recognised on an accruals basis in accordance with the substance of the relevant agreements.

(All amounts in C thousands unless otherwise stated)

18p30(c)   *(f) Dividend income*

Dividend income is recognised when the right to receive payment is established.

Change in accounting policy

7p17
IAS 8p28
The group has changed its accounting policy for dividends paid out of pre-acquisition profits from 1 July 2009 when the revised IAS 27, 'Consolidated and separate financial statements', became effective. Previously, dividends paid out of pre-acquisition profits were deducted from the cost of the investment. The new accounting policy is applied prospectively in accordance with the transition provisions. It was therefore not necessary to make any adjustments to any of the amounts previously recognised in the financial statements.

1p119   **2.25 Leases**

17p33
SIC-15p5
Leases in which a significant portion of the risks and rewards of ownership are retained by the lessor are classified as operating leases. Payments made under operating leases (net of any incentives received from the lessor) are charged to the income statement on a straight-line basis over the period of the lease.

1p119
The group leases certain property, plant and equipment. Leases of property, plant and equipment where the group has substantially all the risks and rewards of ownership are classified as finance leases. Finance leases are capitalised at the lease's commencement at the lower of the fair value of the leased property and the present value of the minimum lease payments.

17p20
17p27
Each lease payment is allocated between the liability and finance charges. The corresponding rental obligations, net of finance charges, are included in other long-term payables. The interest element of the finance cost is charged to the income statement over the lease period so as to produce a constant periodic rate of interest on the remaining balance of the liability for each period. The property, plant and equipment acquired under finance leases is depreciated over the shorter of the useful life of the asset and the lease term.

1p119   **2.26 Dividend distribution**

10p12
Dividend distribution to the company's shareholders is recognised as a liability in the group's financial statements in the period in which the dividends are approved by the company's shareholders.

(All amounts in C thousands unless otherwise stated)

Commentary – Summary of significant accounting policies

Statement of compliance with IFRS

1p16   1   An entity whose financial statements and notes comply with IFRS makes an explicit and unreserved statement of such compliance in the notes. The financial statements and notes are not described as complying with IFRS unless they comply with all the requirements of IFRS.

           2   Where an entity can make the explicit and unreserved statement of compliance in respect of only:

               (a)   the parent financial statements and notes, or

               (b)   the consolidated financial statements and notes,

               it clearly identifies to which financial statements and notes the statement of compliance relates.

Summary of accounting policies

           3   A summary of significant accounting policies includes:

1p117(a)   (a)   the measurement basis (or bases) used in preparing the financial statements; and

1p117(b)   (b)   the other accounting policies used that are relevant to an understanding of the financial statements.

1p116   4   The summary may be presented as a separate component of the financial statements.

1p119   5   In deciding whether a particular accounting policy should be disclosed, management considers whether disclosure would assist users in understanding how transactions, other events and conditions are reflected in the reported financial performance and financial position. Some IFRSs specifically require disclosure of particular accounting policies, including choices made by management between different policies they allow. For example, IAS 16, 'Property, plant and equipment', requires disclosure of the measurement bases used for classes of property, plant and equipment.

Changes in accounting policies

Initial application of IFRS

8p28   6   When initial application of an IFRS:

               (a)   has an effect on the current period or any prior period;

               (b)   would have such an effect except that it is impracticable to determine the amount of the adjustment; or

               (c)   might have an effect on future periods, an entity discloses:
                   (i)   the title of the IFRS;

(All amounts in C thousands unless otherwise stated)

(ii) when applicable, that the change in accounting policy is made in accordance with its transitional provisions;

(iii) the nature of the change in accounting policy;

(iv) when applicable, a description of the transitional provisions;

(v) when applicable, the transitional provisions that might have an effect on future periods;

(vi) for the current period and each prior period presented, to the extent practicable, the amount of the adjustment:
- for each financial statement line item affected;
- if IAS 33, 'Earnings per share', applies to the entity, for basic and diluted earnings per share;

(vii) the amount of the adjustment relating to periods before those presented, to the extent practicable; and

(viii) if retrospective application required by paragraph 19(a) or (b) of IAS 8, 'Accounting policies, changes in accounting estimates and errors', is impracticable for a particular prior period, or for periods before those presented, the circumstances that led to the existence of that condition and a description of how and from when the change in accounting policy has been applied.

Financial statements of subsequent periods need not repeat these disclosures.

Voluntary change in accounting policy

8p29   7   When a voluntary change in accounting policy:

(a) has an effect on the current period or any prior period,

(b) would have an effect on that period except that it is impracticable to determine the amount of the adjustment, or

(c) might have an effect on future periods,
an entity discloses:

(i) the nature of the change in accounting policy;

(ii) the reasons why applying the new accounting policy provides reliable and more relevant information;

(iii) for the current period and each prior period presented, to the extent practicable, the amount of the adjustment:
- for each financial statement line item affected, and
- if IAS 33 applies to the entity, for basic and diluted earnings per share;

(iv) the amount of the adjustment relating to periods before those presented, to the extent practicable; and

(v) if retrospective application is impracticable for a particular prior period, or for periods before those presented, the circumstances that led to the existence of that condition and a description of how and from when the change in accounting policy has been applied.

Financial statements of subsequent periods need not repeat these disclosures.

(All amounts in C thousands unless otherwise stated)

Change during interim periods

1p112(c)   8   There is no longer an explicit requirement to disclose the financial effect of a change in accounting policy that was made during the final interim period on prior interim financial reports of the current annual reporting period. However, where the impact on prior interim reporting periods is significant, an entity should consider explaining this fact and the financial effect.

IFRSs issued but not yet effective

8p30   9   When an entity has not applied a new IFRS that has been issued but is not yet effective, it discloses:

    (a) this fact; and

    (b) known or reasonably estimable information relevant to assessing the possible impact that application of the new IFRS will have on the entity's financial statements in the period of initial application.

8p31   10   An entity considers disclosing:

    (a) the title of the new IFRS;

    (b) the nature of the impending change or changes in accounting policy;

    (c) the date by which application of the IFRS is required;

    (d) the date as at which it plans to apply it initially; and

    (e) either:
      (i) a discussion of the impact that initial application of the IFRS is expected to have on the entity's financial statements, or
      (ii) if that impact is not known or reasonably estimable, a statement to that effect.

    11   The disclosures in the paragraph above are made even if the impact on the entity is not expected to be material. However, there is no need to mention a standard or interpretation if it is clearly not applicable to the entity. For example, if the entity is not operating in the real estate industry, it does not need to refer to IFRIC 15, 'Agreements for the construction of real estates'. Where a pronouncement introduces a new accounting option that was not previously available, management explains whether and/or how it expects to use the option in future.

Disclosures not illustrated in IFRS GAAP plc financial statements

For disclosures relating to IAS 29, 'Financial reporting in hyperinflationary economies', IAS 41, 'Agriculture', and IFRS 6, 'Exploration for and evaluation of mineral resources', please refer to PricewaterhouseCoopers' *IFRS disclosure checklist 2010.*

(All amounts in C thousands unless otherwise stated)

3 Financial risk management

3.1 Financial risk factors

IFRS7p31 The group's activities expose it to a variety of financial risks: market risk (including currency risk, fair value interest rate risk, cash flow interest rate risk and price risk), credit risk and liquidity risk. The group's overall risk management programme focuses on the unpredictability of financial markets and seeks to minimise potential adverse effects on the group's financial performance. The group uses derivative financial instruments to hedge certain risk exposures.

Risk management is carried out by a central treasury department (group treasury) under policies approved by the board of directors. Group treasury identifies, evaluates and hedges financial risks in close co-operation with the group's operating units. The board provides written principles for overall risk management, as well as written policies covering specific areas, such as foreign exchange risk, interest rate risk, credit risk, use of derivative financial instruments and non-derivative financial instruments, and investment of excess liquidity.

(a) Market risk

(i) Foreign exchange risk

IFRS7 p33(a) The group operates internationally and is exposed to foreign exchange risk arising from various currency exposures, primarily with respect to the US dollar and the UK pound. Foreign exchange risk arises from future commercial transactions, recognised assets and liabilities and net investments in foreign operations.

IFRS7 p33(b), 22(c) Management has set up a policy to require group companies to manage their foreign exchange risk against their functional currency. The group companies are required to hedge their entire foreign exchange risk exposure with the group treasury. To manage their foreign exchange risk arising from future commercial transactions and recognised assets and liabilities, entities in the group use forward contracts, transacted with group treasury. Foreign exchange risk arises when future commercial transactions or recognised assets or liabilities are denominated in a currency that is not the entity's functional currency.

IFRS7 p22(c) The group treasury's risk management policy is to hedge between 75% and 100% of anticipated cash flows (mainly export sales and purchase of inventory) in each major foreign currency for the subsequent 12 months. Approximately 90% (2009: 95%) of projected sales in each major currency qualify as 'highly probable' forecast transactions for hedge accounting purposes.

IFRS7 p33(a)(b) IFRS7 p22(c) The group has certain investments in foreign operations, whose net assets are exposed to foreign currency translation risk. Currency exposure arising from the net assets of the group's foreign operations is managed primarily through borrowings denominated in the relevant foreign currencies.

IFRS7p40 IFRS7IG36 At 31 December 2010, if the currency had weakened/strengthened by 11% against the US dollar with all other variables held constant, post-tax profit for the year would have been C362 (2009: C51) higher/lower, mainly as a result of foreign exchange gains/losses on translation of US dollar-denominated trade receivables, financial assets at fair value through profit or loss, debt securities classified as available-for-sale and foreign exchange

(All amounts in C thousands unless otherwise stated)

losses/gains on translation of US dollar-denominated borrowings. Profit is more sensitive to movement in currency/US dollar exchange rates in 2010 than 2009 because of the increased amount of US dollar-denominated borrowings. Similarly, the impact on equity would have been C6,850 (2009: C6,650) higher/lower due to an increase in the volume of cash flow hedging in US dollars.

At 31 December 2010, if the currency had weakened/strengthened by 4% against the UK pound with all other variables held constant, post-tax profit for the year would have been C135 (2009: C172) lower/higher, mainly as a result of foreign exchange gains/losses on translation of UK pound-denominated trade receivables, financial assets at fair value through profit or loss, debt securities classified as available-for-sale and foreign exchange losses/gains on translation of UK pound-denominated borrowings.

(ii) Price risk

IFRS7 p33(a)(b) The group is exposed to equity securities price risk because of investments held by the group and classified on the consolidated balance sheet either as available-for-sale or at fair value through profit or loss. The group is not exposed to commodity price risk. To manage its price risk arising from investments in equity securities, the group diversifies its portfolio. Diversification of the portfolio is done in accordance with the limits set by the group.

The group's investments in equity of other entities that are publicly traded are included in one of the following three equity indexes: DAX equity index, Dow Jones equity index and FTSE 100 UK equity index.

IFRS7p40 IFRS7IG36 The table below summarises the impact of increases/decreases of the three equity indexes on the group's post-tax profit for the year and on equity. The analysis is based on the assumption that the equity indexes had increased/decreased by 5% with all other variables held constant and all the group's equity instruments moved according to the historical correlation with the index:

Index	Impact on post-tax profit in C 2010	2009	Impact on other components of equity in C 2010	2009
DAX	200	120	290	290
Dow Jones	150	120	200	70
FTSE 100 UK	60	30	160	150

Post-tax profit for the year would increase/decrease as a result of gains/losses on equity securities classified as at fair value through profit or loss. Other components of equity would increase/decrease as a result of gains/losses on equity securities classified as available for sale.

(iii) Cash flow and fair value interest rate risk

IFRS7 p33(a)(b), IFRS p22(c) The group's interest rate risk arises from long-term borrowings. Borrowings issued at variable rates expose the group to cash flow interest rate risk which is partially offset by cash held at variable rates. Borrowings issued at fixed rates expose the group to fair value interest rate risk. Group policy is to maintain approximately 60% of its borrowings in fixed rate instruments. During 2010 and 2009, the group's borrowings at variable rate were denominated in the Currency and the UK pound.

IFRS7 p22(b)(c) The group analyses its interest rate exposure on a dynamic basis. Various scenarios are simulated taking into consideration refinancing, renewal of existing positions, alternative financing and hedging. Based on these scenarios, the group calculates the impact on profit and loss of a defined interest rate shift. For each simulation, the same interest rate shift is used for all currencies. The scenarios are run only for liabilities that represent the major interest-bearing positions.

Based on the simulations performed, the impact on post tax profit of a 0.1% shift would be a maximum increase of C41 (2009: C37) or decrease of C34 (2009: C29), respectively. The simulation is done on a quarterly basis to verify that the maximum loss potential is within the limit given by the management.

IFRS7 p22(b)(c) Based on the various scenarios, the group manages its cash flow interest rate risk by using floating-to-fixed interest rate swaps. Such interest rate swaps have the economic effect of converting borrowings from floating rates to fixed rates. Generally, the group raises long-term borrowings at floating rates and swaps them into fixed rates that are lower than those available if the group borrowed at fixed rates directly. Under the interest rate swaps, the group agrees with other parties to exchange, at specified intervals (primarily quarterly), the difference between fixed contract rates and floating-rate interest amounts calculated by reference to the agreed notional amounts.

IFRS7 p22(b)(c) Occasionally the group also enters into fixed-to-floating interest rate swaps to hedge the fair value interest rate risk arising where it has borrowed at fixed rates in excess of the 60% target.

IFRS7p40 IFRS7IG36 At 31 December 2010, if interest rates on Currency-denominated borrowings had been 10 basis points higher/lower with all other variables held constant, post-tax profit for the year would have been C22 (2009: C21) lower/higher, mainly as a result of higher/lower interest expense on floating rate borrowings; other components of equity would have been C5 (2009: C3) lower/higher mainly as a result of a decrease/increase in the fair value of fixed rate financial assets classified as available for sale. At 31 December 2010, if interest rates on UK pound-denominated borrowings at that date had been 0.5% higher/lower with all other variables held constant, post-tax profit for the year would have been C57 (2009: C38) lower/higher, mainly as a result of higher/lower interest expense on floating rate borrowings; other components of equity would have been C6 (2009: C4) lower/higher mainly as a result of a decrease/increase in the fair value of fixed rate financial assets classified as available for sale.

(b) Credit risk

IFRS7 p33(a)(b) IFRS7 p34(a) Credit risk is managed on group basis, except for credit risk relating to accounts receivable balances. Each local entity is responsible for managing and analysing the credit risk for each of their new clients before standard payment and delivery terms and conditions are offered. Credit risk arises from cash and cash equivalents, derivative financial instruments and deposits with banks and financial institutions, as well as credit exposures to wholesale and retail customers, including outstanding receivables and committed transactions. For banks and financial institutions, only independently rated parties with a minimum rating of 'A' are accepted. If wholesale customers are independently rated, these ratings are used. If there is no independent rating, risk control assesses the credit quality of the customer, taking into account its financial position, past experience and other factors. Individual risk limits are set based on internal or external

(All amounts in C thousands unless otherwise stated)

ratings in accordance with limits set by the board. The utilisation of credit limits is regularly monitored. Sales to retail customers are settled in cash or using major credit cards. See note 9(b) for further disclosure on credit risk.

No credit limits were exceeded during the reporting period, and management does not expect any losses from non-performance by these counterparties.

(c) Liquidity risk

**IFRS7
p34(a)**
Cash flow forecasting is performed in the operating entities of the group in and aggregated by group finance. Group finance monitors rolling forecasts of the group's liquidity requirements to ensure it has sufficient cash to meet operational needs while maintaining sufficient headroom on its undrawn committed borrowing facilities (note 22) at all times so that the group does not breach borrowing limits or covenants (where applicable) on any of its borrowing facilities. Such forecasting takes into consideration the group's debt financing plans, covenant compliance, compliance with internal balance sheet ratio targets and, if applicable external regulatory or legal requirements – for example, currency restrictions.

**IFRS7p33,
39(c)
IFRS7B11E**
Surplus cash held by the operating entities over and above balance required for working capital management are transferred to the group treasury. Group treasury invests surplus cash in interest bearing current accounts, time deposits, money market deposits and marketable securities, choosing instruments with appropriate maturities or sufficient liquidity to provide sufficient head-room as determined by the above-mentioned forecasts. At the reporting date, the group held money market funds of C6, 312 (2009: C934) and other liquid assets of C321 (2009: C1,400) that are expected to readily generate cash inflows for managing liquidity risk.

**IFRS7
p39(a)(b)**
The table below analyses the group's non-derivative financial liabilities and net-settled derivative financial liabilities into relevant maturity groupings based on the remaining period at the balance sheet date to the contractual maturity date. Derivative financial liabilities are included in the analysis if their contractual maturities are essential for an understanding of the timing of the cash flows. The amounts disclosed in the table are the contractual undiscounted cash flows[1].

---

[1] IFRS7 p39(a)(b) The amounts included in the table are the contractual undiscounted cash flows, except for trading derivatives, which are included at their fair value (see below). As a result, these amounts will not reconcile to the amounts disclosed on the balance sheet except for short-term payables where discounting is not applied. Entities can choose to add a reconciling column and a final total that ties into the balance sheet, if they wish.

(All amounts in C thousands unless otherwise stated)

At 31 December 2010	Less than 3 months	Between 3 months and 1 year[1]	Between 1 and 2 years[1]	Between 2 and 5 years[1]	Over 5 years[1]
Borrowings (ex finance lease liabilities)	5,112	15,384	22,002	67,457	38,050
Finance lease liabilities	639	2,110	1,573	4,719	2,063
Trading and net settled derivative financial instruments (interest rate swaps)	280	–	10	116	41
Trade and other payables	12,543	3,125[2]	–	–	–
Financial guarantee contracts	21	–	–		
At 31 December 2009					
Borrowings (ex finance lease liability)	4,061	12,197	11,575	58,679	38,103
Finance lease liabilities	697	2,506	1,790	5,370	2,891
Trading and net settled derivative financial instruments (interest rate swaps)	317	–	15	81	50
Trade and other payables	9,214	2,304[2]	–	–	–
Financial guarantee contracts	10	–	–		

IFRS7
B10A(a)

Of the C67,457 disclosed in the 2010 borrowings time band 'Between 2 and 5 years' the company intends to repay C40,000 in the first quarter of 2011 (2009: nil).

IFRS7
p39(b)

The group's trading portfolio derivative instruments with a negative fair value have been included at their fair value of C 268 (2009: C298) within the less than three month time bucket. This is because the contractual maturities are not essential for an understanding of the timing of the cash flows These contracts are managed on a net-fair value basis rather than by maturity date. Net settled derivatives comprise interest rate swaps used by the group to manage the group's interest rate profile.

IFRS7
p39(b)

All of the non-trading group's gross settled derivative financial instruments are in hedge relationships and are due to settle within 12 months of the balance sheet date. These contracts require undiscounted contractual cash inflows of C78,756 (2009: C83,077) and undiscounted contractual cash outflows of C78,241 (2009: C83,366).

1p134,135,
IG10

3.2 Capital risk management

The group's objectives when managing capital are to safeguard the group's ability to continue as a going concern in order to provide returns for shareholders and benefits for other stakeholders and to maintain an optimal capital structure to reduce the cost of capital.

In order to maintain or adjust the capital structure, the group may adjust the amount of dividends paid to shareholders, return capital to shareholders, issue new shares or sell assets to reduce debt.

---

[1] The specific time-buckets presented are not mandated by the standard but are based on a choice by management based on how the business is managed. Sufficient time buckets should be provided to give sufficient granularity to provide the reader with an understanding of the entity's liquidity.
[2] The maturity analysis applies to financial instruments only and therefore statutory liabilities are not included.

(All amounts in C thousands unless otherwise stated)

Consistent with others in the industry, the group monitors capital on the basis of the gearing ratio. This ratio is calculated as net debt divided by total capital. Net debt is calculated as total borrowings (including 'current and non-current borrowings' as shown in the consolidated balance sheet) less cash and cash equivalents. Total capital is calculated as 'equity' as shown in the consolidated balance sheet plus net debt.

During 2010, the group's strategy, which was unchanged from 2009, was to maintain the gearing ratio within 45% to 50% and a BB credit rating. The BB credit rating has been maintained throughout the period. The gearing ratios at 31 December 2010 and 2009 were as follows:

	2010	2009
Total borrowings (note 22)	126,837	114,604
Less: cash and cash equivalents (note 15)	(17,928)	(34,062)
Net debt	108,909	80,542
Total equity	131,773	88,946
Total capital	240,682	169,488
Gearing ratio	45%	48%

The decrease in the gearing ratio during 2010 resulted primarily from the issue of share capital as part of the consideration for the acquisition of a subsidiary (notes 17 and 39).

3.3 Fair value estimation

The table below analyses financial instruments carried at fair value, by valuation method. The different levels have been defined as follows:

- Quoted prices (unadjusted) in active markets for identical assets or liabilities (level 1).

- Inputs other than quoted prices included within level 1 that are observable for the asset or liability, either directly (that is, as prices) or indirectly (that is, derived from prices) (level 2).

- Inputs for the asset or liability that are not based on observable market data (that is, unobservable inputs) (level 3).

IFRS7
p27B(a) The following table presents the group's assets and liabilities that are measured at fair value at 31 December 2010.

	Level 1	Level 2	Level 3	Total
Assets				
Financial assets at fair value through profit or loss				
– Trading derivatives	–	250	111	361
– Trading securities	11,820	–	–	11,820
Derivatives used for hedging	–	1,103	–	1,103
Available-for-sale financial assets				
– Equity securities	18,735	–	–	18,735
– Debt investments	288	347	–	635
Total assets	30,843	1,700	111	32,654

(All amounts in C thousands unless otherwise stated)

	Level 1	Level 2	Level 3	Total
Liabilities				
Financial liabilities at fair value through profit or loss				
– Trading derivatives	–	268	–	268
Derivatives used for hedging	–	327	–	327
Total liabilities	–	595	–	595

The following table presents the group's assets and liabilities that are measured at fair value at 31 December 2009.

	Level 1	Level 2	Level 3	Total
Assets				
Financial assets at fair value through profit or loss				
– Trading derivatives	–	321	–	321
– Trading securities	7,972	–	–	7,972
Derivatives used for hedging	–	875	–	875
Available-for-sale financial assets				
– Equity securities	14,646	–	–	14,646
– Debt investments	–	264	–	264
Total assets	22,618	1,460		24,078
Liabilities				
Financial liabilities at fair value through profit or loss				
– Trading derivatives	–	298	–	298
Derivatives used for hedging	–	449	–	449
Total liabilities	–	747	–	747

IFRS7p27   The fair value of financial instruments traded in active markets is based on quoted market prices at the balance sheet date. A market is regarded as active if quoted prices are readily and regularly available from an exchange, dealer, broker, industry group, pricing service, or regulatory agency, and those prices represent actual and regularly occurring market transactions on an arm's length basis. The quoted market price used for financial assets held by the group is the current bid price. These instruments are included in level 1. Instruments included in level 1 comprise primarily DAX, FTSE 100 and Dow Jones equity investments classified as trading securities or available for sale.

The fair value of financial instruments that are not traded in an active market (for example, over-the-counter derivatives) is determined by using valuation techniques. These valuation techniques maximise the use of observable market data where it is available and rely as little as possible on entity specific estimates. If all significant inputs required to fair value an instrument are observable, the instrument is included in level 2.

If one or more of the significant inputs is not based on observable market data, the instrument is included in level 3.

Specific valuation techniques used to value financial instruments include:

- Quoted market prices or dealer quotes for similar instruments.
- The fair value of interest rate swaps is calculated as the present value of the estimated future cash flows based on observable yield curves.
- The fair value of forward foreign exchange contracts is determined using forward exchange rates at the balance sheet date, with the resulting value discounted back to present value.
- Other techniques, such as discounted cash flow analysis, are used to determine fair value for the remaining financial instruments.

Note that all of the resulting fair value estimates are included in level 2 except for certain forward foreign exchange contracts explained below.

IFRS 7p27B(c) The following table presents the changes in level 3 instruments for the year ended 31 December 2010.

	Trading securities at fair value through profit or loss	Total
Opening balance	–	–
Transfers into level 3	115	115
Gains and losses recognised in profit or loss	(4)	(4)
Closing balance	111	111
Total gains or losses for the period included in profit or loss for assets held at the end of the reporting period	**(4)**	**(4)**

The following table presents the changes in level 3 instruments for the year ended 31 December 2009.

	Trading securities at fair value through profit or loss	Total
Opening balance	62	62
Settlements	(51)	(51)
Gains and losses recognised in profit or loss	(11)	(11)
Closing balance	–	–
Total gains or losses for the period included in profit or loss for assets held at the end of the reporting period	**(0)**	**(0)**

In 2010, the group transferred a held-for-trading forward foreign exchange contract from level 2 into level 3. This is because the counterparty for the derivative encountered significant financial difficulties, which resulted in a significant increase to the discount rate due to increased counterparty credit risk, which is not based on observable inputs.

IFRS7 p27B(e) If the change in the credit default rate would be shifted +/- 5% the impact on profit or loss would be C20.

Commentary – financial risk management

Accounting standard for presentation and disclosure of financial instruments

IFRS7p3 1 IFRS 7, 'Financial instruments: Disclosures', applies to all reporting entities and to all types of financial instruments except:

- Those interests in subsidiaries, associates and joint ventures that are accounted for under IAS 27, 'Consolidated and separate financial statements', IAS 28, 'Investments in associates', or IAS 31, 'Interests in joint ventures'. However, entities should apply IFRS 7 to an interest in a subsidiary, associate or joint venture that according to IAS 27, IAS 28 or IAS 31 is accounted for under IAS 39, 'Financial instruments: Recognition and measurement'. Entities should also apply IFRS 7 to all derivatives on interests in subsidiaries, associates or joint ventures unless the derivative meets the definition of an equity instrument in IAS 32.

- Employers' rights and obligations under employee benefit plans, to which IAS 19, 'Employee benefits', applies.

- Insurance contracts as defined in IFRS 4, 'Insurance contracts'. However, IFRS 7 applies to derivatives that are embedded in insurance contracts if IAS 39 requires the entity to account for them separately. It also applies to financial guarantee contracts if the issuer applies IAS 39 in recognising and measuring the contracts.

- Financial instruments, contracts and obligations under share-based payment transactions to which IFRS 2, 'Share-based payment', applies, except for contracts within the scope of paragraphs 5-7 of IAS 39, which are disclosed under IFRS 7.

- From 1 January 2009 puttable financial instruments that are required to be classified as equity instruments in accordance with paragraphs 16A and 16B or 16C and 16D of IAS 32 (revised).

Parent entity disclosures

IFRS7 2 Where applicable, all disclosure requirements outlined in IFRS 7 should be made for both the parent and consolidated entity. The relief from making parent entity disclosures, which was previously available under IAS 30, 'Disclosures in the financial statements of banks and similar financial institutions', and IAS 32, has not been retained in IFRS 7.

Classes of financial instrument

IFRS7p6, 3 Where IFRS 7 requires disclosures by class of financial instrument, the entity
B1-B3 groups its financial instruments into classes that are appropriate to the nature of the information disclosed and that take into account the characteristics of those financial instruments. The entity should provide sufficient information to permit reconciliation to the line items presented in the balance sheet. Guidance on classes of financial instruments and the level of required disclosures is provided in appendix B of IFRS 7.

(All amounts in C thousands unless otherwise stated)

Level of detail and selection of assumptions – information through the eyes of management

IFRS7
p34(a)

4 The disclosures in relation to an entity's financial risk management should reflect the information provided internally to key management personnel. As such, the disclosures that will be provided by an entity, their level of detail and the underlying assumptions used will vary greatly from entity to entity. The disclosures in this illustrative financial statement are only one example of the kind of information that may be disclosed; the entity should consider carefully what may be appropriate in its individual circumstances.

Nature and extent of risks arising from financial instruments

IFRS7
p31, 32

5 The financial statement should include qualitative and quantitative disclosures that enable users to evaluate the nature and extent of risks arising from financial instruments to which the entity is exposed at the end of the reporting period. These risks typically include, but are not limited to, credit risk, liquidity risk and market risk.

Qualitative disclosures

IFRS7p33

6 An entity should disclose for each type of risk:

(a) the exposures to the risk and how they arise;

(b) the entity's objectives, policies and processes for managing the risk and the methods used to measure the risk; and

(c) any changes in (a) or (b) from the previous period.

Quantitative disclosures

IFRS7
p34(a)(c)

7 An entity should provide for each type of risk, summary quantitative data on risk exposure at the end of the reporting period, based on information provided internally to key management personnel and any concentrations of risk. This information can be presented in narrative form as is done on pages x to x of this publication. Alternatively, entities could provide the data in a table that sets out the impact of each major risk on each type of financial instruments. This table could also be a useful tool for compiling the information that should be disclosed under paragraph 34 of IFRS 7.

IFRS7
p34(b)

8 If not already provided as part of the summary quantitative data, the entity should also provide the information in paragraphs 9-15 below, unless the risk is not material.

Credit risk

IFRS7p36, 37

9 For each class of financial instrument, the entity should disclose:

(a) the maximum exposure to credit risk and any related collateral held;

(b) information about the credit quality of financial assets that are neither past due nor impaired;

(All amounts in C thousands unless otherwise stated)

(c) the carrying amount of financial assets that would otherwise be past due or impaired whose terms have been renegotiated;

(d) an analysis of the age of financial assets that are past due but not impaired; and

(e) an analysis of financial assets that are individually determined to be impaired including the factors in determining that they are impaired.

Liquidity risk

IFRS7 p34(a), 39

10 Information about liquidity risk shall be provided by way of:

(a) a maturity analysis for non-derivative financial liabilities (including issued financial guarantee contracts) that shows the remaining contractual maturities;

(b) a maturity analysis for derivative financial liabilities (see paragraph 12 below for details); and

(c) a description of how the entity manages the liquidity risk inherent in (a) and (b).

IFRS7 B11F

11 In describing how liquidity risk is being managed, an entity should consider discussing whether it:

(a) has committed borrowing facilities or other lines of credit that it can access to meet liquidity needs;

(b) holds deposits at central banks to meet liquidity needs;

(c) has very diverse funding sources;

(d) has significant concentrations of liquidity risk in either its assets or its funding sources;

(e) has internal control processes and contingency plans for managing liquidity risk;

(f) has instruments that include accelerated repayment terms (for example, on the downgrade of the entity's credit rating);

(g) has instruments that could require the posting of collateral (for example, margin calls for derivatives);

(h) has instruments that allow the entity to choose whether it settles its financial liabilities by delivering cash (or another financial asset) or by delivering its own shares; and

(i) has instruments that are subject to master netting agreements.

Maturity analysis

IFRS7 B11B

12 The maturity analysis for derivative financial liabilities should disclose the remaining contractual maturities if these maturities are essential for an understanding of the timing of the cash flows. For example, this will be the case for interest rate swaps in a cash flow hedge of a variable rate financial asset or liability and for all loan commitments. Where the remaining contractual maturities

(All amounts in C thousands unless otherwise stated)

are not essential for an understanding of the timing of the cash flows, the expected maturities may be disclosed instead.

IFRS7p39, B11D 13 For derivative financial instruments where gross cash flows are exchanged and contractual maturities are essential to understanding, the maturity analysis should disclose the contractual amounts that are to be exchanged on a gross basis. The amount disclosed should be the amount expected to be paid in future periods, determined by reference to the conditions existing at the end of the reporting period. However, IFRS 7 does not specify whether current or forward rates should be used. We therefore recommend that entities explain which approach has been chosen. This approach should be applied consistently.

IFRS7B11 14 The specific time buckets presented are not mandated by the standard but are based on what is reported internally to the key management personnel. The entity uses judgement to determine the appropriate number of time bands.

IFRS7 B11D 15 If the amounts included in the maturity tables are the contractual undiscounted cash flows, these amounts will not reconcile to the amounts disclosed on the balance sheet for borrowings, derivative financial instruments and trade and other payables. Entities can choose to add a column with the carrying amounts that ties into the balance sheet and a reconciling column if they so wish, but this is not mandatory.

IFRS7 B10A 16 If an outflow of cash could occur either significantly earlier than indicated or be for significantly different amounts from those indicated in the entity's disclosures about its exposure to liquidity risk, the entity should state that fact and provide quantitative information that enables users of its financial statements to evaluate the extent of this risk. This disclosure is not necessary if that information is included in the contractual maturity analysis.

Financing arrangements

IFRS7 p39(c) 17 Committed borrowing facilities are a major element of liquidity management. Entities should therefore consider providing information about their undrawn facilities. IAS 7, 'Statements of cash flows', also recommends disclosure of undrawn borrowing facilities that may be available for future operating activities and to settle capital commitments, indicating any restrictions on the use of these facilities.

Market risk

IFRS7 p40(a)(b) 18 Entities should disclose a sensitivity analysis for each type of market risk (currency, interest rate and other price risk) to which an entity is exposed at the end of the reporting period, showing how profit or loss and equity would have been affected by 'reasonably possible' changes in the relevant risk variable, as well as the methods and assumptions used in preparing such an analysis.

IFRS7 p40(c) 19 If there have been any changes in methods and assumptions from the previous period, this should be disclosed, together with the reasons for the change.

Foreign currency risk

IFRS7B23 20 Foreign currency risk can only arise on financial instruments that are denominated in a currency other than the functional currency in which they are measured. Translation related risks are therefore not included in the assessment of the entity's exposure to currency risks. Translation exposures arise from financial and non-financial items held by an entity (for example, a subsidiary) with a functional currency different from the group's presentation currency. However, foreign currency denominated inter-company receivables and payables that do not form part of a net investment in a foreign operation are included in the sensitivity analysis for foreign currency risks, because even though the balances eliminate in the consolidated balance sheet, the effect on profit or loss of their revaluation under IAS 21 is not fully eliminated.

Interest rate risk

21 Sensitivity to changes in interest rates is relevant to financial assets or financial liabilities bearing floating interest rates due to the risk that future cash flows will fluctuate. However, sensitivity will also be relevant to fixed rate financial assets and financial liabilities that are re-measured to fair value.

Fair value disclosures

Financial instruments carried at other than fair value

IFRS7p25, 29 22 An entity should disclose the fair value for each class of financial assets and financial liabilities (see paragraph 3 above) in a way that permits it to be compared with its carrying amount. Fair values do not need to be disclosed for the following:

(a) when the carrying amount is a reasonable approximation of fair value;

(b) investments in equity instruments (and derivatives linked to such equity instruments) that do not have a quoted market price in an active market and that are measured at cost in accordance with IAS 39 because their fair value cannot be measured reliably; and

(c) A contract containing a discretionary participation feature (as described in IFRS 4, 'Insurance contracts') where the fair value of that feature cannot be measured reliably.

23 The information about the fair values can be provided either in a combined financial instruments note or in the individual notes. However, fair values should be separately disclosed for each class of financial instrument (see paragraph 3 above), which means that each line item in the table would have to be broken down into individual classes. For that reason, IFRS GAAP plc has chosen to provide the information in the relevant notes.

Methods and assumptions in determining fair value

IFRS7p27 24 An entity should disclose for each class of financial instruments (see paragraph 3 above) the methods and, when a valuation technique is used, the assumptions applied in determining fair values. Examples of assumptions that should be disclosed are assumptions relating to prepayment rates, rates of estimated credit losses, interest rates or discount rates. If the entity has changed a valuation technique, that fact and the reason for the change should also be disclosed.

Financial instruments measured at cost where fair value cannot be determined reliably

IFRS7p30 25 If the fair value of investments in unquoted equity instruments, derivatives linked to such equity instruments or a contract containing a discretionary participation feature (as described in IFRS 4, 'Insurance contracts') cannot be measured reliably, the entity should disclose:

    (a) the fact that fair value information has not been disclosed because it cannot be measured reliably;

    (b) a description of the financial instruments, their carrying amount and an explanation of why fair value cannot be measured reliably;

    (c) information about the market for the instruments;

    (d) information about whether and how the entity intends to dispose of the financial instruments; and

    (e) if the instruments are subsequently derecognised, that fact, their carrying amount at the time of derecognition and the amount of gain or loss recognised.

Fair value measurements recognised in the balance sheet

IFRS7 p27B 26 For fair value measurements recognised in the balance sheet, the entity should also disclose for each class of financial instruments:

    (a) the level in the fair value hierarchy into which the fair value measurements are categorised;

    (b) any significant transfers between level 1 and level 2 of the fair value hierarchy and the reasons for those transfers;

    (c) for fair value measurements in level 3 of the hierarchy, a reconciliation from the beginning balances to the ending balances, showing separately changes during the period attributable to the following:

        (i) total gains or losses for the period recognised in profit or loss, together with a description of where they are presented in the statement of comprehensive income or the income statement (as applicable);

        (ii) total gains or losses recognised in other comprehensive income;

        (iii) purchases, sales issues and settlements (each type disclosed separately); and

        (iv) transfers into or out of level 3 and the reasons for those transfers;

    (d) the amount of total gains or losses for the period included in profit or loss that are attributable to gains or losses relating to assets and liabilities held at the end of the reporting period, together with a description of where the gains and losses are presented in the statement of comprehensive income or the income statement (as applicable); and

    (e) for fair value measurements in level 3, if changing one or more of the inputs to reasonably possible alternative assumptions would change fair value

(All amounts in C thousands unless otherwise stated)

significantly, that fact, the effect of those changes and how the effect was calculated.

IFRS7 p27A 27 Entities should classify fair value measurements using a fair value hierarchy that reflects the significance of the inputs used in making the measurements. The fair value hierarchy should have the following levels:

(a) Level 1: quoted prices (unadjusted) in active markets for identical assets or liabilities.

(b) Level 2: inputs other than quoted prices that are observable for the asset or liability, either directly (for example, as prices) or indirectly (for example, derived from prices).

(c) Level 3: inputs for the asset or liability that are not based on observable market data.

The appropriate level is determined on the basis of the lowest level input that is significant to the fair value measurement.

Additional information where quantitative data about risk exposure is unrepresentative

IFRS7p35, 42 28 If the quantitative data disclosed under paragraphs 7, 9, 10 and 14 above is unrepresentative of the entity's exposure to risk during the period, the entity should provide further information that is representative. If the sensitivity analyses are unrepresentative of a risk inherent in a financial instrument (for example, where the year end exposure does not reflect the exposure during the year), the entity should disclose that fact and the reason why the sensitivity analyses are unrepresentative.

4 Critical accounting estimates and judgements

Estimates and judgements are continually evaluated and are based on historical experience and other factors, including expectations of future events that are believed to be reasonable under the circumstances.

1p125 **4.1 Critical accounting estimates and assumptions**

The group makes estimates and assumptions concerning the future. The resulting accounting estimates will, by definition, seldom equal the related actual results. The estimates and assumptions that have a significant risk of causing a material adjustment to the carrying amounts of assets and liabilities within the next financial year are addressed below.

(a) Estimated impairment of goodwill

The group tests annually whether goodwill has suffered any impairment, in accordance with the accounting policy stated in note 2.6. The recoverable amounts of cash-generating units have been determined based on value-in-use calculations. These calculations require the use of estimates (note 7).

(All amounts in C thousands unless otherwise stated)

1p129,
36p134
(f)(i)-(iii)
An impairment charge of C4,650 arose in the wholesale CGU in Step-land (included in the Russian operating segment) during the course of the 2010 year, resulting in the carrying amount of the CGU being written down to its recoverable amount. If the budgeted gross margin used in the value-in-use calculation for the wholesale CGU in Step-land had been 10% lower than management's estimates at 31 December 2010 (for example, 46% instead of 56%), the group would have recognised a further impairment of goodwill by C100 and would need to reduce the carrying value of property, plant and equipment by C300.

If the estimated cost of capital used in determining the pre-tax discount rate for the wholesale CGU in Step-land had been 1% higher than management's estimates (for example, 13.8% instead of 12.8%), the group would have recognised a further impairment against goodwill of C300.

(b) Income taxes

The group is subject to income taxes in numerous jurisdictions. Significant judgement is required in determining the worldwide provision for income taxes. There are many transactions and calculations for which the ultimate tax determination is uncertain. The group recognises liabilities for anticipated tax audit issues based on estimates of whether additional taxes will be due. Where the final tax outcome of these matters is different from the amounts that were initially recorded, such differences will impact the current and deferred income tax assets and liabilities in the period in which such determination is made.

Were the actual final outcome (on the judgement areas) of expected cash flows to differ by 10% from management's estimates, the group would need to:

- increase the income tax liability by C120 and the deferred tax liability by C230, if unfavourable; or

- decrease the income tax liability by C110 and the deferred tax liability by C215, if favourable.

(c) Fair value of derivatives and other financial instruments

IFRS7p27 The fair value of financial instruments that are not traded in an active market (for example, over-the-counter derivatives) is determined by using valuation techniques. The group uses its judgement to select a variety of methods and make assumptions that are mainly based on market conditions existing at the end of each reporting period. The group has used discounted cash flow analysis for various available-for-sale financial assets that are not traded in active markets.

The carrying amount of available-for-sale financial assets would be an estimated C12 lower or C15 higher were the discount rate used in the discount cash flow analysis to differ by 10% from management's estimates.

(d) Revenue recognition

The group uses the percentage-of-completion method in accounting for its fixed-price contracts to deliver design services. Use of the percentage-of-completion method requires the group to estimate the services performed to date as a proportion of the total services to be performed. Were the proportion of services performed to total services to be performed to differ by 10% from management's estimates, the amount of revenue

(All amounts in C thousands unless otherwise stated)

recognised in the year would be increased by C1175 if the proportion performed were increased, or would be decreased by C1160 if the proportion performed were decreased.

(e) Pension benefits

The present value of the pension obligations depends on a number of factors that are determined on an actuarial basis using a number of assumptions. The assumptions used in determining the net cost (income) for pensions include the discount rate. Any changes in these assumptions will impact the carrying amount of pension obligations.

The group determines the appropriate discount rate at the end of each year. This is the interest rate that should be used to determine the present value of estimated future cash outflows expected to be required to settle the pension obligations. In determining the appropriate discount rate, the group considers the interest rates of high-quality corporate bonds that are denominated in the currency in which the benefits will be paid and that have terms to maturity approximating the terms of the related pension obligation.

Other key assumptions for pension obligations are based in part on current market conditions. Additional information is disclosed in note 24.

Were the discount rate used to differ by 10% from management's estimates, the carrying amount of pension obligations would be an estimated C425 lower or C450 higher.

1p122   **4.2 Critical judgements in applying the entity's accounting policies**

(a) Revenue recognition

The group has recognised revenue amounting to C950 for sales of goods to L&Co in the UK during 2010. The buyer has the right to return the goods if their customers are dissatisfied. The group believes that, based on past experience with similar sales, the dissatisfaction rate will not exceed 3%. The group has, therefore, recognised revenue on this transaction with a corresponding provision against revenue for estimated returns. If the estimate changes by 1%, revenue will be reduced/increased by C10.

(b) Impairment of available-for-sale equity investments

The group follows the guidance of IAS 39 to determine when an available-for-sale equity investment is impaired. This determination requires significant judgement. In making this judgement, the group evaluates, among other factors, the duration and extent to which the fair value of an investment is less than its cost; and the financial health of and short-term business outlook for the investee, including factors such as industry and sector performance, changes in technology and operational and financing cash flow.

If all of the declines in fair value below cost were considered significant or prolonged, the group would suffer an additional loss of C1,300 in its 2010 financial statements, being the transfer of the accumulated fair value adjustments recognised in equity on the impaired available-for-sale financial assets to the income statement.

(All amounts in C thousands unless otherwise stated)

5 Segment information

IFRS8 **p22(a)**	Management has determined the operating segments based on the reports reviewed by the strategic steering committee that are used to make strategic decisions.
IFRS8 **p22(a)**	The committee considers the business from both a geographic and product perspective. Geographically, management considers the performance of wholesale in the UK, US, China, Russia and Europe. The UK and US are further segregated into retail and wholesale, as all of the retail business is located in these two geographic areas.
IFRS8 **p22(a)**	Although the China segment does not meet the quantitative thresholds required by IFRS 8, management has concluded that this segment should be reported, as it is closely monitored by the strategic steering committee as a potential growth region and is expected to materially contribute to group revenue in the future.
IFRS8 **p22(b)**	The reportable operating segments derive their revenue primarily from the manufacture and sale of shoes on a wholesale basis, with the exception of the UK and US, which are further segregated into retail shoe and leather goods sales.
IFRS8p16	Other services included within the European and UK segments include the sale of design services and goods transportation services to other shoe manufacturers. These are not included within the reportable operating segments, as they are not included in the reports provided to the strategic steering committee. The wholesale shoe revenue from the Central American region, mainly Mexico, is also not included, as this information is not reviewed by the strategic steering committee. The results of these operations are included in the 'all other segments' column.
IFRS8 **p27(b), 28**	The strategic steering committee assesses the performance of the operating segments based on a measure of adjusted EBITDA. This measurement basis excludes the effects of non-recurring expenditure from the operating segments such as restructuring costs, legal expenses and goodwill impairments when the impairment is the result of an isolated, non-recurring event. The measure also excludes the effects of equity-settled share-based payments and unrealised gains/losses on financial instruments. Interest income and expenditure are not allocated to segments, as this type of activity is driven by the central treasury function, which manages the cash position of the group. Since the strategic steering committee reviews adjusted EBITDA, the results of discontinued operations are not included in the measure of adjusted EBITDA.

(All amounts in C thousands unless otherwise stated)

The segment information provided to the strategic steering committee for the reportable segments for the year ended 31 December 2010 is as follows:

		UK		US					All other	
		Wholesale	Retail	Wholesale	Retail	Russia	China	Europe	segments	Total
IFRS8 p23(b)	Total segment revenue	46,638	43,257	28,820	42,672	26,273	5,818	40,273	13,155	246,906
	Inter-segment revenue	(11,403)	–	(7,364)	–	(5,255)	(1,164)	(8,055)	(2,631)	(35,872)
IFRS8p23, p33(a)	**Revenue from external customers**	**35,235**	**43,257**	**21,456**	**42,672**	**21,018**	**4,654**	**32,218**	**10,524**	**211,034**
IFRS8p23	Adjusted EBITDA	17,298	9,550	9,146	9,686	12,322	2,323	16,003	3,504	79,832
IFRS8 p23(e)	Depreciation and amortisation	(3,226)	(3,830)	(1,894)	(3,789)	(2,454)	(386)	(2,706)	(269)	(18,554)
IFRS8 p23(i), 36p129(a)	Goodwill impairment	–	–	–	–	(4,650)	–	–	–	(4,650)
IFRS8 p23(i)	Restructuring costs	–	–	–	–	(1,986)	–	–	–	(1,986)
IFRS8 p23(h)	Income tax expense	(2,550)	(2,780)	(1,395)	(3,040)	(1,591)	(365)	(2,490)	(400)	(14,611)
IFRS8 p23(g)	Share of profit/(loss) from associates	200	–	–	–	–	–	(389)	15	(174)
IFRS8p23	**Total assets**	**46,957**	**46,197**	**27,313**	**45,529**	**22,659**	**6,226**	**42,636**	**13,374**	**250,891**
	Total assets includes:									
IFRS8 p24(a)	Investments in associates	7,207	–	–	–	–	–	–	6,166	13,373
IFRS8 p24(b)	Additions to non-current assets (other than financial instruments and deferred tax assets)	–	35,543	–	39,817	–	11,380	–	1,500	88,204
IFRS8p23	**Total liabilities[1]**	**3,207**	**6,700**	**5,900**	**3,500**	**700**	**1,200**	**1,500**	**2,140**	**24,847**

[1] The measure of liabilities has been disclosed for each reportable segment as is regularly provided to the chief operating decision-maker.

(All amounts in C thousands unless otherwise stated)

The segment information for the year ended 31 December 2009 is as follows:

| | | UK | | US | | | | | All other | |
		Wholesale	Retail	Wholesale	Retail	Russia	China	Europe	segments	Total
IFRS8 p23(b)	Total segment revenue	57,284	1,682	33,990	2,390	8,778	3,209	26,223	5,724	139,280
	Inter-segment revenue	(11,457)	–	(6,798)	–	(1,756)	(642)	(5,245)	(1,022)	(26,920)
IFRS8 p23(a), 33(a)	**Revenue from external customers**	**45,827**	**1,682**	**27,192**	**2,390**	**7,022**	**2,567**	**20,978**	**4,702**	**112,360**
IFRS8p23	Adjusted EBITDA	17,183	800	10,369	1,298	3,471	1,506	10,755	1,682	47,064
IFRS8 p23(e)	Depreciation and amortisation	(3,801)	(201)	(2,448)	(199)	(453)	(286)	(2,701)	(138)	(10,227)
IFRS8 p23(h)	Income tax expense	(2,772)	(650)	(1,407)	(489)	(509)	(150)	(2,201)	(687)	(8,865)
IFRS8 p23(g)	Share of profit/(loss) from associates	155	–	–	–	–	–	–	(10)	145
IFRS8p23	**Total assets**	**43,320**	**9,580**	**32,967**	**8,550**	**5,067**	**20,899**	**36,450**	**49,270**	**206,103**
	Total assets includes:									
IFRS8 p24(a)	Investments in associates	7,050	–	–	–	–	–	–	6,194	13,244
IFRS8 p24(b)	Additions to non-current assets (other than financial instruments and deferred tax assets)	–	47	–	46	–	2,971	–	3,678	6,742
IFRS8p23	**Total liabilities**[8]	**4,221**	**55**	**6,054**	**–**	**250**	**800**	**2,537**	**3,464**	**17,381**

IFRS 8 has been amended so that a measure of segment assets is only required to be disclosed if the measure is regularly provided to the chief operating decision-maker. The amendment is effective for periods beginning on or after 1 January 2010.

During 2009, retail did not qualify as a reportable operating segment. However, with the acquisition in 2010 of ABC Group (note 39), retail qualifies as a reportable operating segment; the comparatives are therefore consistent in this regard.

IFRS8 p23(i) See note 7 for details of the impairment of goodwill of C4,650 in the Russian operating segment in 2010 relating to the decision to reduce manufacturing output. There has been no further impact on the measurement of the company's assets and liabilities. There was no impairment charge or restructuring costs recognised in 2009.

IFRS8 p27(a) Sales between segments are carried out at arm's length. The revenue from external parties reported to the strategic steering committee is measured in a manner consistent with that in the income statement.

(All amounts in C thousands unless otherwise stated)

**IFRS8
p28(b)**

A reconciliation of adjusted EBITDA to profit before tax and discontinued operations is provided as follows:

	2010	2009
Adjusted EBITDA for reportable segments	76,328	45,382
Other segments EBITDA	3,504	1,682
Total segments	79,832	47,064
Depreciation	(17,754)	(9,662)
Amortisation	(800)	(565)
Restructuring costs	(1,986)	–
Legal expenses	(737)	(855)
Goodwill impairment	(4,650)	–
Unrealised financial instrument gains	102	101
Share options granted to directors and employees	(690)	(820)
Finance costs – net	(6,443)	(10,588)
Other	802	243
Profit before tax and discontinued operations	**47,676**	**24,918**

The amounts provided to the strategic steering committee with respect to total assets are measured in a manner consistent with that of the financial statements. These assets are allocated based on the operations of the segment and the physical location of the asset.

Investment in shares (classified as available-for-sale financial assets or financial assets at fair value through profit or loss) held by the group are not considered to be segment assets but rather are managed by the treasury function.

**IFRS8
p27(c)**

'Reportable segments' assets are reconciled to total assets as follows:

	2010	2009
Segment assets for reportable segments	198,416	156,833
Other segments assets	61,285	49,270
Unallocated:		
Deferred tax	3,520	3,321
Available-for-sale financial assets	19,370	14,910
Financial assets at fair value through the profit and loss	11,820	7,972
Derivatives	1,464	1,196
Assets of disposal group classified as held for resale	3,333	–
Total assets per the balance sheet	**299,208**	**233,502**

The amounts provided to the strategic steering committee with respect to total liabilities are measured in a manner consistent with that of the financial statements. These liabilities are allocated based on the operations of the segment.

The group's interest-bearing liabilities are not considered to be segment liabilities but rather are managed by the treasury function.

(All amounts in C thousands unless otherwise stated)

IFRS8 p27(d) 'Reportable segments' liabilities are reconciled to total liabilities as follows:

	2010	2009
Segment liabilities for reportable segments	22,707	13,917
Other segments liabilities	2,140	3,464
Unallocated:		
– Deferred tax	12,370	9,053
– Current tax	2,566	2,771
– Current borrowings	11,716	18,258
– Non-current borrowings	115,121	96,346
– Derivatives	595	747
– Liabilities of disposal group classified as held for resale	220	–
Total liabilities per the balance sheet	**167,435**	**144,556**

IFRS8 p27(f) Due to the European operations utilising excess capacity in certain Russian assets that are geographically close to the European region, a portion of the depreciation charge of C197 (2009: C50) relating to the Russian assets has been allocated to the European segment to take account of this.

IFRS8p32 Revenues from external customers are derived from the sales of shoes on a wholesale and retail basis. The breakdown of retail and wholesale results are provided above. The wholesale of shoes relates only to the group's own brand, Footsy Tootsy. The retail sales comprise not only the group's own brand, but other major retail shoe brands.

Breakdown of the revenue from all services is as follows:

Analysis of revenue by category	2010	2009
Sales of goods	202,884	104,495
Revenue from services	8,000	7,800
Royalty income	150	65

IFRS8 p33(a) The entity is domiciled in the UK. The result of its revenue from external customers in the UK is C50,697 (2009: C48,951), and the total of revenue from external customers from other countries is C160,337 (2009: C63,409). The breakdown of the major component of the total of revenue from external customers from other countries is disclosed above.

IFRS8 p33(b) The total of non-current assets other than financial instruments and deferred tax assets (there are no employment benefit assets and rights arising under insurance contracts) located in the UK is C49,696 (2009: C39,567), and the total of these non-current assets located in other countries is C146,762 (2008: C93,299).

IFRS8p34 Revenues of approximately C32,023 (2009: C28,034) are derived from a single external customer. These revenues are attributable to the US retail and wholesale segments.

(All amounts in C thousands unless otherwise stated)

6 Property, plant and equipment

1p78(a)		Land and buildings	Vehicles and machinery	Furniture, fittings and equipment	Total
16p73(d)	**At 1 January 2009**				
	Cost or valuation	39,664	71,072	20,025	130,761
	Accumulated depreciation	(2,333)	(17,524)	(3,690)	(23,547)
	Net book amount	**37,331**	**53,548**	**16,335**	**107,214**
16p73(e)	**Year ended 31 December 2009**				
	Opening net book amount	37,331	53,548	16,335	107,214
16p73 (e)(viii)	Exchange differences	(381)	(703)	(423)	(1,507)
16p73(e)(iv)	Revaluation surplus (note 20)	1,133	–	–	1,133
16p73(e)(i)	Additions	1,588	2,970	1,484	6,042
16p73(e)(ix)	Disposals (note 36)	–	(2,607)	(380)	(2,987)
16p73(e)(vii)	Depreciation charge (note 29)	(636)	(4,186)	(4,840)	(9,662)
	Closing net book amount	**39,035**	**49,022**	**12,176**	**100,233**
16p73(d)	**At 31 December 2009**				
	Cost or valuation	40,232	68,125	20,026	128,383
	Accumulated depreciation	(1,197)	(19,103)	(7,850)	(28,150)
	Net book amount	**39,035**	**49,022**	**12,176**	**100,233**
	Year ended 31 December 2010				
16p73(e)	Opening net book amount	39,035	49,022	12,176	100,233
16p73 (e)(viii)	Exchange differences	1,601	1,280	342	3,223
16p73 (e)(iii)	Acquisition of subsidiary (note 39)	49,072	5,513	13,199	67,784
16p73(e)(i)	Additions	7,126	427	2,202	9,755
16p73(e)(ix)	Disposals (note 36)	(2,000)	(3,729)	(608)	(6,337)
16p73 (e)(vii)	Depreciation charge (note 29)	(3,545)	(4,768)	(9,441)	(17,754)
IFRS5p38	Transferred to disposal group classified as held for sale	(341)	(1,222)	–	(1,563)
	Closing net book amount	**90,948**	**46,523**	**17,870**	**155,341**
16p73(d)	**At 31 December 2010**				
	Cost or valuation	95,129	58,268	26,927	180,324
	Accumulated depreciation	(4,181)	(11,745)	(9,057)	(24,983)
	Net book amount	**90,948**	**46,523**	**17,870**	**155,341**

DV   Property, plant and equipment transferred to the disposal group classified as held for sale amounts to C1,563 and relates to assets that are used by Shoes Limited (part of the wholesale segment). See note 16 for further details regarding the disposal group held for sale.

16p77(a-d) 1p79(b)   The group's land and buildings were last revalued on 1 January 2009 by independent valuers. Valuations were made on the basis of recent market transactions on arm's length terms. The revaluation surplus net of applicable deferred income taxes was credited to other comprehensive income and is shown in 'other reserves in shareholders' equity (note 20).

(All amounts in C thousands unless otherwise stated)

DV, 1p104 Depreciation expense of C8,054 (2009: C5,252) has been charged in 'cost of goods sold', C5,568 (2009: C2,410) in 'selling and marketing costs' and C4,132 (2009: C2,000) in 'administrative expenses'.

17p35(c) Lease rentals amounting to C1,172 (2009: C895) and C9,432 (2009: C7,605) relating to the lease of machinery and property, respectively, are included in the income statement (note 29).

16p77(e) If land and buildings were stated on the historical cost basis, the amounts would be as follows:

	2010	2009
Cost	93,079	37,684
Accumulated depreciation	(6,131)	(2,197)
Net book amount	86,948	35,487

16p74(a) Bank borrowings are secured on land and buildings for the value of C37,680 (2009: C51,306) (note 22).

Vehicles and machinery includes the following amounts where the group is a lessee under a finance lease:

	2010	2009
Cost – capitalised finance leases	13,996	14,074
Accumulated depreciation	(5,150)	(3,926)
Net book amount	8,846	10,148

17p35(d) The group leases various vehicles and machinery under non-cancellable finance lease agreements. The lease terms are between three and 15 years, and ownership of the assets lie within the group.

(All amounts in C thousands unless otherwise stated)

7 Intangible assets

		Goodwill	Trademarks and licences	Contractual customer Relationships	Internally generated software development costs	Total
38p118(c)	**At 1 January 2009**					
IFRS3p75(a)	Cost	12,546	8,301	–	1,455	22,302
IFRS3 p75(a)	Accumulated amortisation and impairment	–	(330)	–	(510)	(840)
	Net book amount	12,546	7,971	–	945	21,462
38p118(e)	**Year ended 31 December 2009**					
IFRS3p74	Opening net book amount	12,546	7,971	–	945	21,462
IFRS3p75(f)	Exchange differences	(546)	(306)	–	(45)	(897)
38p118(e)(i)	Additions	–	700	–	–	700
	Amortisation charge (note 29a)	–	(365)	–	(200)	(565)
	Closing net book amount	12,000	8,000	–	700	20,700
	At 31 December 2009					
38p118(c)	Cost	12,000	8,710	–	1,400	22,110
IFRS3p75(a) IFRS3p75(a)	Accumulated amortisation and impairment	–	(710)	–	(700)	(1,410)
	Net book amount	12,000	8,000	–	700	20,700
38p118(e)	**Year ended 31 December 2010**					
IFRS3p74	Opening net book amount	12,000	8,000	–	700	20,700
IFRS3p75(f)	Exchange differences	341	96	–	134	571
38p118(e)(i)	Additions	–	684	–	2,366	3,050
IFRS3p75(b)	Acquisition of subsidiary (note 39)	4,501	3,000	1,000	–	8,501
IFRS3p75(e)	Impairment charge (note 29a)	(4,650)	–	–	–	(4,650)
	Amortisation charge (note 29a)	–	(402)	(278)	(120)	(800)
IFRS5p38	Transferred to disposal group classified as held for sale	–	(1,000)	–	(100)	(1,100)
	Closing net book amount	12,192	10,378	722	2,980	26,272
38p118(c)	**At 31 December 2010**					
IFRS3p75(h)	Cost	16,842	11,480	1,000	3,800	33,122
IFRS3 p75(h)	Accumulated amortisation and impairment	(4,650)	(1,102)	(278)	(820)	(6,850)
	Net book amount	12,192	10,378	722	2,980	26,272

36p126(a) The carrying amount of the segment has been reduced to its recoverable amount through recognition of an impairment loss against goodwill. This loss has been included in 'cost of goods sold' in the income statement.

38p118(d) Amortisation of C40 (2009: C100) is included in the 'cost of goods sold' the income statement; C680 (2009: C365) in 'distribution costs; and C80 (2009: C100) in 'administrative expenses'.

Additions of internally generated software development cost includes C75 (2009: nil) of interest capitalised at an average borrowing rate of 8.0%.

(All amounts in C thousands unless otherwise stated)

DV The trademark transferred to the disposal group classified as held for sale relates to the Shoes Limited trademark (part of the wholesale segment), which was previously recognised by the group on the acquisition of the entity in 2006. A further net book amount of C100 transferred to the disposal group relates to software that was specifically developed for Shoes Limited. See note 16 for further details regarding the disposal group held for sale.

Impairment tests for goodwill

36p134(d) Goodwill is allocated to the group's cash-generating units (CGUs) identified according to operating segment.

An operating segment-level summary of the goodwill allocation is presented below.

36p134(a)

	2010			2009		
	Wholesale	**Retail**	**Total**	**Wholesale**	**Retail**	**Total**
UK	6,250	1,051	7,301	5,970	120	6,090
US	325	2,501	2,826	125	30	155
Europe	1,609	–	1,609	705	–	705
Russia	100	–	100	4,750	–	4,750
China	146	–	146	100	–	100
All other segments	210	–	210	200	–	200
	8,640	3,552	12,192	11,850	150	12,000

During 2009, retail did not qualify as a reportable operating segment. However, with the acquisition in 2010 of ABC Group (note 39), retail qualifies as a separate reportable operating segment; the comparatives have therefore been restated to be consistent.

36p130(e)
36p134(c)
36p134
(d)(iii)
The recoverable amount of all CGUs has been determined based on value-in-use calculations. These calculations use pre-tax cash flow projections based on financial budgets approved by management covering a five-year period. Cash flows beyond the five-year period are extrapolated using the estimated growth rates stated below. The growth rate does not exceed the long-term average growth rate for the shoe business in which the CGU operates.

36p134
(d)(i)
The key assumptions used for value-in-use calculations in 2010 are as follows[1]:

		Wholesale						Retail	
		UK	**US**	**Europe**	**Russia**	**China**	**All Other Segments**	**UK**	**US**
36p134(d) 36p134	Gross margin[2]	60.0%	59.0%	60.0%	55.5%	57.0%	56.0%	58.0%	56.0%
(d)(iv) 36p134 (d)(v)	Growth rate[3]	1.8%	1.8%	1.8%	2.0%	2.0%	1.9%	1.1%	1.3%
36p130(g)	Discount rate[4]	10.5%	10.0%	10.7%	12.8%	12.0%	12.8%	11.5%	11.0%

[1] Disclosure of long-term growth rates and discount rates is required. Other key assumptions are required to be disclosed and quantified where a reasonably possible change in the key assumption would remove any remaining headroom in the impairment calculation. Otherwise the additional disclosures are encouraged but not required.
[2] Budgeted gross margin.
[3] Weighted average growth rate used to extrapolate cash flows beyond the budget period.
[4] Pre-tax discount rate applied to the cash flow projections.

(All amounts in C thousands unless otherwise stated)

36p134(d)(i) The key assumptions used for value-in-use calculations in 2009 are as follows[1]:

		Wholesale				Retail		
						All Other		
		UK	US	Europe	Russia	China	Segments	UK	US
36p134(d)	Gross margin[2]	62.5%	61.0%	62.5%	58.0%	59.0%	58.0%	60.0%	58.0%
36p134 (d)(iv)	Growth rate[3]	2.0%	2.0%	2.0%	2.5%	2.5%	2.3%	1.3%	1.5%
36p134 (d)(v) 36p130(g)	Discount rate[4]	10.0%	9.5%	10.1%	11.5%	11.0%	11.0%	11.0%	10.4%

36p134 (d)(ii) These assumptions have been used for the analysis of each CGU within the operating segment.

36p134 (d)(ii) Management determined budgeted gross margin based on past performance and its expectations of market development. The weighted average growth rates used are consistent with the forecasts included in industry reports. The discount rates used are pre-tax and reflect specific risks relating to the relevant operating segments.

36p130(a) The impairment charge arose in a wholesale CGU in Step-land (included in the Russian operating segment) following a decision in early 2010 to reduce the manufacturing output allocated to these operations (note 25). This was a result of a redefinition of the group's allocation of manufacturing volumes across all CGUs in order to benefit from advantageous market conditions. Following this decision, the group reassessed the depreciation policies of its property, plant and equipment in this country and estimated that their useful lives would not be affected. No class of asset other than goodwill was impaired. The pre-tax discount rate used in the previous years for the wholesale CGU in Step-land was 11.5%.

36p134(f) In European Wholesale, the recoverable amount calculated based on value in use exceeded carrying value by C205,000. A reduction in gross margin of 1.5%, a fall in growth rate to 1.6% or a rise in discount rate to 10.9% would remove the remaining headroom.

8 Investments in associates

		2010	2009
	At 1 January	**13,244**	13,008
	Acquisition of subsidiary (note 39)	389	–
28p38	Share of (loss)/profit[5]	(174)	145
	Exchange differences (note 20)	(74)	105
	Other equity movements: available-for-sale reserve (note 20)	(12)	(14)
28p38	**At 31 December**	**13,373**	13,244

28p37(b) The group's share of the results of its principal associates, all of which are unlisted, and its aggregated assets (including goodwill) and liabilities, are as follows[6]:

[1] Disclosure of long-term growth rates and discount rates is required. Other key assumptions are required to be disclosed and quantified where a reasonably possible change in the key assumption would remove any remaining headroom in the impairment calculation. Otherwise the additional disclosures are encouraged but not required.
[2] Budgeted gross margin.
[3] Weighted average growth rate used to extrapolate cash flows beyond the budget period.
[4] Pre-tax discount rate applied to the cash flow projections.
[5] Share of profit/(loss) is after tax and Non-controlling interest in associates (IG14).
[6] An alternative method of presentation is to give the gross amounts of assets and liabilities (excluding goodwill) of associates and not of the group's share.

(All amounts in C thousands unless otherwise stated)

Name	Country of incorporation	Assets	Liabilities	Revenues	Profit/(Loss)	% interest held
2009						
Alfa Limited	Cyprus	27,345	20,295	35,012	155	25
Beta SA	Greece	9,573	3,379	10,001	(10)	30
		36,918	23,674	45,013	145	
2010						
Alfa Limited	Cyprus	32,381	25,174	31,123	200	25
Beta SA	Greece	12,115	5,949	9,001	15	30
Delta Limited	UK	15,278	15,278	25,741	(389)	42
		59,774	**46,401**	**65,865**	**(174)**	

28p37(g) The group has not recognised losses amounting to C20 (2009: nil) for Delta Limited. The accumulated losses not recognised were C20 (2009: nil).

9a Financial instruments by category

IFRS7p6

	Loans and receivables	Assets at fair value through the profit and loss	Derivatives used for hedging	Available-for-sale	Total
31 December 2010					
Assets as per balance sheet					
Available-for-sale financial assets	–	–	–	19,370	19,370
Derivative financial instruments	–	361	1,103	–	1,464
Trade and other receivables excluding pre-payments[1]	20,787	–	–	–	20,787
Financial assets at fair value through profit or loss	–	11,820	–	–	11,820
Cash and cash equivalents	17,928	–	–	–	17,928
Total	**38,715**	**12,181**	**1,103**	**19,370**	**71,369**

	Liabilities at fair value through the profit and loss	Derivatives used for hedging	Other financial liabilities at amortised cost	Total
Liabilities as per balance sheet				
Borrowings (excluding finance lease liabilities)	–	–	117,839	117,839
Finance lease liabilities			8,998	8,998
Derivative financial instruments	268	327	–	595
Trade and other payables excluding statutory liabilities[2]	–	–	15,668	15,668
Total	**268**	**327**	**142,505**	**143,100**

[1] Pre-payments are excluded from the trade and other receivables balance, as this analysis is required only for financial instruments.

[2] Statutory liabilities are excluded from the trade payables balance, as this analysis is required only for financial instruments.

(All amounts in C thousands unless otherwise stated)

	Loans and receivables	Assets at fair value through the profit and loss	Derivatives used for hedging	Available for sale	Total
31 December 2009					
Assets as per balance sheet					
Available-for-sale financial assets	–	–	–	14,910	14,910
Derivative financial instruments	–	321	875	–	1,196
Trade and other receivables excluding prepayments[1]	18,536	–	–	–	18,536
Financial assets at fair value through profit or loss	–	7,972	–	–	7,972
Cash and cash equivalents	34,062	–	–	–	34,062
Total	**52,598**	**8,293**	**875**	**14,910**	**76,676**

	Liabilities at fair value through the profit and loss	Derivatives used for hedging	Other financial liabilities	Total
Liabilities as per balance sheet				
Borrowings (excluding finance lease liabilities)	–	–	104,006	104,006
Finance lease liabilities			10,598	10,598
Derivative financial instruments	298	449	–	747
Trade and other payables excluding statutory liabilities[2]	–	–	11,518	11,518
Total	**298**	**449**	**126,122**	**126,869**

[1] Pre-payments are excluded from the trade and other receivables balance, as this analysis is required only for financial instruments.
[2] Statutory liabilities are excluded from the trade payables balance, as this analysis is required only for financial instruments.

(All amounts in C thousands unless otherwise stated)

9b Credit quality of financial assets

IFRS7
p36(c)

The credit quality of financial assets that are neither past due nor impaired can be assessed by reference to external credit ratings (if available) or to historical information about counterparty default rates:

	2010	2009
Trade receivables		
Counterparties with external credit rating (Moody's)		
A	**5,895**	5,757
BB	**3,200**	3,980
BBB	**1,500**	1,830
	10,595	11,567
Counterparties without external credit rating		
Group 1	**750**	555
Group 2	**4,832**	3,596
Group 3	**1,770**	1,312
	7,352	5,463
Total unimpaired trade receivables	**17,947**	17,030
Cash at bank and short-term bank deposits[1]		
AAA	**8,790**	15,890
AA	**5,300**	7,840
A	**6,789**	11,257
	20,879	34,987

DV

Available-for-sale debt securities		
AA	**347**	264
	347	264

DV

Derivative financial assets		
AAA	**1,046**	826
AA	**418**	370
	1,464	1,196
Loans to related parties		
Group 2	**2,501**	1,301
Group 3	**167**	87
	2,668	1,388

- Group 1 – new customers/related parties (less than 6 months).

- Group 2 – existing customers/related parties (more than 6 months) with no defaults in the past.

- Group 3 – existing customers/related parties (more than 6 months) with some defaults in the past. All defaults were fully recovered.

Note: None of the financial assets that are fully performing has been renegotiated in the last year. None of the loans to related parties is past due but not impaired.

[1] The rest of the balance sheet item 'cash and cash equivalents' is cash in hand.

(All amounts in C thousands unless otherwise stated)

10 Available-for-sale financial assets

		2010	2009
	At 1 January	**14,910**	14,096
	Exchange differences	**646**	(435)
	Acquisition of subsidiary (note 39)	**473**	–
	Additions	**4,037**	1,126
	Disposals	**(1,256)**	–
	Net gains/(losses) transfer from equity (note 20)	**(130)**	(152)
1p79(b)	Net gains/(losses) transfer to equity (note 20)	**690**	275
	At 31 December	**19,370**	14,910
1p66	Less: non-current portion	**(17,420)**	(14,910)
1p66	**Current portion**	**1,950**	–

IFRS7
p20(a)(ii)   The group removed profits of C217 (2009: C187) and losses C87 (2009: C35) from equity into the income statement. Losses in the amount of C55 (2009: C20) were due to impairments.

IFRS7p,31, Available-for-sale financial assets include the following:
34

	2010	2009
Listed securities:		
– Equity securities – UK	**8,335**	8,300
– Equity securities – Europe	**5,850**	2,086
– Equity securities – US	**4,550**	4,260
– Debentures with fixed interest of 6.5% and maturity date of		
27 August 2012	**210**	–
– Non-cumulative 9.0% non-redeemable preference shares	**78**	–
Unlisted securities:		
– Debt securities with fixed interest ranging from 6.3% to		
6.5% and maturity dates between July 2011 and May 2013	**347**	264
	19,370	14,910

IFRS7
p34(c)   Available-for-sale financial assets are denominated in the following currencies:

	2010	2009
UK pound	**7,897**	8,121
Euro	**5,850**	2,086
US dollar	**4,550**	4,260
Other currencies	**1,073**	443
	19,370	14,910

IFRS7p27   The fair values of unlisted securities are based on cash flows discounted using a rate based on the market interest rate and the risk premium specific to the unlisted securities (2010: 6%; 2009: 5.8%).

IFRS7
p36(a)   The maximum exposure to credit risk at the reporting date is the carrying value of the debt securities classified as available for sale.

IFRS7
p36(c)   None of these financial assets is either past due or impaired.

(All amounts in C thousands unless otherwise stated)

11 Derivative financial instruments

		2010		2009	
		Assets	**Liabilities**	**Assets**	**Liabilities**
IFRS7 p22(a)(b)	Interest rate swaps – cash flow hedges	**351**	**110**	220	121
IFRS7 p22(a)(b)	Interest rate swaps – fair value hedges	**57**	**37**	49	11
IFRS7 p22(a)(b)	Forward foreign exchange contracts – cash flow hedges	**695**	**180**	606	317
	Forward foreign exchange contracts – held-for-trading	**361**	**268**	321	298
	Total	**1,464**	**595**	1,196	747
1p66	Less non-current portion:				
	Interest rate swaps – cash flow hedges	**345**	**100**	200	120
	Interest rate swaps – fair value hedges	**50**	**35**	45	9
		395	**135**	245	129
1p66	**Current portion**	**1,069**	**460**	951	618

Trading derivatives are classified as a current asset or liability. The full fair value of a hedging derivative is classified as a non-current asset or liability if the remaining maturity of the hedged item is more than 12 months and, as a current asset or liability, if the maturity of the hedged item is less than 12 months.

IFRS7p24 The ineffective portion recognised in the profit or loss that arises from fair value hedges amounts to a loss of C1 (2009: loss of C1) (note 26). The ineffective portion recognised in the profit or loss that arises from cash flow hedges amounts to a gain of C17 (2009: a gain of C14) (note 26). There was no ineffectiveness to be recorded from net investment in foreign entity hedges.

(a) Forward foreign exchange contracts

IFRS7p31 The notional principal amounts of the outstanding forward foreign exchange contracts at 31 December 2010 were C92,370 (2009: C89,689).

IFRS7 p23(a) 39p100, 1p79(b) The hedged highly probable forecast transactions denominated in foreign currency are expected to occur at various dates during the next 12 months. Gains and losses recognised in the hedging reserve in equity (note 20) on forward foreign exchange contracts as of 31 December 2010 are recognised in the income statement in the period or periods during which the hedged forecast transaction affects the income statement. This is generally within 12 months of the end of the reporting period unless the gain or loss is included in the initial amount recognised for the purchase of fixed assets, in which case recognition is over the lifetime of the asset (five to 10 years).

(b) Interest rate swaps

IFRS7p31 The notional principal amounts of the outstanding interest rate swap contracts at 31 December 2010 were C4,314 (2009: C3,839).

IFRS7 p23(a) At 31 December 2010, the fixed interest rates vary from 6.9% to 7.4% (2009: 6.7% to 7.2%), and the main floating rates are EURIBOR and LIBOR. Gains and losses recognised in the hedging reserve in equity (note 20) on interest rate swap contracts as of

(All amounts in C thousands unless otherwise stated)

31 December 2010 will be continuously released to the income statement within finance cost until the repayment of the bank borrowings (note 22).

(c) Hedge of net investment in foreign entity

IFRS7p22,
1p79(b) A proportion of the group's US dollar-denominated borrowing amounting to C321 (2009: C321) is designated as a hedge of the net investment in the group's US subsidiary. The fair value of the borrowing at 31 December 2010 was C370 (2009: C279). The foreign exchange loss of C45 (2009: gain of C40) on translation of the borrowing to currency at the end of the reporting period is recognised in other comprehensive income .

IFRS7
p36(a) The maximum exposure to credit risk at the reporting date is the fair value of the derivative assets in the balance sheet.

12 Trade and other receivables

		2010	2009
IFRS7p36, **1p77**	Trade receivables	**18,174**	17,172
	Less: provision for impairment of trade receivables	**(109)**	(70)
1p78(b)	Trade receivables – net	**18,065**	17,102
1p78(b)	Prepayments	**1,300**	1,146
1p78(b), **24p17(b)**	Receivables from related parties (note 40)	**54**	46
1p78(b), **24p17(b)**	Loans to related parties (note 40)	**2,668**	1,388
		22,087	19,682
1p78(b), **1p66**	Less non-current portion: loans to related parties	**(2,322)**	(1,352)
1p66	**Current portion**	**19,765**	18,330

All non-current receivables are due within five years from the end of the reporting period.

IFRS7p25 The fair values of trade and other receivables are as follows:

	2010	2009
Trade receivables	**18,065**	17,172
Receivables from related parties	**54**	46
Loans to related parties	**2,722**	1,398
	20,841	18,616

IFRS7p27 The fair values of loans to related parties are based on cash flows discounted using a rate based on the borrowings rate of 7.5% (2009: 7.2%). The discount rate equals to LIBOR plus appropriate credit rating.

24p17(b)(i) The effective interest rates on non-current receivables were as follows:

	2010	2009
Loans to related parties (note 40)	**6.5-7.0%**	6.5-7.0%

(All amounts in C thousands unless otherwise stated)

IFRS7p14 Certain European subsidiaries of the group transferred receivable balances amounting to C1,014 to a bank in exchange for cash during the year ended 31 December 2010. The transaction has been accounted for as a collateralised borrowing (note 22). In case the entities default under the loan agreement, the bank has the right to receive the cash flows from the receivables transferred. Without default, the entities will collect the receivables and allocate new receivables as collateral.

DV As of 31 December 2010, trade receivables of C17,670 (2009: C16,595) were fully performing.

IFRS7 p37(a) As of 31 December 2010, trade receivables of C277 (2009: C207) were past due but not impaired. These relate to a number of independent customers for whom there is no recent history of default. The ageing analysis of these trade receivables is as follows:

	2010	2009
Up to 3 months	177	108
3 to 6 months	100	99
	277	207

IFRS7 p37(b) As of 31 December 2010, trade receivables of C227 (2009: C142) were impaired and provided for. The amount of the provision was C109 as of 31 December 2010 (2009: C70). The individually impaired receivables mainly relate to wholesalers, which are in unexpectedly difficult economic situations. It was assessed that a portion of the receivables is expected to be recovered. The ageing of these receivables is as follows:

	2010	2009
3 to 6 months	177	108
Over 6 months	50	34
	227	142

The carrying amounts of the group's trade and other receivables are denominated in the following currencies:

	2010	2009
UK pound	9,846	8,669
Euros	5,987	6,365
US dollar	6,098	4,500
Other currencies	156	148
	22,087	19,682

IFRS7p16 Movements on the group provision for impairment of trade receivables are as follows:

	2010	2009
At 1 January	70	38
Provision for receivables impairment	74	61
Receivables written off during the year as uncollectible	(28)	(23)
Unused amounts reversed	(10)	(8)
Unwind of discount	3	2
At 31 December	109	70

IFRS7 p20(e)

(All amounts in C thousands unless otherwise stated)

The creation and release of provision for impaired receivables have been included in 'other expenses' in the income statement (note 29). Unwind of discount is included in 'finance costs' in the income statement (note 31). Amounts charged to the allowance account are generally written off, when there is no expectation of recovering additional cash.

IFRS7p16 The other classes within trade and other receivables do not contain impaired assets.

IFRS7 p36(a) The maximum exposure to credit risk at the reporting date is the carrying value of each class of receivable mentioned above. The group does not hold any collateral as security.

13 Inventories

	2010	2009
2p36(b), 1p78(c)		
Raw materials	7,622	7,612
Work in progress	1,810	1,796
Finished goods[1]	15,268	8,774
	24,700	18,182

2p36(d), 38 The cost of inventories recognised as expense and included in 'cost of sales' amounted to C60,252 (2009: C29,545).

2p36(f)(g) The group reversed C603 of a previous inventory write-down in July 2010. The group has sold all the goods that were written down to an independent retailer in Australia at original cost. The amount reversed has been included in 'cost of sales' in the income statement.

14 Financial assets at fair value through profit or loss

	2010	2009
IFRS7p8(a), 31, 34(c) Listed securities – held for trading		
– Equity securities – UK	5,850	3,560
– Equity securities – Europe	4,250	3,540
—Equity securities – US	1,720	872
	11,820	7,972

7p15 Financial assets at fair value through profit or loss are presented within 'operating activities' as part of changes in working capital in the statement of cash flows (note 36).

Changes in fair values of financial assets at fair value through profit or loss are recorded in 'other (losses)/gains – net' in the income statement (note 26).

IFRS7p27 The fair value of all equity securities is based on their current bid prices in an active market.

[1] Separate disclosure of finished goods at fair value less cost to sell is required, where applicable.

(All amounts in C thousands unless otherwise stated)

15 Cash and cash equivalents

	2010	2009
Cash at bank and on hand	8,398	28,648
Short-term bank deposits	9,530	5,414
Cash and cash equivalents (excluding bank overdrafts)	17,928	34,062

7p45   Cash and cash equivalents include the following for the purposes of the statement of cash flows:

	2010	2009
Cash and cash equivalents	17,928	34,062
Bank overdrafts (note 22)	(2,650)	(6,464)
Cash and cash equivalents	15,278	27,598

7p8 is shown beside the "Bank overdrafts (note 22)" line.

16 Non-current assets held for sale and discontinued operations

IFRS5p41 (a)(b)(d)   The assets and liabilities related to company Shoes Limited (part of the wholesale segment) have been presented as held for sale following the approval of the group's management and shareholders on 23 September 2010 to sell company Shoes Limited in the UK. The completion date for the transaction is expected by May 2011.

	2010	2009
IFRS5p33(c) Operating cash flows[1]	300	190
IFRS5p33(c) Investing cash flows[1]	(103)	(20)
IFRS5p33(c) Financing cash flows[1]	(295)	(66)
Total cash flows	(98)	104

IFRS5p38   *(a) Assets of disposal group classified as held for sale*

	2010	2009
Property, plant and equipment	1,563	–
Intangible assets	1,100	–
Inventory	442	–
Other current assets	228	–
Total	3,333	–

[1] Under this approach, the entity presents the statement of cash flows as if no discontinued operation has occurred and makes the required IFRS 5 para 33 disclosures in the notes. It would also be acceptable to present the three categories separately on the face of the statement of cash flows and present the line-by-line breakdown of the categories, either in the notes or on the face of the statement of cash flows. It would not be acceptable to present all cash flows from discontinued operations in one line either as investing or operating activity.

IFRS GAAP plc – Illustrative corporate consolidated financial statements 2010

(All amounts in C thousands unless otherwise stated)

IFRS5p38 *(b) Liabilities of disposal group classified as held for sale*

	2010	2009
Trade and other payables	104	–
Other current liabilities	20	–
Provisions	96	–
Total	**220**	**–**

IFRS5p38 *(c) Cumulative income or expense recognised in other comprehensive income relating to disposal group classified as held for sale*

	2010	2009
Foreign exchange translation adjustments[1]	–	–
Total	**–**	**–**

IFRS5p33 (b) Analysis of the result of discontinued operations, and the result recognised on the re-measurement of assets or disposal group, is as follows[2]:

	2010	2009
Revenue	1,200	1,150
Expenses	(960)	(950)
Profit before tax of discontinued operations	240	200
12p81(h)(ii) Tax	(96)	(80)
Profit after tax of discontinued operations	**144**	**120**
Pre-tax gain/(loss) recognised on the re-measurement of assets of disposal group	(73)	–
12p81(h)(ii) Tax	29	–
After tax gain/(loss) recognised on the re-measurement of assets of disposal group	(44)	–
Profit for the year from discontinued operations	**100**	**120**

---

[1] IFRS 5 requires the separate presentation of any cumulative income or expense recognised in other comprehensive income relating to a non-current asset (or disposal group) classified as held for sale. There are no items recognised in equity relating to the disposal group classified as held-for-sale, but the line items are shown for illustrative purposes.
[2] These disclosures can also be given on the face of the primary financial statements.

(All amounts in C thousands unless otherwise stated)

Fair value estimation

The following table presents the group's assets and liabilities that are measured at fair value at 31 December 2010.

**IFRS7
p27B(a)**

	Level 1	Level 2	Level 3	Total balance
Assets				
Financial assets at fair value through profit or loss				
– Trading derivatives	–	4.9	–	4.9
Derivatives used for hedging	–	15.8	–	15.8
Available-for-sale financial assets				
– Equity securities	459.3	–	–	459.3
– Debt investments	39.2	–	24.6	63.8
Total assets	**498.5**	**20.7**	**24.6**	**543.8**
Liabilities				
Financial liabilities at fair value through profit or loss				
– Trading derivatives	–	2.2	–	2.2
Derivatives used for hedging	–	13.6	–	13.6
Total liabilities	–	**15.8**	–	**15.8**

The following table presents the group's assets and liabilities that are measured at fair value at 31 December 2009.

**IFRS7
p27B(a)**

	Level 1	Level 2	Level 3	Total balance
Assets				
Financial assets at fair value through profit or loss				
– Trading derivatives		3.1		3.1
Derivatives used for hedging		4.0		4.0
Available-for-sale financial assets				
– Equity securities	377.0			377.0
– Debt investments	21.1	–	11.9	33.0
Total assets	**398.1**	**7.1**	**11.9**	**417.1**
Liabilities				
Financial liabilities at fair value through profit or loss				
– Trading derivatives		3.3		3.3
Derivatives used for hedging		13.8		13.8
Total liabilities		**17.1**		**17.1**

The fair value of financial instruments traded in active markets is based on quoted market prices at the balance sheet date. A market is regarded as active if quoted prices are readily and regularly available from an exchange, dealer, broker, industry group, pricing service, or regulatory agency, and those prices represent actual and regularly occurring market transactions on an arm's length basis. The quoted market price used for financial assets held by the group is the current bid price. These instruments are included in level 1. Instruments included in level 1 comprise listed equity investments classified as available for sale.

(All amounts in C thousands unless otherwise stated)

IFRS7p27 The fair value of financial instruments that are not traded in an active market (for example, over-the-counter derivatives) is determined by using valuation techniques. These valuation techniques maximise the use of observable market data where it is available and rely as little as possible on entity specific estimates. If all significant inputs required to fair value an instrument are observable, the instrument is included in level 2.

If one or more of the significant inputs is not based on observable market data, the instrument would be included in level 3.

The following table presents the changes in level 3 instruments for the year ended 31 December 2010.

IFRS7 p27B(c)	**Available for sale – Unlisted debt securities Total balance**
Opening balance	11.9
Transfers into level 3	–
Additions	9.7
Gains and losses recognised in the statement of total recognised gains and losses	3
Closing balance	**24.6**

The following table presents the changes in level 3 instruments for the year ended 31 December 2009.

IFRS7 p27B(c)	**Available for sale – Unlisted debt securities Total balance**
Opening balance	–
Additions	11.9
Gains and losses recognised in the statement of total recognised gains and losses	–
Closing balance	**11.9**

(All amounts in C thousands unless otherwise stated)

<table>
<tr><td>1p79</td><td colspan="5">17 Share capital and premium</td></tr>
</table>

	Number of shares (thousands)	Ordinary shares	Share premium	Total
At 1 January 2009	20,000	20,000	10,424	30,424
Employee share option scheme:				
– Proceeds from shares issued	1,000	1,000	70	1,070
At 31 December 2009	21,000	21,000	10,494	31,494
Employee share option scheme:				
– Proceeds from shares issued	750	750	200	950
Acquisition of subsidiary (note 39)	3,550	3,550	6,450	10,000
At 31 December 2010	**25,300**	**25,300**	**17,144**	**42,444**

Row references (left margin):
- 1p106 (d)(iii) — – Proceeds from shares issued (2009)
- 1p106 (d)(iii) — – Proceeds from shares issued (2010)
- IFRS3 p67(d)(ii) — Acquisition of subsidiary (note 39)
- 1p79(a) — At 31 December 2010

1p79(a) The company acquired 875,000 of its own shares through purchases on the EuroMoney stock exchange on 18 April 2010. The total amount paid to acquire the shares, net of income tax, was C2,564 and has been deducted from retained earnings[1] within shareholders' equity (note 19). The shares are held as 'treasury shares'. The company has the right to re-issue[2] these shares at a later date. All shares issued by the company were fully paid.

The group issued 3,550,000 shares on 1 March 2010 (14.0% of the total ordinary share capital issued) to the shareholders of ABC group as part of the purchase consideration for 70% of its ordinary share capital. The ordinary shares issued have the same rights as the other shares in issue. The fair value of the shares issued amounted to C10.05 million (C2.83 per share). The related transaction costs amounting to C50 have been netted off with the deemed proceeds.

The company reissued 500,000 treasury shares for a total consideration of C1,500 on 15 January 2010.

18 Share-based payment

IFRS2 p45(a) Share options are granted to directors and to selected employees. The exercise price of the granted options is equal to the market price of the shares less 15% on the date of the grant. Options are conditional on the employee completing three years' service (the vesting period). The options are exercisable starting three years from the grant date, subject to the group achieving its target growth in earnings per share over the period of inflation plus 4%; the options have a contractual option term of five years. The group has no legal or constructive obligation to repurchase or settle the options in cash.

---

[1] The accounting treatment of treasury shares should be recorded in accordance with local company law and practice. Treasury shares may be disclosed separately on the balance sheet or deducted from retained earnings or a specific reserve.
[2] Depending on local Company Law, the company could have the right to resell the treasury shares.

(All amounts in C thousands unless otherwise stated)

Movements in the number of share options outstanding and their related weighted average exercise prices are as follows:

		2010		2009	
		Average exercise price in C per share	Options (thousands)	Average exercise price in C per share	Options (thousands)
IFRS2 p45(b)(i)	At 1 January	1.73	4,744	1.29	4,150
IFRS2 p45(b)(ii)	Granted	2.95	964	2.38	1,827
IFRS2 p45(b)(iii)	Forfeited	–	–	2.00	(200)
IFRS2 p45(b)(iv)	Exercised	1.28	(750)	1.08	(1,000)
IFRS2 p45(b)(v)	Expired	2.30	(125)	0.80	(33)
IFRS2p45 (b)(vi)	At 31 December	2.03	4,833	1.73	4,744

IFRS2p45 (b)(vii), IFRS2 p45(c) — Out of the 4,833,000 outstanding options (2009: 4,744,000 options), 400,000 options (2009: 600,000) were exercisable. Options exercised in 2010 resulted in 750,000 shares (2009: 1,000,000 shares) being issued at a weighted average price of C1.28 each (2009: C1.08 each). The related weighted average share price at the time of exercise was C2.85 (2009: C2.65) per share. The related transaction costs amounting to C10 (2009: C10) have been netted off with the proceeds received.

IFRS2 p45(d) — Share options outstanding at the end of the year have the following expiry date and exercise prices:

Expiry date – 1 July	Exercise price in C per share	Shares 2010	2009
2010	1.10	–	500
2011	1.20	800	900
2012	1.35	1,075	1,250
2013	2.00	217	267
2014	2.38	1,777	1,827
2015	2.95	964	–
		4,833	4,744

IFRS2p46 IFRS2 p47(a) — The weighted average fair value of options granted during the period determined using the Black-Scholes valuation model was C0.86 per option (2009: C0.66). The significant inputs into the model were weighted average share price of C3.47 (2009: C2.80) at the grant date, exercise price shown above, volatility of 30% (2009: 27%), dividend yield of 4.3% (2009: 3.5%), an expected option life of three years (2009: 3 years) and an annual risk-free interest rate of 5% (2009: 4%). The volatility measured at the standard deviation of continuously compounded share returns is based on statistical analysis of daily share prices over the last three years. See note 30a for the total expense recognised in the income statement for share options granted to directors and employees.

(All amounts in C thousands unless otherwise stated)

33p71(e)
10p21,
22(f)
On 1 January 2011, 1,200,000 share options were granted to directors and employees with an exercise price set at the market share prices less 15% on that date of C3.20 per share (share price: C3.68) (expiry date: 31 December 2015).

19 Retained earnings

1p106(d)	At 1 January 2009	48,470
	Profit for the year	15,512
1p106(d)	Dividends paid relating to 2008	(15,736)
IFRS2p50	Value of employee services[1]	822
16p41	Depreciation transfer on land and buildings net of tax	87
12p68C	Tax credit relating to share option scheme	20
19p93A	Actuarial loss on post employment benefit obligations net of tax	(494)
	At 31 December 2009	**48,681**
1p106(d)	At 1 January 2010	48,681
	Profit for the year	30,617
1p106(d)	Dividends relating to 2009	(10,102)
IFRS2p50	Value of employee services[1]	690
16p41	Depreciation transfer on land and buildings net of tax	100
12p68C	Tax credit relating to share option scheme	30
1p106(d)	Purchase of treasury shares[2]	(2,564)
19p93A **12p81** **(a),(b)**	Actuarial loss on post employment benefit obligations net of tax	–
	Impact of change in Euravian tax rate on deferred tax[3]	(10)
	At 31 December 2010	**67,442**

[1] The credit entry to equity in respect of the IFRS 2 charge should be recorded in accordance with local company law and practice. This may be a specific reserve, retained earnings or share capital.
[2] The accounting treatment of treasury shares should be recorded in accordance with local company law and practice. Treasury shares may be disclosed separately on the balance sheet or deducted from retained earnings or a specific reserve.
[3] Solely for illustrative purposes, a change in Euravian tax rates has been assumed to have taken place in 2010. i UK Companies with 31 December 2010 year ends will need to consider the impact of the reduction in tax rates in the Finance (No.2) Act 2010.

(All amounts in C thousands unless otherwise stated)

20 Other reserves

		Convertible bond	Land and buildings revalu-ation[1]	Hedging reserve	Available-for-sale Invest-ments	Trans-lation	Total
	At 1 January 2009	–	1,152	65	1,320	3,827	6,364
16p39, IFRS7 p20(a)(ii)	Revaluation – gross (notes 6 and 10)	–	1,133	–	275	–	1,408
	Revaluation transfer -- gross				(152)		(152)
12p61A, 81(a)(b)	Revaluation – tax (note 32)	–	(374)	–	(61)	–	(435)
28p39	Revaluation – associates (note 8)	–	–	–	(14)	–	(14)
16p41	Depreciation transfer -- gross	–	(130)	–	–	–	(130)
16p41	Depreciation transfer – tax	–	43	–	–	–	43
1p96(b)	Cash flow hedges:						
IFRS7p23(c)	– Fair value gains in year	–	–	300	–	–	300
12p61, 81(a)	– Tax on fair value gains (note 32)	–	–	(101)	–	–	(101)
IFRS7p23(d)	– Transfers to sales	–	–	(236)	–	–	(236)
12p61A, 81(a)(b)	– Tax on transfers to sales (note 32)	–	–	79	–	–	79
IFRS7p23(e)	– Transfers to inventory	–	–	(67)	–	–	(67)
12p61, 81(a)	– Tax on transfers to inventory (note 32)	–	–	22	–	–	22
39p102(a)	Net investment hedge (note 11)	–	–	–	–	40	40
1p106(d)	Currency translation differences:						
21p52(b)	– Group	–	(50)	–	–	(171)	(221)
28p39	– Associates	–	–	–	–	105	105
	At 31 December 2009	–	1,774	62	1,368	3,801	7,005

[1] An entity should disclose in its financial statements whether there are any restrictions on the distribution of the 'land and buildings' fair value reserve to the equity holders of the company (IAS16p77(f)).

(All amounts in C thousands unless otherwise stated)

16p39, IFRS7							
p20(a)(ii)	Revaluation – gross (note 10)	–	–	–	690	–	690
	Revaluation transfer -- gross				(130)		(130)
12p61A,							
81(a)(b)	Revaluation – tax (note 32)	–	–	–	(198)	–	(198)
	Revaluation – associates						
28p39	(note 8)	–	–	–	(12)	–	(12)
16p41	Depreciation transfer -- gross	–	(149)	–	–	–	(149)
16p41	Depreciation transfer – tax	–	49	–	–	–	49
1p96(b)	Cash flow hedges:						
IFRS7p23(c)	– Fair value gains in year	–	–	368	–	–	368
12p61A,	– Tax on fair value gains						
81(a)(b)	(note 32)	–	–	(123)	–	–	(123)
IFRS7p23(d)	– Transfers sales	–	–	(120)	–	–	(120)
12p61A,	– Tax on transfers to sales						
81(a)(b)	(note 32)	–	–	40	–	–	40
IFRS7p23(e)	– Transfers to inventory	–	–	(151)	–	–	(151)
12p61A,	– Tax on transfers to						
81(a)(b)	inventory (note 32)	–	–	50	–	–	50
39p102(a)	Net investment hedge (note 11)	–	–	–	–	(45)	(45)
1p106(d)	Currency translation differences:						
21p52(b)	– Group	–	15	–	–	2,051	2,066
28p39	– Associates	–	–	–	–	(74)	(74)
	Convertible bond – equity component (note 22)	7,761	–	–	–	–	7,761
12p61A,	Tax on equity component						
81(a),	on convertible bond (note 32)	(2,328)	–	–	–	–	(2,328)
	At 31 December 2010	**5,433**	**1,689**	**126**	**1,718**	**5,733**	**14,699**

Note: It is assumed that the tax base on the convertible bond is not split between the debt and equity elements. If the tax base were split, this would impact the deferred tax position.

21 Trade and other payables

		2010	2009
1p77	Trade payables	**8,983**	9,495
24p17	Amounts due to related parties (note 40)	**2,202**	1,195
	Social security and other taxes	**2,002**	960
	Other liabilities – contingent consideration (Note 39)	**2,000**	–
	Accrued expenses	**1,483**	828
		16,670	12,478

(All amounts in C thousands unless otherwise stated)

22 Borrowings

	2010	2009
Non-current		
Bank borrowings	**32,193**	40,244
Convertible bond	**42,822**	–
Debentures and other loans	**3,300**	18,092
Redeemable preference shares	**30,000**	30,000
Finance lease liabilities	**6,806**	8,010
	115,121	96,346
Current		
Bank overdrafts (note 15)	**2,650**	6,464
Collateralised borrowings	**1,014**	–
Bank borrowings	**3,368**	4,598
Debentures and other loans	**2,492**	4,608
Finance lease liabilities	**2,192**	2,588
	11,716	18,258
Total borrowings	**126,837**	114,604

(a) Bank borrowings

IFRS7p31 Bank borrowings mature until 2015 and bear average coupons of 7.5% annually (2009: 7.4% annually).

IFRS7p14 Total borrowings include secured liabilities (bank and collateralised borrowings) of C37,680 (2009: C51,306). Bank borrowings are secured by the land and buildings of the group (note 6). Collateralised borrowings are secured by trade receivables (note 12).

IFRS7p31 The exposure of the group's borrowings to interest rate changes and the contractual repricing dates at the end of the reporting period are as follows:

	2010	2009
6 months or less	**10,496**	16,748
6-12 months	**36,713**	29,100
1-5 years	**47,722**	38,555
Over 5 years	**31,906**	30,201
	126,837	114,604

IFRS7p25 The carrying amounts and fair value of the non-current borrowings are as follows:

	Carrying amount		Fair value	
	2010	2009	**2010**	2009
Bank borrowings	**32,193**	40,244	**32,590**	39,960
Redeemable preference shares	**30,000**	30,000	**28,450**	28,850
Debentures and other loans	**3,300**	18,092	**3,240**	17,730
Convertible bond	**42,822**	–	**42,752**	–
Finance lease liabilities	**6,806**	8,010	**6,205**	7,990
	115,121	96,346	**113,237**	94,530

(All amounts in C thousands unless otherwise stated)

IFRS7
p29(a)
IFRS7p25
The fair value of current borrowings equals their carrying amount, as the impact of discounting is not significant. The fair values are based on cash flows discounted using a rate based on the borrowing rate of 7.5% (2009: 7.2%).

IFRS7p31,
34(c)
The carrying amounts of the group's borrowings are denominated in the following currencies:

	2010	2009
UK pound	80,100	80,200
Euro	28,353	16,142
US dollar	17,998	17,898
Other currencies	386	364
	126,837	114,604

DV7p50(a) The group has the following undrawn borrowing facilities:

	2010	2009
Floating rate:		
– Expiring within one year	6,150	4,100
– Expiring beyond one year	14,000	8,400
Fixed rate:		
– Expiring within one year	18,750	12,500
	38,900	25,000

The facilities expiring within one year are annual facilities subject to review at various dates during 2011. The other facilities have been arranged to help finance the proposed expansion of the group's activities in Europe.

(b) Convertible bonds

IFRS7p17,
1p79(b)
The company issued 500,000 5.0% convertible bonds at a par value of C50 million[1] on 2 January 2010. The bonds mature five years from the issue date at their nominal value of C50 million or can be converted into shares at the holder's option at the maturity date at the rate of 33 shares per C5,00. The values of the liability component and the equity conversion component were determined at issuance of the bond.

32p28,
32p31,
1p79(b)
The fair value of the liability component, included in non-current borrowings, was calculated using a market interest rate for an equivalent non-convertible bond. The residual amount, representing the value of the equity conversion option, is included in shareholders' equity in other reserves (note 20), net of income taxes.

---

[1] These amounts are not in C thousands.

IFRS GAAP plc – Illustrative corporate consolidated financial statements 2010

(All amounts in C thousands unless otherwise stated)

The convertible bond recognised in the balance sheet is calculated as follows:

	2010	2009
Face value of convertible bond issued on 2 January 2010	50,000	–
Equity component (note 20)	(7,761)	–
Liability component on initial recognition at 2 January 2010	42,239	–
Interest expense (note 31)	3,083	–
Interest paid	(2,500)	–
Liability component at 31 December 2010	**42,822**	–

12Appx BEx4 labels apply to rows above.

IFRS7p27 The fair value of the liability component of the convertible bond at 31 December 2010 amounted to C42,617. The fair value is calculated using cash flows discounted at a rate based on the borrowings rate of 7.5%.

(c) Redeemable preference shares

32p15, 32p18(a) The group issued 30 million cumulative redeemable preference shares with a par value of C1 per share on 4 January 2009. The shares are mandatorily redeemable at their par value on 4 January 2014, and pay dividends at 6.5% annually.

10p21 On 1 February 2010, the group issued C6,777 6.5% US dollar bonds to finance its expansion programme and working capital requirements in the US. The bonds are repayable on 31 December 2015.

(d) Finance lease liabilities

Lease liabilities are effectively secured as the rights to the leased asset revert to the lessor in the event of default.

	2010	2009
17p31(b) Gross finance lease liabilities – minimum lease payments		
No later than 1 year	2,749	3,203
Later than 1 year and no later than 5 years	6,292	7,160
Later than 5 years	2,063	2,891
	11,104	13,254
Future finance charges on finance leases	(2,106)	(2,656)
Present value of finance lease liabilities	**8,998**	**10,598**

17p31(b) The present value of finance lease liabilities is as follows:

	2010	2009
No later than 1 year	2,192	2,588
Later than 1 year and no later than 5 years	4,900	5,287
Later than 5 years	1,906	2,723
	8,998	10,598

(All amounts in C thousands unless otherwise stated)

23 Deferred income tax

The analysis of deferred tax assets and deferred tax liabilities is as follows:

	2010	2009
1p61 Deferred tax assets:		
– Deferred tax asset to be recovered after more than 12 months	**(2,873)**	(3,257)
– Deferred tax asset to be recovered within 12 months	**(647)**	(64)
	(3,520)	(3,321)
Deferred tax liabilities:		
– Deferred tax liability to be recovered after more than 12 months	**10,743**	8,016
– Deferred tax liability to be recovered within 12 months	**1,627**	1,037
	12,370	9,053
Deferred tax liabilities (net)	**8,850**	5,732

The gross movement on the deferred income tax account is as follows:

	2010	2009
At 1 January	**5,732**	3,047
Exchange differences	**(1,753)**	(154)
Acquisition of subsidiary (note 39)	**1,953**	–
Income statement charge (note 32)	**379**	2,635
Tax charge/(credit) relating to components of other comprehensive income (note 32)	**241**	224
Tax charged/(credited) directly to equity (note 20)	**2,298**	(20)
At 31 December	**8,850**	5,732

12p81 (g)(i), (ii) The movement in deferred income tax assets and liabilities during the year, without taking into consideration the offsetting of balances within the same tax jurisdiction, is as follows:

Deferred tax liabilities	Accelerated tax depreciation	Fair value gains	Convertible bond	Other	Total
At 1 January 2009	6,058	272	–	284	6,614
12p81(g)(ii) Charged/(credited) to the income statement	1,786	–	–	799	2,585
Charged/(credited) to other comprehensive income	–	435	–	–	435
12p81(a) Charged directly to equity	–	–	–	–	–
Exchange differences	241	100	–	–	341
12p81(g)(i) At 31 December 2009	8,085	807	–	1,083	9,975
12p81(g)(ii) Charged/(credited) to the income statement	425	–	(193)	138	370
Charged/(credited) to other comprehensive income	–	231	–	–	231
12p81(a) Charged directly to equity	–	–	2,328	–	2,328
Acquisition of subsidiary	553	1,375	–	275	2,203
Exchange differences	(571)	(263)	–	(123)	(957)
12p81(g)(i) At 31 December 2010	8,492	2,150	2,135	1,373	14,150

(All amounts in C thousands unless otherwise stated)

Deferred tax assets	Retirement benefit obligation	Provisions	Impairment losses	Tax losses	Other	Total
At 1 January 2009	(428)	(962)	(732)	(1,072)	(373)	(3,567)
12p81(g)(ii) Charged/(credited) to the income statement	–	181	–	–	(131)	50
Charged/(credited) to other comprehensive income	(211)	–	–	–		(211)
12p81(a) Charged/(credited) directly to equity	–	–	–	–	(20)	(20)
Exchange differences	–	(35)	–	(460)	–	(495)
12p81(g)(i) At 31 December 2009	(639)	(816)	(732)	(1,532)	(524)	(4,243)
(Credited)/charged to the income statement	–	(538)	(322)	1,000	(131)	9
Charged/(credited) to other comprehensive income	10	–	–	–	–	10
12p81(a) Charged/(credited) directly to equity	–	–	–	–	(30)	(30)
Acquisition of subsidiary (note 39)	(250)	–	–	–	–	(250)
Exchange differences	–	(125)	(85)	(350)	(236)	(796)
12p81(g)(i) **At 31 December 2010**	**(879)**	**(1,479)**	**(1,139)**	**(882)**	**(921)**	**(5,300)**

12p81(e) Deferred income tax assets are recognised for tax loss carry-forwards to the extent that the realisation of the related tax benefit through future taxable profits is probable. The group did not recognise deferred income tax assets of C333 (2009: C1,588) in respect of losses amounting to C1,000 (2009: C5,294) that can be carried forward against future taxable income. Losses amounting to C900 (2009: C5,294) and C100 (2009: nil) expire in 2013 and 2014 respectively.

12p81(f) Deferred income tax liabilities of C3,141 (2009: C2,016) have not been recognised for the withholding tax and other taxes that would be payable on the unremitted earnings of certain subsidiaries. Such amounts are permanently reinvested. Unremitted earnings totalled C30,671 at 31 December 2010 (2009: C23,294).

24 Retirement benefit obligations

	2010	2009
Balance sheet obligations for:		
Pension benefits	**3,225**	1,532
Post-employment medical benefits	**1,410**	701
Liability in the balance sheet	**4,635**	2,233
Income statement charge for (note 30a):		
Pension benefits	**755**	488
Post-employment medical benefits	**149**	107
	904	595
19p120A(h) Actuarial losses recognised in the statement of other comprehensive income in the period	–	705
19p120A(i) Cumulative actuarial losses recognised in the statement of other comprehensive income	**908**	203

(All amounts in C thousands unless otherwise stated)

(a) Pension benefits

DV The group operates defined benefit pension plans in the UK and the US based on employee pensionable remuneration and length of service. The majority of plans are externally funded. Plan assets are held in trusts, foundations or similar entities, governed by local regulations and practice in each country, as is the nature of the relationship between the group and the trustees (or equivalent) and their composition.

19p120A (d)(f) The amounts recognised in the balance sheet are determined as follows:

	2010	2009
Present value of funded obligations	6,155	2,943
Fair value of plan assets	(5,991)	(2,797)
Deficit of funded plans	164	146
Present value of unfunded obligations	3,206	1,549
Unrecognised past service cost	(145)	(163)
Liability in the balance sheet	3,225	1,532

19p120A(c) The movement in the defined benefit obligation over the year is as follows:

	2010	2009
At 1 January	4,492	3,479
Current service cost	751	498
Interest cost	431	214
Employee contributions	55	30
Actuarial losses/(gains)	(15)	706
Exchange differences	(61)	(330)
Past service cost 28	18	16
Benefits paid	(66)	(121)
Liabilities acquired in a business combination (note 39)	3,691	–
Curtailments	65	–
Settlements 28	–	–
At 31 December	9,361	4,492

19p120A(e) The movement in the fair value of plan assets of the year is as follows:

	2010	2009
At 1 January	2,797	2,264
Expected return on plan assets	510	240
Actuarial (losses)/gains	(15)	1
Exchange differences	25	(22)
Employer contributions	908	411
Employee contributions	55	30
Benefits paid	(66)	(127)
Assets acquired in a business combination (note 39)	1,777	–
Settlements (note 28)	–	–
At 31 December	5,991	2,797

IFRS GAAP plc – Illustrative corporate consolidated financial statements 2010

(All amounts in C thousands unless otherwise stated)

19p120A(g) The amounts recognised in the income statement are as follows:

	2010	2009
Current service cost	**751**	498
Interest cost	**431**	214
Expected return on plan assets	**(510)**	(240)
Past service cost	**18**	16
Losses on curtailment footnote as per suggested text.	**65**	–
Total, included in staff costs (note 30[1])	**755**	488

19p120A(g) Of the total charge, C516 (2009: C319) and C239 (2009: C169) were included in 'cost of goods sold' and 'administrative expenses' respectively.

19p120A(m) The actual return on plan assets was C495 (2009: C419).

19p120A(n) The principal actuarial assumptions were as follows:

	2010		2009	
	UK	**US**	UK	US
Discount rate	**6.0%**	**6.1%**	5.5%	5.6%
Inflation rate	**3.6%**	**3.0%**	3.3%	2.7%
Expected return on plan assets	**8.5%**	**8.3%**	8.7%	8.7%
Future salary increases	**5.0%**	**4.5%**	4.5%	4.0%
Future pension increases	**3.6%**	**2.8%**	3.1%	2.7%

Assumptions regarding future mortality experience are set based on actuarial advice in accordance with published statistics and experience in each territory. Mortality assumptions for the most important countries are based on the following post-retirement mortality tables: (i) UK: PNMA 00 and PNFA 00 with medium cohort adjustment subject to a minimum annual improvement of 1% and scaling factors of 110% for current male pensioners, 125% for current female pensioners and 105% for future male and female pensioners; and (ii) US: RP2000 with a projection period of 10-15 years.

These tables translate into an average life expectancy in years of a pensioner retiring at age 65:

	2010		2009	
	UK	**US**	UK	US
Retiring at the end of the reporting period:				
– Male	**22**	**20**	22	20
– Female	**25**	**24**	25	24
– Retiring 20 years after the end of the reporting period:				
– Male	**24**	**23**	24	23
– Female	**27**	**26**	27	26

---

[1] The gain or loss on curtailment is in principle the resulting change in surplus (or deficit) plus related unrecognised actuarial gains and losses and past service cost attributable to the reporting employer.

(All amounts in C thousands unless otherwise stated)

DV The sensitivity of the overall pension liability to changes in the weighted principal assumptions is:

	Change in assumption	Impact on overall liability
Discount rate	Increase/decrease by 0.5%	Increase/decrease by 7.2%
Inflation rate	Increase/decrease by 0.5%	Increase/decrease by 5.1%
Salary growth rate	Increase/decrease by 0.5%	Increase/decrease by 3.3%
Life expectancy	Increase by 1 year	Increase by 5.2%

19p122(b) *(b) Post-employment medical benefits*

The group operates a number of post-employment medical benefit schemes, principally in the US. The method of accounting, assumptions and the frequency of valuations are similar to those used for defined benefit pension schemes. The majority of these plans are unfunded.

19p120A(n) In addition to the assumptions set out above, the main actuarial assumption is a long-term increase in health costs of 8.0% a year (2009: 7.6%).

19p120A (d)(f) The amounts recognised in the balance sheet were determined as follows:

	2010	2009
Present value of funded obligations	705	340
Fair value of plan assets	(620)	(302)
Deficit of the funded plans	85	38
Present value of unfunded obligations	1,325	663
Liability in the balance sheet	1,410	701

19p120A(c) Movement in the defined benefit obligation is as follows:

	2010	2009
At 1 January	1,003	708
Current service cost	153	107
Interest cost	49	25
Employee contributions by plan participants[1]	–	
Actuarial losses/(gains)	(2)	204
Exchange differences	25	(41)
Benefits paid[2]	–	–
Past service costs[1]	–	–
Liabilities acquired in a business combination (note 39)	802	–
Curtailments[1]	–	–
Settlements[1]	–	–
At 31 December	2,030	1,003

[1] IAS 19 requires the disclosure of employee contributions, benefits paid and settlements as part of the reconciliation of the opening and closing balances of plan assets. There is no such movement on the plan assets relating to post-employment medical benefits in these financial statements, but the line items have been shown for illustrative purposes.
[2] IAS 19 requires the disclosure of employee contributions, benefits paid, past service costs, settlements and curtailments as part of the reconciliation of the opening and closing balances of the present value of the defined benefit obligation. There is no such movement on the defined benefit obligation relating to pension plans in these financial statements, but the line item has been shown for illustrative purposes.

(All amounts in C thousands unless otherwise stated)

19p120A(e) The movement in the fair value of plan assets of the year is as follows:

	2010	2009
At 1 January	302	207
Expected return on plan assets	53	25
Actuarial gains/(losses)	(2)	(1)
Exchange differences	5	(2)
Employer contributions	185	73
Employee contributions[3]	–	–
Benefits paid[36]	–	–
Assets acquired in a business combination (note 39)	77	–
Settlements [36]	–	–
At 31 December	**620**	**302**

19p120A(g) The amounts recognised in the income statement were as follows:

	2010	2009
Current service cost	153	107
Interest cost	49	25
Expected return on plan assets	(53)	(25)
Total, included in staff costs (note 30a)	**149**	**107**

19p120A(g) Of the total charge, C102 (2009: C71) and C47 (2009: C36) respectively were included in cost of goods sold and administrative expenses.

19p120A(m) The actual return on plan assets was C51 (2009: C24).

19p120A(o) The effect of a 1% movement in the assumed medical cost trend rate is as follows:

	Increase	Decrease
Effect on the aggregate of the current service cost and interest cost	24	(20)
Effect on the defined benefit obligation	366	(313)

(c) Post-employment benefits (pension and medical)

19p120A(j) Plan assets are comprised as follows:

	2010		2009	
Equity instruments	3,256	49%	1,224	40%
Debt instruments	1,524	23%	571	18%
Property	1,047	16%	943	30%
Other	784	12%	361	12%
	6,611	**100%**	**3,099**	**100%**

DV Investments are well diversified, such that the failure of any single investment would not have a material impact on the overall level of assets. The largest proportion of assets is invested in equities, although the group also invests in property, bonds, hedge funds and cash. The group believes that equities offer the best returns over the long term with an acceptable level of risk. The majority of equities are in a globally diversified portfolio of international blue chip entities, with a target of 60% of equities held in the UK and Europe, 30% in the US and the remainder in emerging markets.

(All amounts in C thousands unless otherwise stated)

19p120A(k) Pension plan assets include the company's ordinary shares with a fair value of C136 (2009: C126) and a building occupied by the group with a fair value of C612 (2009: C609).

19p120A(l) The expected return on plan assets is determined by considering the expected returns available on the assets underlying the current investment policy. Expected yields on fixed interest investments are based on gross redemption yields as at the end of the reporting period. Expected returns on equity and property investments reflect long-term real rates of return experienced in the respective markets.

19p120(q) Expected contributions to post-employment benefit plans for the year ending 31 December 2011 are C1,150.

DV The group has agreed that it will aim to eliminate the deficit over the next nine years. Funding levels are monitored on an annual basis and the current agreed regular contribution rate is 14% of pensionable salaries in the UK and 12% in the US. The next triennial valuation is due to be completed as at 31 December 2011. The group considers that the contribution rates set at the last valuation date are sufficient to eliminate the deficit over the agreed period and that regular contributions, which are based on service costs, will not increase significantly.

DV An alternative method of valuation to the projected unit credit method is a buy-out valuation. This assumes that the entire post-employment benefit obligation will be settled by transferring all obligations to a suitable insurer. The group estimates the amount required to settle the post-employment benefit obligation at the end of the reporting period would be C15,500

19p120A(p)

	2010	2009	2008	2007	2006
At 31 December					
Present value of defined benefit obligation	**11,391**	5,495	4,187	3,937	3,823
Fair value of plan assets	**6,611**	3,099	2,471	2,222	2,102
Deficit in the plan	**4,780**	2,396	1,716	1,715	1,721
Experience adjustments on plan liabilities	**(25)**	125	55	18	32–
Experience adjustments on plan assets	**(17)**	(0)	(197)	(50)–	(16)–

(All amounts in C thousands unless otherwise stated)

25 Provisions for other liabilities and charges

		Environmental restoration	Restructuring	Legal claims	Profit-sharing and bonuses	Contingent liability arising on a business combination	Total
37p84(a)	At 1 January 2010	842	–	828	1,000	–	2,670
	Charged/(credited) to the income statement:						
37p84(b)	– Additional provisions/ fair value adjustment on acquisition of ABC Group	316	1,986	2,405	500	1,000	6,207
37p84(d)	– Unused amounts reversed	(15)	–	(15)	(10)	–	(40)
37p84(e)	– Unwinding of discount	40	–	–	–	4	44
37p84(c)	Used during year	(233)	(886)	(3,059)	(990)	–	(5,168)
	Exchange differences	(7)	–	(68)	–	–	(75)
IFRS5p38	Transferred to disposal group/classified as held for sale	(96)	–	–	–	–	(96)
37p84(a)	**At 31 December 2010**	**847**	**1,100**	**91**	**500**	**1,004**	**3,542**

1p78(d)

		2010	2009
	Analysis of total provisions:		
1p69	Non-current (environmental restoration)	1,320	274
1p69	Current	2,222	2,396
		3,542	2,670

(a) Environmental restoration

37p85 (a)-(c) The group uses various chemicals in working with leather. A provision is recognised for the present value of costs to be incurred for the restoration of the manufacturing sites. It is expected that C531 will be used during 2011 and C320 during 2012. Total expected costs to be incurred are C880 (2009: C760).

DV The provision transferred to the disposal group classified as held for sale amounts to C96 and relates to an environmental restoration provision for Shoes Limited (part of the wholesale segment). See note 16 for further details regarding the disposal group held for sale.

(b) Restructuring

37p85(a)-(c) The reduction of the volumes assigned to manufacturing operations in Step-land (a subsidiary) will result in the reduction of a total of 155 jobs at two factories. An agreement was reached with the local union representatives, which specifies the number of staff involved and the voluntary redundancy compensation package offered by the group, as well as amounts payable to those made redundant, before the financial year-end. The estimated staff restructuring costs to be incurred are C799 at 31 December 2010 (note 30). Other direct costs attributable to the restructuring, including lease termination, are C1,187. These costs were fully provided for in 2010. The provision of C1,100 at 31 December 2010 is expected to be fully utilised during the first half of 2011.

(All amounts in C thousands unless otherwise stated)

36p130 A goodwill impairment charge of C4,650 was recognised in the cash-generating unit relating to Step-land as a result of this restructuring (note 7).

(c) Legal claims

37p85(a)- The amounts represent a provision for certain legal claims brought against the group by
(c) customers of the wholesale segment. The provision charge is recognised in profit or loss within 'administrative expenses'. The balance at 31 December 2010 is expected to be utilised in the first half of 2011. In the directors' opinion, after taking appropriate legal advice, the outcome of these legal claims will not give rise to any significant loss beyond the amounts provided at 31 December 2010.

(d) Profit-sharing and bonuses

19p8(c),10
DV, The provision for profit-sharing and bonuses is payable within three month of finalisation
37p85(a) of the audited financial statements.

(e) Contingent liability

A contingent liability of C1,000 has been recognised on the acquisition of ABC Group for a pending lawsuit in which the entity is a defendant. The claim has arisen from a customer alleging defects on products supplied to them. It is expected that the courts will have reached a decision on this case by the end of 2012. The potential undiscounted amount of all future payments that the group could be required to make if there was an adverse decision related to the lawsuit is estimated to be between C500 and C1,500. As of 31 December 2010, there has been no change in the amount recognised (except for the unwinding of the discount of C4) for the liability at 31 March 2010, as there has been no change in the probability of the outcome of the lawsuit.

The selling shareholders of ABC Group have contractually agreed to indemnify IFRS GAAP plc for the claim that may become payable in respect of the above-mentioned lawsuit. This possible compensation will not be recognised until virtually certain and will be adjusted against goodwill once received from the vendor.

26 Other (losses)/gains – net

	2010	2009
IFRS7 **p20(a)(i)** Financial assets at fair value through profit or loss (note 14):		
– Fair value losses	**(508)**	(238)
– Fair value gains	**593**	–
IFRS7 **p20(a)(i)** Foreign exchange forward contracts:		
– Held for trading	**86**	88
21p52(a) – Net foreign exchange gains/(losses) (note 33)	**(277)**	200
IFRS7 **p24(a)** Ineffectiveness on fair value hedges (note 11)	**(1)**	(1)
IFRS7 **p24(b)** Ineffectiveness on cash flow hedges (note 11)	**17**	14
	(90)	63

(All amounts in C thousands unless otherwise stated)

27 Other income

	2010	2009
Gain on remeasuring existing interest in ABC Group on acquisition (note 39)	850	–
18p35(b)(v) Dividend income on available-for-sale financial assets	1,100	883
18p35(b)(v) Dividend income on financial assets at fair value through profit or loss	800	310
Investment income	2,750	1,193
Insurance reimbursement	–	66
	2,750	1,259

The insurance reimbursement relates to the excess of insurance proceeds over the carrying values of goods damaged.

28 Loss on expropriated land

During 2010, undeveloped land owned by the group in the UK was expropriated following works for the enlargement of a motorway adjacent to the group's manufacturing facilities. Losses relating to the expropriation are C1,117 as of 31 December 2010 (2009: nil).

29 Expenses by nature

	2010	2009
1p104 Changes in inventories of finished goods and work in progress	6,950	(2,300)
1p104 Raw materials and consumables used	53,302	31,845
1p104 Employee benefit expense (note 30a)	40,082	15,492
1p104 Depreciation, amortisation and impairment charges (notes 6 and 7)	23,204	10,227
1p104 Transportation expenses	8,584	6,236
1p104 Advertising costs	12,759	6,662
1p104 Operating lease payments (note 6)	10,604	8,500
1p104 Other expenses	2,799	1,659
Total cost of sales, distribution costs and administrative expenses	**158,284**	78,321

30 Employee benefit expense

	2010	2009
19p142 Wages and salaries, including restructuring costs C799 (2009: nil) (note 25) and other termination benefits C1,600 (2009: nil)	28,363	10,041
Social security costs	9,369	3,802
IFRS2 p51(a) Share options granted to directors and employees notes 18/19)	690	822
19p46 Pension costs – defined contribution plans	756	232
19p120A(g) Pension costs – defined benefit plans (note 24)	755	488
19p120A(g) Other post-employment benefits (note 24)	149	107
	40,082	15,492

(All amounts in C thousands unless otherwise stated)

31 Finance income and costs

		2010	2009
IFRS7 p20(b)	Interest expense:		
	– Bank borrowings	**(5,317)**	(10,646)
	– Dividend on redeemable preference shares (note 22)	**(1,950)**	(1,950)
	– Convertible bond (note 22)	**(3,083)**	–
	– Finance lease liabilities	**(550)**	(648)
37p84(e)	– Provisions: unwinding of discount (note 25)	**(44)**	(37)
21p52(a)	Net foreign exchange gains on financing activities (note 33)	**2,594**	996
	Fair value gains on financial instruments:		
IFRS7 p23(d)	– Interest rate swaps: cash flow hedges, transfer from equity	**102**	88
IFRS7 p24(a)(i)	– Interest rate swaps: fair value hedges	**16**	31
IFRS7 p24(a)(ii)	Fair value adjustment of bank borrowings attributable to interest rate risk	**(16)**	(31)
	Finance costs	**(8,248)**	(12,197)
	Less: amounts capitalised on qualifying assets	**75**	–
	Total finance cost	**(8,173)**	–
	Finance income:		
	– Interest income on short-term bank deposits	**550**	489
IFRS7 p20(b)	– Interest income on available-for-sale financial assets	**963**	984
IFRS7 p20(b)	– Interest income on loans to related parties (note 40)	**217**	136
	Finance income	**1,730**	1,609
	Net finance costs	**(6,443)**	(10,588)

32 Income tax expense

		2010	2009
	Current tax:		
12p80(a)	Current tax on profits for the year	**14,082**	6,035
12p80(b)	Adjustments in respect of prior years	**150**	–
	Total current tax	**14,232**	6,035
	Deferred tax (note 23):		
12p80(c)	Origination and reversal of temporary differences	**476**	2,635
12p80(d)	Impact of change in the Euravian tax rate[1]	**(97)**	–
	Total deferred tax	**379**	2,635
	Income tax expense	**14,611**	8,670

[1] The impact of change in Euravian tax rate is shown for illustrative purposes.

(All amounts in C thousands unless otherwise stated)

12p81(c) The tax on the group's profit before tax differs from the theoretical amount that would arise using the weighted average tax rate applicable to profits of the consolidated entities as follows:

	2010	2009
Profit before tax	**47,676**	24,918
Tax calculated at domestic tax rates applicable to profits in the respective countries	**15,453**	7,475
Tax effects of:		
– Associates' results reported net of tax	**57**	(44)
– Income not subject to tax	**(1,072)**	(212)
– Expenses not deductible for tax purposes	**1,540**	1,104
– Utilisation of previously unrecognised tax losses	**(1,450)**	–
– Tax losses for which no deferred income tax asset was recognised	**30**	347
Re-measurement of deferred tax – change in the Euravian tax rate	**(97)**	–
Adjustment in respect of prior years	**150**	–
Tax charge	**14,611**	8,670

12p81(d) The weighted average applicable tax rate was 33% (2009: 30%). The increase is caused by a change in the profitability of the group's subsidiaries in the respective countries partially offset by the impact of the reduction in the Euravian tax rate (see below).

12p81(d) During the year, as a result of the change in the Euravian corporation tax rate from 30% to 28% that was substantively enacted on 26 June 2010 and that will be effective from 1 April 2011, the relevant deferred tax balances have been re-measured. Deferred tax expected to reverse in the year to 31 December 2011 has been measured using the effective rate that will apply in Euravia for the period (28.5%).[1]

1p125
10p21 Further reductions to the Euravian tax rate have been announced. The changes, which are expected to be enacted separately each year, propose to reduce the rate by 1% per annum to 24% by 1 April 2014. The changes had not been substantively enacted at the balance sheet date and, therefore, are not recognised in these financial statements.[2]

---

[1] If the effect of the proposed changes is material, disclosure should be given of the effect of the changes, either as disclosure of events after the reporting period or as future material adjustment to the carrying amounts of assets and liabilities. This disclosure does not need to be totalled or reconciled to the income statement.
[2] Disclosure in respect of the impact of change in Euravian tax rate is shown for illustrative purposes.

(All amounts in C thousands unless otherwise stated)

12p81(ab) The tax (charge)/credit relating to components of other comprehensive income is as follows:

		2010			2009	
	Before tax	**Tax (charge) credit**	**After tax**	**Before tax**	**Tax (charge) credit**	**After tax**
Fair value gains:						
1p90 -- Land and buildings	–	–	–	1,133	(374)	759
1p90 -- Available-for-sale financial assets	**560**	**(198)**	**362**	123	(61)	62
1p90 Share of other comprehensive income of associates	**(12)**	**–**	**(12)**	(14)	–	(14)
1p90 Actuarial loss on retirement benefit obligations	–	–	–	(705)	211	(494)
1p90 Impact of change in the Euravian tax rate on deferred tax[1]	–	**(10)**	**(10)**	–	–	–
1p90 Cash flow hedges	**97**	**(33)**	**64**	(3)	–	(3)
1p90 Net investment hedge	**(45)**	**–**	**(45)**	40	–	40
1p90 Currency translation differences	**2,244**	**–**	**2,244**	(156)	–	(156)
IFRS3p59 Increase in fair values of proportionate holding of ABC Group (note 39)	**850**	**–**	**850**	–	–	–
Other comprehensive income	**3,694**	**(241)**	**3,453**	418	(224)	194
Current tax[2]		–			–	
Deferred tax (note 23)		**(241)**			(224)	
		(241)			(224)	

12p81(a) The income tax (charged)/credited directly to equity during the year is as follows:

	2010	**2009**
Current tax[3]		
Share option scheme	–	–
Deferred tax		
Share option scheme	**30**	20
Convertible bond – equity component[4] (note 20)	**(2,328)**	–
	(2,298)	20

In addition, deferred income tax of C49 (2009: C43) was transferred from other reserves (note 20) to retained earnings (note 19). This represents deferred tax on the difference between the actual depreciation on buildings and the equivalent depreciation based on the historical cost of buildings.

[1] The impact of change in Euravian tax rate is shown for illustrative purposes. UK companies with 31 December 2010 year ends will need to consider the impact of the reduction in tax rates from 28% to 27% in the Finance (No. 2) Act 2010.
[2] There are no current tax items relating to other comprehensive income in these financial statements, but the line item is shown for illustrative purposes.
[3] IAS 12 requires disclosure of current tax charged/credited directly to equity, in addition to deferred tax. There are no current tax items shown directly in equity in these financial statements, but the line item is shown for illustrative purposes.
[4] It is assumed that the tax base on the convertible bond is not split between the debt and equity elements. If the tax base were split, this would impact the deferred tax position

(All amounts in C thousands unless otherwise stated)

33 Net foreign exchange gains/(losses)

21p52(a)   The exchange differences (charged)/credited to the income statement are included as
follows:

	2010	2009
Other (losses)/gains – net (note 26)	(277)	200
Net finance costs (note 31)	2,594	996
	2,317	1,196

34 Earnings per share

(a) Basic

Basic earnings per share is calculated by dividing the profit attributable to equity holders
of the company by the weighted average number of ordinary shares in issue during the
year excluding ordinary shares purchased by the company and held as treasury shares
(note 17).

		2010	2009
33p70(a)	Profit attributable to equity holders of the company	30,617	15,512
	Profit from discontinued operation attributable to equity holders of the company	100	120
		30,717	15,632
33p70(b)	Weighted average number of ordinary shares in issue (thousands)	23,454	20,500

(b) Diluted

Diluted earnings per share is calculated by adjusting the weighted average number of
ordinary shares outstanding to assume conversion of all dilutive potential ordinary shares.
The company has two categories of dilutive potential ordinary shares: convertible debt
and share options. The convertible debt is assumed to have been converted into ordinary
shares, and the net profit is adjusted to eliminate the interest expense less the tax effect.
For the share options, a calculation is done to determine the number of shares that could
have been acquired at fair value (determined as the average annual market share price of
the company's shares) based on the monetary value of the subscription rights attached to
outstanding share options. The number of shares calculated as above is compared with
the number of shares that would have been issued assuming the exercise of the share
options.

(All amounts in C thousands unless otherwise stated)

	2010	2009
Earnings		
Profit attributable to equity holders of the company	**30,617**	15,512
Interest expense on convertible debt (net of tax)	**2,158**	–
33p70(a) Profit used to determine diluted earnings per share	**32,775**	15,512
Profit from discontinued operations attributable to equity holders of the company	**100**	120
	32,825	15,632
Weighted average number of ordinary shares in issue (thousands)	**23,454**	20,500
Adjustments for:		
– Assumed conversion of convertible debt (thousands)	**3,030**	–
– Share options (thousands)	**1,213**	1,329
33p70(b) Weighted average number of ordinary shares for diluted earnings per share (thousands)	**27,697**	21,829

35 Dividends per share

1p107
1p137(a)
10p12

The dividends paid in 2010 and 2009 were C10,102 (C0.48 per share) and C15,736 (C0.78 per share) respectively. A dividend in respect of the year ended 31 December 2010 of C0.51 per share, amounting to a total dividend of C12,945, is to be proposed at the annual general meeting on 30 April 2010. These financial statements do not reflect this dividend payable.

36 Cash generated from operations

	2010	2009
7p18(b), 20 Profit before income tax including discontinued operations	**47,916**	25,118
Adjustments for:		
– Depreciation (note 6)	**17,754**	9,662
– Amortisation (note 7)	**800**	565
– Goodwill impairment charge (note 7)	**4,650**	–
– (Profit)/loss on disposal of property, plant and equipment (see below)	**(17)**	8
– Share-based payment and increase in retirement benefit obligations	**509**	1,470
– Fair value gains on derivative financial instruments (note 26)	**(86)**	(88)
– Fair value (gains)/losses on financial assets at fair value through profit or loss (note 26)	**(85)**	238
– Dividend income on available-for-sale financial assets (note 27)	**(1,100)**	(883)
– Dividend income on financial assets at fair value through profit or loss (note 27)	**(800)**	(310)
– Finance costs – net (note 31)	**6,443**	10,588
– Share of loss/(profit) from associates (note 8)	**174**	(145)
– Foreign exchange losses/(gains) on operating activities (note 33)	**(277)**	(200)
Gains on revaluation of existing investments (Note 39)	**(850)**	–
Changes in working capital (excluding the effects of acquisition and exchange differences on consolidation):		
– Inventories	**(6,077)**	(966)
– Trade and other receivables	**(1,339)**	(2,966)
– Financial assets at fair value through profit or loss	**(3,747)**	(858)
– Trade and other payables	**(7,634)**	543
Cash generated from operations	**56,234**	41,776

(All amounts in C thousands unless otherwise stated)

In the statement of cash flows, proceeds from sale of property, plant and equipment comprise:

	2010	2009
Net book amount (note 6)	6,337	2,987
Profit/(loss) on disposal of property, plant and equipment	17	(8)
Proceeds from disposal of property, plant and equipment	**6,354**	2,979

Non-cash transactions

7p43   The principal non-cash transaction is the issue of shares as consideration for the acquisition discussed in note 39.

37 Contingencies

37p86   The group has contingent liabilities in respect of legal claims arising in the ordinary course of business.

It is not anticipated that any material liabilities will arise from the contingent liabilities other than those provided for (note 25).

In respect of the acquisition of ABC Group on 1 March 2010 (note 39), additional consideration of 5% of the profit of ABC Group may be payable in cash if the acquired operations achieve sales in excess of C7,500 for 2010, up to a maximum undiscounted amount of C2,500. For details of the amount provided at acquisition and subsequent movements, see note 39.

38 Commitments

(a) Capital commitments

Capital expenditure contracted for at the end of the reporting period but not yet incurred is as follows:

	2010	2009
16p74(c) Property, plant and equipment	3,593	3,667
38p122(e) Intangible assets	460	474
Total	**4,053**	4,141

(b) Operating lease commitments – group company as lessee

17p35(d)   The group leases various retail outlets, offices and warehouses under non-cancellable operating lease agreements. The lease terms are between five and 10 years, and the majority of lease agreements are renewable at the end of the lease period at market rate.

17p35(d)   The group also leases various plant and machinery under cancellable operating lease agreements. The group is required to give a six-month notice for the termination of these agreements. The lease expenditure charged to the income statement during the year is disclosed in note 29.

(All amounts in C thousands unless otherwise stated)

17p35(a)   The future aggregate minimum lease payments under non-cancellable operating leases are as follows:

	2010	2009
No later than 1 year	11,664	10,604
Later than 1 year and no later than 5 years	45,651	45,651
Later than 5 years	15,710	27,374
Total	**73,025**	83,629

39 Business combinations

IFRS3R
B64(a-d)   On 30 June 2009, the group acquired 15% of the share capital of ABC Group for C1,126. On 1 March 2010, the group acquired a further 55% of the share capital and obtained the control of ABC Group, a shoe and leather goods retailer operating in the US and most western European countries. As a result of the acquisition, the group is expected to increase its presence in these markets. It also expects to reduce costs through economies of scale.

IFRS3R
B64(e)   The goodwill of C7,360 arising from the acquisition is attributable to acquired customer base and economies of scale expected from combining the operations of the group and ABC Group.

IFRS3R
B64(k)   None of the goodwill recognised is expected to be deductible for income tax purposes. The following table summarises the consideration paid for ABC Group and the amounts of the assets acquired and liabilities assumed recognised at the acquisition date, as well as the fair value at the acquisition date of the non-controlling interest in ABC Group.

(All amounts in C thousands unless otherwise stated)

	Consideration at 1 March 2010	
IFRS3 B64(f)(i), B64(f)(iv)	Cash	4,050
IFRS3 B64(f)(iii)	Equity instruments (3,550 ordinary shares)	10,000
IFRS3 B64(g)(i)	Contingent consideration	1,000
IFRS3 B64(f)	**Total consideration transferred**	**15,050**
	Indemnification asset	(1,000)
IFRS3 B64(p)(i)	Fair value of equity interest in ABC Group held before the business combination	2,000
	Total consideration	**16,050**
IFRS3 B64(m)	**Acquisition-related costs** (included in administrative expenses in the consolidated income statement for the year ended 31 December 2010)	200
IFRS3 B64(i)	**Recognised amounts of identifiable assets acquired and liabilities assumed**	
	Cash and cash equivalents	300
	Property, plant and equipment (note 6)	67,784
	Trademarks (included in intangibles) (note 7)	2,000
	Licences (included in intangibles) (note 7)	1,000
	Contractual customer relationship (included in intangibles) (note 7)	1,000
	Investment in associates (note 8)	389
	Available-for-sale financial assets (note 10)	473
	Inventories	1,122
	Trade and other receivables	585
	Trade and other payables	(12,461)
	Retirement benefit obligations:	
	– Pensions (note 24)	(1,914)
	– Other post-retirement obligations (note 24)	(725)
	Borrowings	(41,459)
	Contingent liability	(1,000)
	Deferred tax liabilities (note 23)	(1,953)
	Total identifiable net assets	**15,141**
IFRS3 B64(o)(i)	**Non-controlling interest**	(6,451)
	Goodwill	7,360
		16,050

IFRS3 B64(f)(iv) IFRS3 B64(m)	The fair value of the 3,550 ordinary shares issued as part of the consideration paid for ABC Group (C10,050) was based on the published share price on 1 March 2010. Issuance costs totalling C50 have been netted against the deemed proceeds.
IFRS3 B64(f)(iii) IFRS3 B64(g) IFRS3 B67(b)	The contingent consideration arrangement requires the group to pay the former owners of ABC Group 5% of the profit of ABC Group, in excess of C7,500 for 2010, up to a maximum undiscounted amount of C2,500.

The potential undiscounted amount of all future payments that the group could be required to make under this arrangement is between C0 and C2,500.

The fair value of the contingent consideration arrangement of C1,000 was estimated by applying the income approach. The fair value estimates are based on a discount

(All amounts in C thousands unless otherwise stated)

rate of 8% and assumed probability-adjusted profit in ABC Group of C20,000 to C40,000.

As of 31 December 2010, there was an increase of C500 recognised in the income statement for the contingent consideration arrangement, as the assumed probability-adjusted profit in ABC Group was recalculated to be approximately C30,000-50,000.

IFRS3
B64(h) The fair value of trade and other receivables is C585 and includes trade receivables with a fair value of C510. The gross contractual amount for trade receivables due is C960, of which C450 is expected to be uncollectible.

IFRS3
B67(a) The fair value of the acquired identifiable intangible assets of C4,000 (including trademarks and licences) is provisional pending receipt of the final valuations for those assets.

IFRS3
B64(j)
B67(c),
37p84, 85 A contingent liability of C1,000 has been recognised for a pending lawsuit in which ABC Group is a defendant. The claim has arisen from a customer alleging defects on products supplied to them. It is expected that the courts will have reached a decision on this case by the end of 2012. The potential undiscounted amount of all future payments that the group could be required to make if there was an adverse decision related to the lawsuit is estimated to be between C500 and C1,500. As of 31 December 2010, there has been no change in the amount recognised (except for unwinding of the discount C4) for the liability at 31 March 2010, as there has been no change in the range of outcomes or assumptions used to develop the estimates.

IFRS3
B64(g),
p57 The selling shareholders of ABC Group have contractually agreed to indemnify IFRS GAAP plc for the claim that may become payable in respect of the above-mentioned lawsuit. An indemnification asset of C1,000, equivalent to the fair value of the indemnified liability, has been recognised by the group. The indemnification asset is deducted from consideration transferred for the business combination. As is the case with the indemnified liability, there has been no change in the amount recognised for the indemnification asset as at 31 December 2010, as there has been no change in the range of outcomes or assumptions used to develop the estimate of the liability.

IFRS3
B64(o) The fair value of the non-controlling interest in ABC Group, an unlisted company, was estimated by applying a market approach and an income approach. The fair value estimates are based on:

(a) an assumed discount rate of 11%;

(b) an assumed terminal value based on a range of terminal EBITDA multiples between three and five times;

(c) long-term sustainable growth rate of 2%;

(d) assumed financial multiples of companies deemed to be similar to ABC group; and

(e) assumed adjustments because of the lack of control or lack of marketability that market participants would consider when estimating the fair value of the non-controlling interest in ABC Group.

(All amounts in C thousands unless otherwise stated)

IFRS3 B64(p)(ii)	The group recognised a gain of C850 as a result of measuring at fair value its 15% equity interest in ABC Group held before the business combination. The gain is included in other income in the group's statement of comprehensive income for the year ending 31 December 2010.
IFRS3 B64(q)(i)	The revenue included in the consolidated statement of comprehensive income since 1 March 2010 contributed by ABC Group was C44,709. ABC Group also contributed profit of C12,762 over the same period.
IFRS3 B64(q)(ii)	Had ABC Group been consolidated from 1 January 2010, the consolidated statement of comprehensive income would show revenue of C220,345 and profit of C33,126.

40 Related-party transactions

1p138(c) 24p12 The group is controlled by M Limited (incorporated in the UK), which owns 57% of the company's shares. The remaining 43% of the shares are widely held. The group's ultimate parent is G Limited (incorporated in the UK). The group's ultimate controlling party is Mr Power.

24p17, 18, 22 The following transactions were carried out with related parties:

24p17(a) *(a) Sales of goods and services*

	2010	2009
Sales of goods:		
– Associates	1,123	291
Sales of services:		
– Ultimate parent (legal and administration services)	67	127
– Close family members of the ultimate controlling party (design services)	100	104
Total	**1,290**	522

Goods are sold based on the price lists in force and terms that would be available to third parties[1]. Sales of services are negotiated with related parties on a cost-plus basis, allowing a margin ranging from 15% to 30% (2009: 10% to 18%).

24p17(a) *(b) Purchases of goods and services*

	2010	2009
Purchases of goods:		
– Associates	3,054	3,058
Purchases of services:		
– Entity controlled by key management personnel	83	70
– Immediate parent (management services)	295	268
Total	**3,432**	3,396

[1] Management should disclose that related-party transactions were made on an arm's length basis only when such terms can be substantiated (IAS24p21).

(All amounts in C thousands unless otherwise stated)

24p21 Goods and services are bought from associates and an entity controlled by key management personnel on normal commercial terms and conditions. The entity controlled by key management personnel is a firm belonging to Mr Chamois, a non-executive director of the company. Management services are bought from the immediate parent on a cost-plus basis, allowing a margin ranging from 15% to 30% (2009: 10% to 24%).

24p16 *(c) Key management compensation*

Key management includes directors (executive and non-executive), members of the Executive Committee, the Company Secretary and the Head of Internal Audit. The compensation paid or payable to key management for employee services is shown below:

	2010	2009
24p16(a) Salaries and other short-term employee benefits	2,200	1,890
24p16(d) Termination benefits	1,600	–
24p16(b) Post-employment benefits	123	85
24p16(c) Other long-term benefits	26	22
24p16(e) Share-based payments	150	107
Total	4,099	2,104

24p17(b),
1p77 *(d) Year-end balances arising from sales/purchases of goods/services*

	2010	2009
Receivables from related parties (note 12):		
– Ultimate parent	50	40
– Close family members of key management personnel	4	6
Payables to related parties (note 21):		
– Immediate parent	200	190
– Associates	1,902	1, 005
– Entity controlled by key management personnel	100	–

The receivables from related parties arise mainly from sale transactions and are due two months after the date of sales. The receivables are unsecured in nature and bear no interest. No provisions are held against receivables from related parties (2009: nil).

The payables to related parties arise mainly from purchase transactions and are due two months after the date of purchase. The payables bear no interest.

(All amounts in C thousands unless otherwise stated)

24p17,
1p77 *(e) Loans to related parties*

	2010	2009
Loans to key management of the company (and their families)[1]:		
At 1 January	196	168
Loans advanced during year	343	62
Loan repayments received	(49)	(34)
Interest charged	30	16
Interest received	(30)	(16)
At 31 December	**490**	196
Loans to associates:		
At 1 January	1,192	1,206
Loans advanced during year	1,000	50
Loan repayments received	(14)	(64)
Interest charged	187	120
Interest received	(187)	(120)
At 31 December	**2,178**	1,192
Total loans to related parties:		
At 1 January	1,388	1,374
Loans advanced during year	1,343	112
Loan repayments received	(63)	(98)
Interest charged	217	136
Interest received (note 31)	(217)	(136)
At 31 December (note 12)	**2,668**	1,388

24p17(b)(i) The loans advanced to key management have the following terms and conditions:

Name of key management	Amount of loan	Term	Interest rate
2010			
Mr Brown	173	Repayable monthly over 2 years	6.3%
Mr White	170	Repayable monthly over 2 years	6.3%
2009			
Mr Black	20	Repayable monthly over 2 years	6.5%
Mr White	42	Repayable monthly over 1 year	6.5%

IFRS7p15 Certain loans advanced to associates during the year amounting to C1,500 (2009: C500) are collateralised by shares in listed companies. The fair value of these shares was C65 at the end of the reporting period (2009: C590).

The loans to associates are due on 1 January 2011 and carry interest at 7.0% (2009:8%). The fair values and the effective interest rates of loans to associates are disclosed in note 12.

24p17(c) No provision was required in 2010 (2009: nil) for the loans made to key management personnel and associates.

---

[1] None of the loans made to members of key management has been made to directors.

(All amounts in C thousands unless otherwise stated)

41 Events after the reporting period

(a) Business combinations

10p21
IFRS3
B64(a)-(d) The group acquired 100% of the share capital of K&Co, a group of companies specialising in the manufacture of shoes for extreme sports, for a cash consideration of C5, 950 on 1 February 2011.

Details of net assets acquired and goodwill are as follows:

		2010
IFRS3 **B64 (f),(i)**	Purchase consideration:	
	– Cash paid	**5,950**
IFRS3 **B64(m)**	– Direct cost relating to the acquisition – charged in P&L	150
7p40(a)	Total purchase consideration	5,950
	Fair value of assets acquired (see below)	(5,145)
	Goodwill	**805**

IFRS3
B64(e) The above goodwill is attributable to K&Co's strong position and profitability in trading in the niche market for extreme-sports equipment.

IFRS3
B64(i) The assets and liabilities arising from the acquisition, provisionally determined, are as follows:

	Fair value
Cash and cash equivalents	195
Property, plant and equipment	29,056
Trademarks	1,000
Licences	700
Customer relationships	1,850
Favourable lease agreements	800
Inventories	995
Trade and other receivables	855
Trade and other payables	(9,646)
Retirement benefit obligations	(1,425)
Borrowings	(19,259)
Deferred tax assets	24
Net assets acquired	**5,145**

(b) Associates

10p21 The group acquired 40% of the share capital of L&Co, a group of companies specialising in the manufacture of leisure shoes, for a cash consideration of C2, 050 on 25 January 2011.

(All amounts in C thousands unless otherwise stated)

Details of net assets acquired and goodwill are as follows:

	2010
Purchase consideration:	
– Cash paid	2,050
– Direct cost relating to the acquisition	70
Total purchase consideration	2,120
Share of fair value of net assets acquired (see below)	(2,000)
Goodwill	**120**

DV   The goodwill is attributable to L&Co's strong position and profitability in trading in the market of leisure shoes and to its workforce, which cannot be separately recognised as an intangible asset.

DV   The assets and liabilities arising from the acquisition, provisionally determined, are as follows:

	Fair value
Contractual customer relationships	380
Property, plant and equipment	3,200
Inventory	500
Cash	220
Trade creditors	(420)
Borrowings	(1,880)
Net assets acquired	**2,000**

(c) Equity transactions

10p21
33p71(e)
10p21,
22(f)

On 1 January 2011, 1,200 thousand share options were granted to directors and employees with an exercise price set at the market share prices less 15% on that date of C3.13 per share (share price: C3.68) (expiry date: 31 December 2015).

The company re-issued 500,000 treasury shares for a total consideration of C1,500 on 15 January 2011.

(d) Borrowings

10p21   On 1 February 2011, the group issued C6,777 6.5% US dollar bonds to finance its expansion programme and working capital requirements in the US. The bonds are repayable on 31 December 2015.

(All amounts in C thousands unless otherwise stated)

Independent auditor's report to the shareholders of IFRS GAAP plc

Report on the consolidated financial statements

We have audited the accompanying consolidated financial statements of IFRS GAAP plc, which comprise the consolidated balance sheet as of 31 December 2010 and the consolidated statements of income, comprehensive income, changes in equity and cash flows for the year then ended, and a summary of significant accounting policies and other explanatory notes.

Management's responsibility for the consolidated financial statements

Management is responsible for the preparation of consolidated financial statements that give a true and fair view in accordance with International Financial Reporting Standards (IFRSs)[1], and for such internal control as management determines necessary to enable the preparation of consolidated financial statements that are free from material misstatement, whether due to fraud or error.

Auditor's responsibility

Our responsibility is to express an opinion on these consolidated financial statements based on our audit. We conducted our audit in accordance with International Standards on Auditing. Those standards require that we comply with ethical requirements and plan and perform the audit to obtain reasonable assurance whether the consolidated financial statements are free from material misstatement.

An audit involves performing procedures to obtain audit evidence about the amounts and disclosures in the consolidated financial statements. The procedures selected depend on the auditor's judgement, including the assessment of the risks of material misstatement of the consolidated financial statements, whether due to fraud or error. In making those risk assessments, the auditor considers internal control relevant to the entity's preparation of consolidated financial statements that give a true and fair view[2] in order to design audit procedures that are appropriate in the circumstances, but not for the purpose of expressing an opinion on the effectiveness of the entity's internal control. An audit also includes evaluating the appropriateness of accounting policies used and the reasonableness of accounting estimates made by management, as well as evaluating the overall presentation of the consolidated financial statements.

We believe that the audit evidence we have obtained is sufficient and appropriate to provide a basis for our audit opinion.

Opinion

In our opinion, the accompanying consolidated financial statements give a true and fair view[3] of the financial position of IFRS GAAP plc and its subsidiaries as of 31 December 2010, and of their financial performance and cash flows for the year then ended in accordance with International Financial Reporting Standards (IFRSs)

---

[1] This can be changed to say, 'Management is responsible for the preparation and fair presentation of these financial statements in accordance...' where the term 'true and fair view' is not used.

[2] This can be changed to say '...relevant to the entity's preparation and fair presentation of the consolidated financial statements in order...' where the term 'true and fair view' is not used.

[3] The term 'give a true and fair view' can be changed to 'present fairly, in all material aspects'.

(All amounts in C thousands unless otherwise stated)

Report on other legal and regulatory requirements

[Form and content of this section of the auditor's report will vary depending on the nature of the auditor's other reporting responsibilities, if any.]

Auditor's signature
Date of the auditor's report
Auditor's address

[The format of the audit report will need to be tailored to reflect the legal framework of particular countries. In certain countries, the audit report covers both the current year and the comparative year.]

(All amounts in C thousands unless otherwise stated)

Appendices

Appendix I – Operating and financial review

Contents

International Organization of Securities Commissions

In 1998, the International Organization of Securities Commissions (IOSCO) issued 'International disclosure standards for cross-border offerings and initial listings by foreign issuers', comprising recommended disclosure standards, including an operating and financial review and discussion of future prospects. IOSCO standards for prospectuses are not mandatory, but they are increasingly incorporated in national stock exchange requirements for prospectuses and annual reports. The text of IOSCO's standard on operating and financial reviews and prospects is reproduced below. Although the standard refers to a 'company' throughout, we consider that, where a company has subsidiaries, it should be applied to the group.

Standard

Discuss the company's financial condition, changes in financial condition and results of operations for each year and interim period for which financial statements are required, including the causes of material changes from year to year in financial statement line items, to the extent necessary for an understanding of the company's business as a whole. Information provided also shall relate to all separate segments of the group. Provide the information specified below as well as such other information that is necessary for an investor's understanding of the company's financial condition, changes in financial condition and results of operations.

A Operating results. Provide information regarding significant factors, including unusual or infrequent events or new developments, materially affecting the company's income from operations, indicating the extent to which income was so affected. Describe any other significant component of revenue or expenses necessary to understand the company's results of operations.

(1) To the extent that the financial statements disclose material changes in net sales or revenues, provide a narrative discussion of the extent to which such changes are attributable to changes in prices or to changes in the volume or amount of products or services being sold or to the introduction of new products or services.

(2) Describe the impact of inflation, if material. If the currency in which financial statements are presented is of a country that has experienced hyperinflation, the existence of such inflation, a five-year history of the annual rate of inflation and a discussion of the impact of hyperinflation on the company's business shall be disclosed.

(3) Provide information regarding the impact of foreign currency fluctuations on the company, if material, and the extent to which foreign currency net investments are hedged by currency borrowings and other hedging instruments.

(4) Provide information regarding any governmental economic, fiscal, monetary or political policies or factors that have materially affected, or could materially affect, directly or indirectly, the company's operations or investments by host country shareholders.

(All amounts in C thousands unless otherwise stated)

B Liquidity and capital resources. The following information shall be provided:

(1) Information regarding the company's liquidity (both short and long term), including:

    (a) a description of the internal and external sources of liquidity and a brief discussion of any material unused sources of liquidity. Include a statement by the company that, in its opinion, the working capital is sufficient for the company's present requirements, or, if not, how it proposes to provide the additional working capital needed.

    (b) an evaluation of the sources and amounts of the company's cash flows, including the nature and extent of any legal or economic restrictions on the ability of subsidiaries to transfer funds to the parent in the form of cash dividends, loans or advances and the impact such restrictions have had or are expected to have on the ability of the company to meet its cash obligations.

    (c) information on the level of borrowings at the end of the period under review, the seasonality of borrowing requirements and the maturity profile of borrowings and committed borrowing facilities, with a description of any restrictions on their use.

(2) Information regarding the type of financial instruments used, the maturity profile of debt, currency and interest rate structure. The discussion also should include funding and treasury policies and objectives in terms of the manner in which treasury activities are controlled, the currencies in which cash and cash equivalents are held, the extent to which borrowings are at fixed rates, and the use of financial instruments for hedging purposes.

(3) Information regarding the company's material commitments for capital expenditures as of the end of the latest financial year and any subsequent interim period and an indication of the general purpose of such commitments and the anticipated sources of funds needed to fulfil such commitments.

C Research and development, patents and licenses, etc. Provide a description of the company's research and development policies for the last three years, where it is significant, including the amount spent during each of the last three financial years on group-sponsored research and development activities.

D Trend information. The group should identify the most significant recent trends in production, sales and inventory, the state of the order book and costs and selling prices since the latest financial year. The group also should discuss, for at least the current financial year, any known trends, uncertainties, demands, commitments or events that are reasonably likely to have a material effect on the group's net sales or revenues, income from continuing operations, profitability, liquidity or capital resources, or that would cause reported financial information not necessarily to be indicative of future operating results or financial condition.

(All amounts in C thousands unless otherwise stated)

IASB's exposure draft on management commentary

The IASB published an exposure draft on management commentary (MC) in June 2009. The exposure draft sets out a non-binding framework for preparing and presenting management commentary. MC provides an opportunity for management to outline how an entity's financial position, financial performance and cash flows relate to management's objectives and its strategies for achieving those objectives. The exposure draft was open for comment until 1 March 2010.

Many of the principles and proposed disclosures in the draft standard are consistent with those of the ASB's reporting statement on the OFR. For example, the principles for the preparation of MC are to:

- provide management's view of the entity's performance, position and development;

- supplement and complement information presented in the financial statements; and

- have an orientation to the future.

The proposed standard states that a decision-useful MC includes information that is essential to an understanding of:

- The nature of the business.

- Management's objectives and strategies for meeting those objectives.

- The entity's most significant resources, risks and relationships.

- Results of operations and prospects.

- Critical performance measures and indicators that management uses to evaluate the entity's performance against stated objectives.

The exposure draft acknowledges that management commentary is already an important part of communication with the market. The proposals present a broad framework for MC reporting, and management will need to decide how best to apply this reporting framework to the particular circumstances of the business.

Appendix II – Alternative presentation of primary statements

IAS 19 – Employee benefits

Included below is the illustrative disclosure for post-employment benefits using the option in IAS 19 to recognise actuarial gains and losses using the corridor approach.

Note – Accounting policies

Employee benefits

1p119   *(a) Pension obligations*

19p27
19p25
19p7
19p120A(b)
     Group companies operate various pension schemes. The schemes are generally funded through payments to insurance companies or trustee-administered funds, determined by periodic actuarial calculations. The group has both defined benefit and defined contribution plans. A defined contribution plan is a pension plan under which the group pays fixed contributions into a separate entity. The group has no legal or constructive obligations to pay further contributions if the fund does not hold sufficient assets to pay all employees the benefits relating to employee service in the current and prior periods. A defined benefit plan is a pension plan that is not a defined contribution plan. Typically, defined benefit plans define an amount of pension benefit that an employee will receive on retirement, usually dependent on one or more factors such as age, years of service and compensation.

19p79
19p80
19p64
     The liability recognised in the balance sheet in respect of defined benefit pension plans is the present value of the defined benefit obligation at the end of the reporting period less the fair value of plan assets, together with adjustments for unrecognised actuarial gains or losses and past service costs. The defined benefit obligation is calculated annually by independent actuaries using the projected unit credit method. The present value of the defined benefit obligation is determined by discounting the estimated future cash outflows using interest rates of high-quality corporate bonds that are denominated in the currency in which the benefits will be paid and that have terms to maturity approximating to the terms of the related pension liability. In countries where there is no deep market in such bonds, the market rates on government bonds are used.

19p92
19p93
19p120A(a)
     Actuarial gains and losses arising from experience adjustments and changes in actuarial assumptions in excess of the greater of 10% of the fair value of plan assets or 10% of the present value of the defined benefit obligation are charged or credited to income over the employees' expected average remaining working lives.

19p96   Past-service costs are recognised immediately in income, unless the changes to the pension plan are conditional on the employees remaining in service for a specified period of time (the vesting period). In this case, the past-service costs are amortised on a straight-line basis over the vesting period.

19p44   For defined contribution plans, the group pays contributions to publicly or privately administered pension insurance plans on a mandatory, contractual or voluntary basis. The group has no further payment obligations once the contributions have been paid. The contributions are recognised as employee benefit expense when they are due. Prepaid contributions are recognised as an asset to the extent that a cash refund or a reduction in the future payments is available.

(All amounts in C thousands unless otherwise stated)

1p119 *(b) Other post-employment obligations*

19p120A(a) Some group companies provide post-retirement healthcare benefits to their retirees. The
19p120A(b) entitlement to these benefits is usually conditional on the employee remaining in service
up to retirement age and the completion of a minimum service period. The expected costs
of these benefits are accrued over the period of employment using the same accounting
methodology as used for defined benefit pension plans. Actuarial gains and losses arising
from experience adjustments, and changes in actuarial assumptions in excess of the
greater of 10% of the fair value of plan assets or 10% of the present value of the defined
benefit obligation, are charged or credited to income over the expected average
remaining working lives of the related employees. These obligations are valued annually
by independent qualified actuaries.

1p119 *(c) Termination benefits*

19p133 Termination benefits are payable when employment is terminated by the group before the
normal retirement date, or whenever an employee accepts voluntary redundancy in
19p134 exchange for these benefits. The group recognises termination benefits when it is
19p139 demonstrably committed to a termination when the entity has a detailed formal plan to
terminate the employment of current employees without possibility of withdrawal. In the
case of an offer made to encourage voluntary redundancy, the termination benefits are
measured based on the number of employees expected to accept the offer. Benefits
falling due more than 12 months after the end of the reporting period are discounted to
their present value.

The group recognises termination benefits when it is demonstrably committed to either:
terminating the employment of current employees according to a detailed formal plan
without possibility of withdrawal; or providing termination benefits as a result of an offer
made to encourage voluntary redundancy. Benefits falling due more than 12 months after
the end of the reporting period are discounted to present value.

1p119 *(d) Profit-sharing and bonus plans*

19p17 The group recognises a liability and an expense for bonuses and profit-sharing, based on
a formula that takes into consideration the profit attributable to the company's
shareholders after certain adjustments. The group recognises a provision where
contractually obliged or where there is a past practice that has created a constructive
obligation.

Appendix II – Alternative presentation of primary statements

(All amounts in C thousands unless otherwise stated)

Note – Retirement benefit obligation

	2010	2009
Balance sheet obligations for:	**3,138**	1,438
Pension benefits		
Post-employment medical benefits	**1,402**	692
	4,540	2,130
Income statement charge for		
Pension benefits	**762**	496
Post-employment medical benefits	**150**	107
	912	603

(a) Pension benefits

The group operates defined benefit pension plans in the UK and the US based on employee pensionable remuneration and length of service. The majority of plans are externally funded. Plan assets are held in trusts, foundations or similar entities, governed by local regulations and practice in each country, as is the nature of the relationship between the group and the trustees (or equivalent) and their composition.

19p120A (d)(f) The amounts recognised in the balance sheet are determined as follows:

	2010	2009
Present value of funded obligations	**6,155**	2,943
Fair value of plan assets	**(5,991)**	(2,797)
Deficit of funded plans	**164**	146
Present value of unfunded obligations	**3,206**	1,549
Unrecognised actuarial losses	**(87)**	(94)
Unrecognised past service cost	**(145)**	(163)
Liability in the balance sheet	**3,138**	1,438

19p120A(c) The movement in the defined benefit obligation over the year is as follows:

	2010	2009
At 1 January	**4,492**	3,479
Current service cost	**751**	498
Interest cost	**431**	214
Employee contributions	**55**	30
Actuarial losses/(gains)	**(15)**	495
Exchange differences	**(43)**	(103)
Benefits paid	**(66)**	(121)
Liabilities acquired in a business combination (note 39)	**3,691**	–
Curtailments	**65**	–
At 31 December	**9,361**	4,492

(All amounts in C thousands unless otherwise stated)

19p120A(e) The movement in the fair value of plan assets of the year is as follows:

	2010	2009
At 1 January	2,797	2,264
Expected return on plan assets	510	240
Actuarial gains/(losses)	(15)	(5)
Exchange differences	25	(22)
Employer contributions	908	411
Employee contributions	55	30
Benefits paid	(66)	(121)
Assets acquired in a business combination (note 39)	1,777	–
At 31 December	**5,991**	**2,797**

19p120A(g) The amounts recognised in the income statement are as follows:

	2010	2009
Current service cost	751	498
Interest cost	431	214
Expected return on plan assets	(510)	(240)
Net actuarial losses recognised during the year	7	8
Past service cost	18	16
Losses on curtailment	65	–
Total, included in staff costs	**762**	**496**

19p120A(g) Of the total charge, C521 (2009: C324) and C241 (2009: C172) were included in cost of goods sold and administrative expenses respectively.

19p120A(m) The actual return on plan assets was C495 (2009: C235).

19p120A(n) The principal actuarial assumptions used were as follows:

	2010		2009	
19p120A(n)	**UK**	**US**	**UK**	**US**
Discount rate	6.0%	6.1%	5.5%	5.6%
Inflation rate	3.6%	3.0%	3.3%	2.7%
Expected return on plan assets	8.5%	8.3%	8.7%	8.7%
Future salary increases	5.0%	4.5%	4.5%	4.0%
Future pension increases	3.6%	2.8%	3.1%	2.7%

19p120A (n)(vi) Assumptions regarding future mortality experience are set based on actuarial advice, published statistics and experience in each territory. Mortality assumptions for the most important countries are based on the following post-retirement mortality tables: (i) UK: PNMA 00 and PNFA 00 with medium cohort adjustment subject to a minimum annual improvement of 1% and scaling factors of 110% for current male pensioners, 125% for current female pensioners and 105% for future male and female pensioners; and (ii) US: RP2000 with a projection period of 10-15 years.

Appendix II – Alternative presentation of primary statements

(All amounts in C thousands unless otherwise stated)

These tables translate into an average life expectancy in years of a pensioner retiring at age 65 of:

19p120A(n)	2010 UK	2010 US	2009 UK	2009 US
Retiring at the end of the reporting period:				
– Male	22	20	22	20
– Female	25	24	25	24
– Retiring 20 years after the end of the reporting period:				
– Male	25	23	24	23
– Female	28	26	27	26

DV The sensitivity of the overall pension liability to changes in the weighted principal assumptions is:

	Change in assumption	Impact on overall liability
Discount rate	Increase/decrease by 0.5%	Increase/decrease by 7.2%
Inflation rate	Increase/decrease by 0.5%	Increase/decrease by 5.1%
Salary growth rate	Increase/decrease by 0.5%	Increase/decrease by 3.3%
Life expectancy	Increase by 1 year	Increase by 5.2%

19p122(b) *(b) Post-employment medical benefits*

The group operates a number of post-employment medical benefit schemes, principally in the US. The method of accounting, assumptions and the frequency of valuations are similar to those used for defined benefit pension schemes. The majority of these plans are unfunded.

19p120A(n) In addition to the assumptions set out above, the main actuarial assumption is a long-term increase in health costs of 8.0% a year (2009: 7.6%).

19p120A(d) The amounts recognised in the balance sheet were determined as follows:

19p120A(f)	2010	2009
Present value of funded obligations	705	340
Fair value of plan assets	(620)	(302)
Deficit of funded plans	85	38
Present value of unfunded obligations	1,325	663
Unrecognised actuarial losses	(8)	(9)
Liability in the balance sheet	**1,402**	692

(All amounts in C thousands unless otherwise stated)

19p120A(c) The movement in the defined benefit obligation is as follows:

	2010	2009
At 1 January	**1,003**	708
Current service cost	153	107
Interest cost	49	25
Actuarial losses/(gains)	(2)	204
Exchange differences	25	(41)
Liabilities acquired in a business combination (note 39)	802	–
At 31 December	**2,030**	1,003

19p120A(e) The movement in the fair value of plan assets of the year is as follows:

	2010	2009
At 1 January	302	207
Expected return on plan assets	53	25
Actuarial gains/(losses)	(2)	(1)
Exchange differences	5	(2)
Employer contributions	185	73
Assets acquired in a business combination (note 30)	77	–
At 31 December	**620**	302

19p120A(g) The amounts recognised in the income statement were as follows:

Current service cost	153	107
Interest cost	49	25
Expected return on plan assets	(53)	(25)
Net actuarial losses recognised in year	1	–
Total, included in employee benefits expense	**150**	107

19p120A(g) Of the total charge, C102 (2009:C71) and C48 (2009:C36) respectively were included in cost of goods sold and administrative expenses.

19p120A(m) The actual return on plan assets was C51 (2009: C24)

19p120A(o) The effect of a 1% movement in the assumed medical cost trend rate is as follows:

	Increase	Decrease
Effect on the aggregate of the current service cost and interest cost	24	(20)
Effect on the defined benefit obligation	366	(313)

(All amounts in C thousands unless otherwise stated)

(c) Post-employment benefits (pension and medical)

19p120A(j) Plan assets are comprised as follows:

	2010		2009	
Equity instruments	3,256	49%	1,224	40%
Debt instruments	1,524	23%	571	18%
Property	1,047	16%	943	30%
Other	784	12%	361	12%
	6,611	100%	3,099	100%

DV   Investments are well diversified, such that the failure of any single investment would not have a material impact on the overall level of assets. The largest proportion of assets is invested in equities, although the group also invests in property, bonds, hedge funds and cash. The group believes that equities offer the best returns over the long-term with an acceptable level of risk. The majority of equities are in a globally diversified portfolio of international blue chip entities, with a target of 60% of equities held in the UK and Europe, 30% in the US and the remainder in emerging markets.

19p120A(k) Pension plan assets include the company's ordinary shares with a fair value of C136 (2009: C126) and a building occupied by the group with a fair value of C612 (2009: C609).

19p120A(l) The expected return on plan assets is determined by considering the expected returns available on the assets underlying the current investment policy. Expected yields on fixed interest investments are based on gross redemption yields as at the end of the reporting period. Expected returns on equity and property investments reflect long-term real rates of return experienced in the respective markets.

19p120(q) Expected contributions to post-employment benefit plans for the year ending 31 December 2011 are C1,150.

DV   The group has agreed that it will aim to eliminate the deficit over the next nine years. Funding levels are monitored on an annual basis and the current agreed regular contribution rate is 14% of pensionable salaries in the UK and 12% in the US. The next triennial valuation is due to be completed as at 31 December 2011. The group considers that the contribution rates set at the last valuation date are sufficient to eliminate the deficit over the agreed period and that regular contributions, which are based on service costs, will not increase significantly.

DV   An alternative method of valuation to the projected unit credit method is a buy-out valuation. This assumes that the entire post-employment benefit liability will be settled by transferring all obligations to a suitable insurer. The group estimates the amount required to settle the post-employment benefit liabilities at the end of the reporting period would be C15,500.

(All amounts in C thousands unless otherwise stated)

19p120A(p)	2010	2009	2008	2007	2006
At 31 December					
Present value of defined benefit obligation	**11,391**	5,495	4,187	3,937	3,823
Fair value of plan assets	**6,611**	3,099	2,471	2,222	2,102
Deficit in the plan	**4,780**	2,396	1,716	1,715	1,721
Experience adjustments on plan liabilities	**(25)**	125	55	18	32
Experience adjustments on plan assets	**(17)**	(0)	(197)	(50)	(16)

(All amounts in C thousands unless otherwise stated)

Consolidated statement of cash flows – direct method

IAS 7 encourages the use of the 'direct method' for the presentation of cash flows from operating activities. The presentation of cash flows from operating activities using the direct method in accordance with IAS 7, paragraph 18, is as follows:

Consolidated statement of cash flows

			Year ended 31 December	
1p113, 7p10		Note	**2010**	2009
7p18(a)	**Cash flows from operating activities**			
	Cash receipts from customers		**212,847**	114,451
	Cash paid to suppliers and employees		**(156,613)**	(72,675)
	Cash generated from operations		**56,234**	41,776
	Interest paid		**(7,835)**	14,773)
	Income taxes paid		**(14,317)**	(10,526)
	Net cash flows from operating activities		**34,082**	16,477
7p21	**Cash flows from investing activities**			
7p39	Acquisition of subsidiary, net of cash acquired	39	**(3,950)**	–
7p16(a)	Purchases of property, plant and equipment (PPE)	6	**(9,755)**	(6,042)
7p16(b)	Proceeds from sale of PPE	36	**6,354**	2,979
7p16(a)	Purchases of intangible assets	7	**(3,050)**	(700)
7p16(c)	Purchases of available-for-sale financial assets	10	**(2,781)**	(1,126)
7p16(e)	Loans granted to associates	40	**(1,000)**	(50)
7p16(f)	Loan repayments received from associates	40	**14**	64
7p31	Interest received		**1,254**	1,193
7p31	Dividends received		**1,180**	1,120
	Net cash used in investing activities		**(11,734)**	(2,562)
7p21	**Cash flows from financing activities**			
7p17(a)	Proceeds from issuance of ordinary shares	17	**950**	1,070
7p17(b)	Purchase of treasury shares	17	**(2,564)**	–
7p17(c)	Proceeds from issuance of convertible bond		**50,000**	–
7p17(c)	Proceeds from issuance of redeemable preference shares		–	30,000
7p17(c)	Proceeds from borrowings		**8,500**	18,000
7p17(d)	Repayments of borrowings		**(78,117)**	(34,674)
7p31	Dividends paid to group shareholders		**(10,102)**	(15,736)
7p31	Dividends paid to holders of redeemable preference shares		**(1,950)**	(1,950)
7p31	Dividends paid to non-controlling interests		**(1,920)**	(550)
	Net cash used in financing activities		**(35,203)**	(3,840)
	Net (decrease)/increase in cash, cash equivalents and bank overdrafts		**(12,855)**	10,075
	Cash, cash equivalents and bank overdrafts at beginning of the year		**27,598**	17,587
	Exchange gains/(losses) on cash, cash equivalents and bank overdrafts		**535**	(64)
	Cash, cash equivalents and bank overdrafts at end of the year	15	**15,278**	27,598

The notes on pages 1 to 116 are an integral part of these consolidated financial statements.

(All amounts in C thousands unless otherwise stated)

Consolidated statement of comprehensive income – single statement, by function of expense

		Note	Year ended 31 December 2010	Year ended 31 December 2009
1p81-83, 1p103, 1p38, 1p113				
	Continuing operations			
1p82(a), 103	Revenue	5	**211,034**	112,360
1p99,103	Cost of sales		**(77,366)**	(46,68)
1p99,103	**Gross profit**		**133,668**	65,678
1p99,103	Distribution costs		**(52,140))**	(21,213)
1p99,103	Administrative expenses		**(28,778))**	(10,426)
1p99,103	Other income	27	**1,900**	1,259
1p85	Other (losses)/gains – net	26	**(90)**	63
1p85	Loss on expropriated land	28	**(1,117)**	–
1p85	**Operating profit**		**53,443**	35,361
1p85	Finance income	31	**1,730**	1,609
1p82(b)	Finance costs	31	**(8,173)**	(12,197)
1p85	Finance costs – net	31	**(6,443))**	(10,558)
1p82(c)	Share of (loss)/profit of associates	8	**(174)**	145
1p85 1p82(d), 12p77	**Profit before income tax**		**46,826**	24,918
12p77	Income tax expense	32	**(14,611))**	(8,670)
1p85 IFRS5p34, 12p81(b)	Profit for the year from continuing operations	16	**32,215**	16,248
	Discontinued operations:			
	Profit for the year from discontinued operations		**100**	120
1p82(f)	**Profit for the year**		**32,315**	16,368
1p82(g), 1p82(g), 16p77(f)	**Other comprehensive income:**			
	Gains on revaluation of land and buildings	20	**–**	1,133
1p82(g), IFRS7 p20(a)(ii) 28p39,	Available-for-sale financial assets	20	**560**	123
1p82(h)	Share of other comprehensive income of associates	20	**(12)**	(14)
1p82(g), 19p93A	Actuarial loss on retirement benefit obligations		**–**	(70)
12p80(d)	Impact of change in the Euravian tax rate on deferred tax	23	**(10)**	
1p82(g), IFRS7p23(c)	Cash flow hedges	20	**97**	(3)
1p82(g)	Net investment hedge	20	**(45)**	40
1p82(g)	Currency translation differences	20	**2,244**	(156)
IFRS3p59	Increase in fair values of proportionate holding of ABC Group	20	**850**	–
1p91(b)	Income tax relating to components of other comprehensive income		**(231)**	(224)
	Other comprehensive income for the year, net of tax		**3,453**	194
1p82(i)	**Total comprehensive income for the year**		**35,768**	16,562

Appendix II – Alternative presentation of primary statements

(All amounts in C thousands unless otherwise stated)

		Year ended 31 December	
		2010	2009
1p83(a)	**Profit attributable to:**		
1p83(a)(ii)	Owners of the parent	**29,767**	15,512
1p83(a)(i)	Non-controlling interest	**2,548**	856
		32,315	16,368
1p83(b)	**Total comprehensive income attributable to:**		
1p83(b)(ii)	Owners of the parent	**32,968**	15,746
1p83(b)(i)	Non-controlling interest	**2,800**	816
		35,768	16,562

Earnings per share from continuing and discontinued operations to the equity holders of the company during the year (expressed in C per share)

			2010	2009
	Basic earnings per share			
33p66	From continuing operations	34	**1.26**	0.75
33p68	From discontinued operations		**0.01**	0.01
			1.27	0.76
	Diluted earnings per share[1]			
33p66	From continuing operations	34	**1.15**	0.71
33p68	From discontinued operations		**0.01**	0.01
			1.16	0.72

The income tax effect has been presented on an aggregate basis; therefore an additional note disclosure resents the income tax effect of each component. Alternatively, this information could be presented within the statement of comprehensive income.

The notes on pages 1 to 116 are an integral part of these consolidated financial statements.

---

[1] EPS for discontinued operations may be given in the notes to the accounts instead of the face of the income statement.

(All amounts in C thousands unless otherwise stated)

Note – Income tax expense

Tax effects of components of other comprehensive income

Year ended 31 December

1p90			2010 Tax			2009 Tax	
		Before tax	(charge) credit	After tax	Before tax	(charge) credit	After tax
1p90	Fair value gains:						
1p90	– Land and buildings	–	–	–	1,133	(374)	759
1p90	– Available-for-sale financial assets	560	(198)	362	123	(61)	62
1p90	Share of other comprehensive income of associates	(12)	–	(12)	(14)	–	(14)
1p90	Actuarial loss on retirement benefit obligations	–	–	–	(705)	211	(494)
1p90	Impact of change in the Euravaian tax rate on deferred tax	–	(10)	(10)	–	–	–
1p90	Cash flow hedges	97	(33)	64	(3)	–	(3)
1p90	Net investment hedge	(45)	–	(45)	40	–	40
1p90	Currency translation differences	2,244	–	2,244	(156)	–	(156)
IFRS3p59	Increase in fair values of proportionate holding of ABC Group (note 39)	850	–	850	–	–	–
	Other comprehensive income	**3,694**	**(241)**	**3,453**	418	(224)	194

Appendix III – Policies and disclosures for areas not relevant to IFRS GAAP plc

Construction contracts

Note – Accounting policies

11p3   A construction contract is defined by IAS 11 as a contract specifically negotiated for the construction of an asset.

11p39(b)(c) Contract costs are recognised as expenses in the period in which they are incurred.

When the outcome of a construction contract cannot be estimated reliably, contract revenue is recognised only to the extent of contract costs incurred that are likely to be recoverable.

11p31   When the outcome of a construction contract can be estimated reliably and it is probable that the contract will be profitable, contract revenue is recognised over the period of the contract. When it is probable that total contract costs will exceed total contract revenue, the expected loss is recognised as an expense immediately.

Variations in contract work, claims and incentive payments are included in contract revenue to the extent that may have been agreed with the customer and are capable of being reliably measured.

The group uses the 'percentage-of-completion method' to determine the appropriate amount to recognise in a given period. The stage of completion is measured by reference to the contract costs incurred up to the end of the reporting period as a percentage of total estimated costs for each contract. Costs incurred in the year in connection with future activity on a contract are excluded from contract costs in determining the stage of completion. They are presented as inventories, prepayments or other assets, depending on their nature.

The group presents as an asset the gross amount due from customers for contract work for all contracts in progress for which costs incurred plus recognised profits (less recognised losses) exceed progress billings. Progress billings not yet paid by customers and retention are included within 'trade and other receivables'.

The group presents as a liability the gross amount due to customers for contract work for all contracts in progress for which progress billings exceed costs incurred plus recognised profits (less recognised losses).

(All amounts in C thousands unless otherwise stated)

Consolidated balance sheet (extracts)

	Note	2010	2009
1p60 **Current assets**			
1p54(h) Trade and other receivables	12	**23,303**	20,374
1p54(g) Inventories	13	**24,885**	18,481
1p60 **Current liabilities**			
1p54(k) Trade and other payables	21	**17,667**	13,733

Consolidated income statement (extracts)

	Note	2010	2009
11p39(a) Contract revenue		**58,115**	39,212
11p16 Contract costs		**(54,729)**	(37,084)
1p103 Gross profit		**3,386**	2,128
1p103 Selling and marketing costs		**(386)**	(128)
1p103 Administrative expenses		**(500)**	(400)

Note – Trade and other receivables (extracts)

	2010	2009
IFRS7p36, 1p78(b) Trade receivables	**18,174**	16,944
Less: Provision for impairment of receivables	**(109)**	(70)
Trade receivables – net	**18,065**	16,874
11p42(a) Amounts due from customers for contract work	**984**	788
11p40(c) Retentions	**232**	132
Prepayments	**1,300**	1,146
1p77, 24p17 Receivables from related parties (note 40)	**54**	46
1p77, 24p17 Loans to related parties (note 40)	**2,668**	
Total	**23,303**	20,374

Note – Trade and other payables (extracts)

	2010	2009
1p77 Trade payables	**10,983**	9,495
24p17 Amounts due to related parties (note 40)	**2,202**	1,195
11p42(b) Amounts due to customers for contract work	**855**	900
11p40(b) Advances received for contract work	**142**	355
Social security and other taxes	**2,002**	960
Accrued expenses	**1,483**	828
	17,667	13,733

Note – Inventories (extract)

	2010	2009
1p78(c) Raw materials	**7,622**	7,612
Work in progress (not related to construction contracts)	**1,810**	1,796
Finished goods	**15,268**	8,774
Costs capitalised in relation to construction contracts	**185**	299
	24,885	18,481

(All amounts in C thousands unless otherwise stated)

Note – Construction contracts

	2010	2009
11p40(a) The aggregate costs incurred and recognised profits (less recognised losses) to date	69,804	56,028
Less: Progress billings	(69,585)	(56,383)
Net balance sheet position for ongoing contracts	**219**	(355)

Leases: Accounting by lessor

17p4   A lease is an agreement whereby the lessor conveys to the lessee in return for a payment, or series of payments, the right to use an asset for an agreed period of time.

Note – Accounting policies

1p119   When assets are leased out under a finance lease, the present value of the lease payments is recognised as a receivable. The difference between the gross receivable and the present value of the receivable is recognised as unearned finance income.

Additional disclosure is required of the following for a lease:

(a)   reconciliation between the gross investment in the lease and the present value of the minimum lease payments receivable at the end of the reposting period. An entity discloses the gross investment in the lease and the present value of the minimum lease payments receivable at the end of the reporting periods:

    (i)   not later than one year;

    (ii)   ater than one year and not later than five years;

    (iii) later than five years.

(b)   unearned finance income

(c)   the unguaranteed residual values accruing to the benefit of the lessor

(d)   the accumulated allowance for uncollectible minimum lease payments receivable.

(e)   contingent rents recognised as income in the period.

(f)   a general description of the lessor's material leasing arrangements.

The method for allocating gross earnings to accounting periods is referred to a as the 'actuarial method'. The actuarial method allocated rentals between finance income and repayment of capital in each accounting period in such a way that finance income will emerge as a constant rate of return on the lessor's net investment in the lease.

17p49   When assets are leased out under an operating lease, the asset is included in the balance sheet based on the nature of the asset.

17p50   Lease income is recognised over the term of the lease on a straight-line basis.

(All amounts in C thousands unless otherwise stated)

Note – Property, plant and equipment

The category of vehicles and equipment includes vehicles leased by the group to third parties under operating leases with the following carrying amounts:

17p57		2010	2009
	Cost	70,234	–
	Accumulated depreciation at 1 January	(14,818)	–
	Depreciation charge for the year	(5,058)	–
	Net book amount	**50,358**	**–**

Note – Trade and other receivables

1p78(b)		2010	2009
	Non-current receivables		
17p47(a)	Finance leases – gross receivables	1,810	630
17p47(b)	Unearned finance income	(222)	(98)
		1,588	532
1p78(b)	**Current receivables**		
17p47(a)	Finance leases – gross receivables	1,336	316
17p47(b)	Unearned finance income	(300)	(98)
		1,036	218
1p78(b)	Gross receivables from finance leases:		
17p47(a)	No later than 1 year	1,336	316
	Later than 1 year and no later than 5 years	1,810	630
	Later than 5 years	–	-
		3,146	946
1p78(b), 17p47(b)	Unearned future finance income on finance leases	(522)	(196)
	Net investment in finance leases	**2,624**	**750**

1p78(b) The net investment in finance leases may be analysed as follows:

17p47(a)		2010	2009
	– No later than 1 year	1,036	218
	– Later than 1 year and no later than 5 years	1,588	532
	– Later than 5 years	–	–
		2,624	750

Note – Operating leases

17p56(a) **Operating leases commitments – group company as lessor**

The future minimum lease payments receivable under non-cancellable operating leases are as follows:

	2010	2009
No later than 1 year	12,920	12,920
Later than 1 year and no later than 5 years	41,800	41,800
Later than 5 years	840	10,840
	55,560	65,560

17p56(b) Contingent-based rents recognised in the income statement were C235 (2009: C40).

17p56(c) The company leases vehicles under various agreements which terminate between 2011 and 2016. The agreements do not include an extension option.

(All amounts in C thousands unless otherwise stated)

Investments: held-to-maturity financial assets

Note – Accounting policies

Investments

Held-to-maturity financial assets

1p119
39p9
Held-to-maturity financial assets are non-derivative financial assets with fixed or determinable payments and fixed maturities that the group's management has the positive intention and ability to hold to maturity. If the group were to sell other than an insignificant amount of held-to-maturity financial assets, the whole category would be tainted and reclassified as available for sale. Held-to-maturity financial assets are included in non-current assets, except for those with maturities less than 12 months from the end of the reporting period, which are classified as current assets.

Consolidated balance sheet

	2010	2009
1p60 **Non-current assets**		
1p54(d) Held-to-maturity financial assets	**3,999**	1,099

Note – Held-to-maturity financial assets

IFRS7
p27(b) *Held-to-maturity financial assets*

	2010	2009
39AG71-73 Listed securities:		
– Debentures with fixed interest of 5% and maturity date of 15 June 2015 – UK	**4,018**	984
– Debentures with fixed interest of 5.5% and maturity date of 15 June 2010 – US	**–**	160
Allowance for impairment	**(19)**	(45)
	3,999	1,099

The movement in held to maturity of financial assets may be summarised as follows:

	2010	2009
At 1 January	**1,009**	390
Exchange differences	**81**	56
Additions	**3,003**	978
Disposals	**(165)**	(280)
Provision for impairment	**(19)**	(45)
At 31 December	**3,999**	1,009
1p66 Less: non-current portion	**(3,999)**	(1,009)
1p66 **Current portion**	**–**	160

(All amounts in C thousands unless otherwise stated)

IFRS7p16 Movements on the provision for impairment of held-to-maturity financial assets are as follows:

	2010	2009
At 1 January	**45**	30
Provision for impairment	**–**	16
Unused amounts reversed	**(26)**	(3)
Unwind of discount (note 31)	**–**	2
At 31 December	**19**	45

IFRS7 appears at left margin: IFRS7 p20(e)

IFRS7 p12(b) The group has not reclassified any financial assets measured amortised cost rather than fair value during the year (2009: nil).

IFRS7 p20(a)(iii) There were no gains or losses realised on the disposal of held to maturity financial assets in 2010 and 2009, as all the financial assets were disposed of at their redemption date.

IFRS7p25 The fair value of held to maturity financial assets is based on quoted market bid prices (2010: C3,901; 2009: C976).

IFRS7 p34(c) Held-to-maturity financial assets are denominated in the following currencies:

	2010	2009
UK pound	**2,190**	990
US dollar	**1,809**	109
Total	**3,999**	1,099

IFRS7p36(a) The maximum exposure to credit risk at the reporting date is the carrying amount of held to maturity financial assets.

Government grants[1]

Note – Accounting policies

Government grants

**20p39(a)
20p12** Grants from the government are recognised at their fair value where there is a reasonable assurance that the grant will be received and the group will comply with all attached conditions.

Government grants relating to costs are deferred and recognised in the income statement over the period necessary to match them with the costs that they are intended to compensate.

Government grants relating to property, plant and equipment are included in non-current liabilities as deferred government grants and are credited to the income statement on a straight-line basis over the expected lives of the related assets.

---

[1] There are two approaches to accounting for government grants namely the capital approach, under which a grant is credited directly to shareholder's interest and the income approach, under which a grant is taken to income over one or more periods. The accounting policy and disclosure below reflects the income approach.

(All amounts in C thousands unless otherwise stated)

Note – Other (losses)/gains

20p39(b)
20p39(c)
The group obtained and recognised as income a government grant of C100 (2009: nil) to compensate for losses caused by flooding incurred in the previous year. The group is obliged not to reduce its average number of employees over the next three years under the terms of this government grant.

The group benefits from government assistance for promoting in international markets products made in the UK; such assistance includes marketing research and similar services provided by various UK government agencies free of charge.

Joint ventures

Note – Accounting policies

1p119 **Consolidation**

(c) Joint ventures

31p57
The group's interests in jointly controlled entities are accounted for by proportionate consolidation. The group combines its share of the joint ventures' individual income and expenses, assets and liabilities and cash flows on a line-by-line basis with similar items in the group's financial statements. The group recognises the portion of gains or losses on the sale of assets by the group to the joint venture that is attributable to the other venturers. The group does not recognise its share of profits or losses from the joint venture that result from the group's purchase of assets from the joint venture until it re-sells the assets to an independent party. However, a loss on the transaction is recognised immediately if the loss provides evidence of a reduction in the net realisable value of current assets, or an impairment loss.

Note – Interest in joint venture

31p56
The group has a 50% interest in a joint venture, JV&Co, which provides products and services to the automotive industry. The following amounts represent the group's 50% share of the assets and liabilities, and sales and results of the joint venture. They are included in the balance sheet and income statement:

	2010	2009
Assets:		
Long-term assets	**2,730**	2,124
Current assets	**803**	717
	3,533	2,841
Liabilities:		
Long-term liabilities	**1,114**	1,104
Current liabilities	**355**	375
	1,469	1,479
Net assets	**2,064**	1,362
Income	**5,276**	5,618
Expenses	**(3,754)**	(4,009)
Profit after income tax	**1,522**	1,609
31p55(b) **Proportionate interest in joint venture's commitments**	**90**	92

(All amounts in C thousands unless otherwise stated)

31p54   There are no contingent liabilities relating to the group's interest in the joint venture, and no contingent liabilities of the venture itself.

Oil and gas exploration assets

Note – Accounting policies

IFRS6p24   Oil and natural gas exploration and evaluation expenditures are accounted for using the 'successful efforts' method of accounting. Costs are accumulated on a field-by-field basis. Geological and geophysical costs are expensed as incurred. Costs directly associated with an exploration well, and exploration and property leasehold acquisition costs, are capitalised until the determination of reserves is evaluated. If it is determined that commercial discovery has not been achieved, these costs are charged to expense.

Capitalisation is made within property, plant and equipment or intangible assets according to the nature of the expenditure.

Once commercial reserves are found, exploration and evaluation assets are tested for impairment and transferred to development tangible and intangible assets. No depreciation and/or amortisation is charged during the exploration and evaluation phase.

(a) Development tangible and intangible assets

Expenditure on the construction, installation or completion of infrastructure facilities such as platforms, pipelines and the drilling of commercially proven development wells, is capitalised within property, plant and equipment and intangible assets according to nature. When development is completed on a specific field, it is transferred to production or intangible assets. No depreciation or amortisation is charged during the exploration and evaluation phase.

(b) Oil and gas production assets

Oil and gas production properties are aggregated exploration and evaluation tangible assets, and development expenditures associated with the production of proved reserves.

(c) Depreciation/amortisation

Oil and gas properties intangible assets are depreciated or amortised using the unit-of-production method. Unit-of-production rates are based on proved developed reserves, which are oil, gas and other mineral reserves estimated to be recovered from existing facilities using current operating methods. Oil and gas volumes are considered produced once they have been measured through meters at custody transfer or sales transaction points at the outlet valve on the field storage tank.

(d) Impairment – exploration and evaluation assets

Exploration and evaluation assets are tested for impairment when reclassified to development tangible or intangible assets, or whenever facts and circumstances indicate impairment. An impairment loss is recognised for the amount by which the exploration and evaluation assets' carrying amount exceeds their recoverable amount. The recoverable amount is the higher of the exploration and evaluation assets' fair value less costs to sell and their value in use. For the purposes of assessing impairment, the

(All amounts in C thousands unless otherwise stated)

exploration and evaluation assets subject to testing are grouped with existing cash-generating units of production fields that are located in the same geographical region.

(e) Impairment – proved oil and gas production properties and intangible assets

Proven oil and gas properties and intangible assets are reviewed for impairment whenever events or changes in circumstances indicate that the carrying amount may not be recoverable. An impairment loss is recognised for the amount by which the asset's carrying amount exceeds its recoverable amount. The recoverable amount is the higher of an asset's fair value less costs to sell and value in use. For the purposes of assessing impairment, assets are grouped at the lowest levels for which there are separately identifiable cash flows.

Property, plant and equipment[1]

	Capitalised exploration and evaluation expenditure	Capitalised development expenditure	Subtotal – assets under construction	Production assets	Other businesses and corporate assets	Total
At 1 January 2010						
Cost	218	12,450	12,668	58,720	3,951	75,339
Accumulated amortisation and impairment	(33)	–	(33)	(5,100)	(77)	(5,210)
Net book amount	185	12,450	12,635	53,620	3,874	70,129
Year ended 31 December 2010						
Opening net book amount	185	12,450	12,635	53,620	3,874	70,129
Exchange differences	17	346	363	1,182	325	1,870
Acquisitions	–	386	386	125	4	515
Additions	45	1,526	1,571	5,530	95	7,196
Transfers	(9)	(958)	(967)	1,712	–	745
Disposals	(12)	(1,687)	(1,699)	–	–	(1,699)
Depreciation charge	–	–	–	(725)	(42)	(767)
Impairment charge	(7)	(36)	(43)	(250)	(3)	(296)
Closing net book amount	**219**	**12,027**	**12,246**	**61,194**	**4,253**	**77,693**
At 31 December 2010						
Cost	264	12,027	12,291	67,019	4,330	83,640
Accumulated amortisation and impairment	(45)	–	(45)	(5,825)	(77)	(5,947)
Net book amount	**219**	**12,027**	**12,246**	**61,194**	**4,253**	**77,693**

[1] For the purpose of this illustrative appendix, comparatives for the year ended 31 December 2009 are not disclosed, although they are required by IAS 1.

(All amounts in C thousands unless otherwise stated)

Intangible assets[1]

	Capitalised exploration and evaluation expenditure	Capitalised development expenditure	Subtotal – intangible assets in progress expenditure	Production assets	Goodwill	Other	Total
At 1 January 2010							
Cost	5,192	750	5,942	3,412	9,475	545	19,374
Accumulated amortisation and impairment	(924)	–	(924)	(852)	(75)	(19)	(1,870)
Net book amount	4,268	750	5,018	2,560	9,400	526	17,504
Year ended 31 December 2010							
Opening net book amount	4,268	750	5,018	2,560	9,400	526	17,504
Exchange differences	152	8	160	195	423	28	806
Acquisitions	26	32	58	5	–	5	68
Additions	381	8	389	15	–	86	490
Transfers	(548)	548	–	–	–	–	-
Transfers to production	–	(850)	(850)	105	–	–	(745)
Disposals	–	(28)	(28)	(15)	–	–	(43)
Amortisation charge	–	–	–	(98)	–	(42)	(140)
Impairment charge	(45)	–	(45)	–	(175)	(5)	(225)
Closing net book amount	**4,234**	**468**	**4,702**	**2,767**	**9,648**	**598**	**17,715**
At 31 December 2010							
Cost	5,203	468	5,671	3,717	9,898	659	19,945
Accumulated amortisation and impairment	(969)	–	(969)	(950)	(250)	(61)	(2,230)
Net book amount	**4,234**	**468**	**4,702**	**2,767**	**9,648**	**598**	**17,715**

Assets and liabilities related to the exploration and evaluation of mineral resources other than those presented above are as follows:

	2010	2009
Receivables from joint venture partners	**25**	22
Payable to subcontractors and operators	**32**	34

Exploration and evaluation activities have led to total expenses of C59,000 (2009: C57,000), of which C52,000 (2009: C43,000) are impairment charges.

In 2010, the disposal of a 16.67% interest in an offshore exploration stage 'Field X' resulted in post-tax profits on sale of C3000 (2009: nil).

Cash payments of C415,000 (2009: C395,000) have been incurred related to exploration and evaluation activities. The cash proceeds due to the disposal of the interest in Field X were C8,000 (2009: nil).

---

[1] For the purpose of this illustrative appendix, comparatives for the year ended 31 December 2009 are not disclosed, although they are required by IAS 1.

(All amounts in C thousands unless otherwise stated)

Revenue recognition: multiple-element arrangements

Note – Accounting policies

The group offers certain arrangements whereby a customer can purchase a personal computer together with a two-year servicing agreement. When such multiple-element arrangements exist, the amount recognised as revenue upon the sale of the personal computer is the fair value of the computer in relation to the fair value of the arrangement taken as a whole. The revenue relating to the service element, which represents the fair value of the servicing arrangement in relation to the fair value of the arrangement, is recognised over the service period. The fair values of each element are determined based on the current market price of each of the elements when sold separately.

Where the group is unable to determine the fair value of each of the elements in an arrangement, it uses the residual value method. Under this method, the group determines the fair value of the delivered element by deducting the fair value of the undelivered element from the total contract consideration.

To the extent that there is a discount on the arrangement, such discount is allocated between the elements of the contract in such a manner as to reflect the fair value of the elements.

Defaults and breaches of loans payable[1]

Borrowings (extract)

IFRS7p18 The company was overdue paying interest on bank borrowings with a carrying amount of C10,000. The company experienced a temporary shortage of currencies because cash outflows in the second and third quarters for business expansions in the UK were higher than anticipated. As a result, interest payables of C700 due by 30 September 2011 remained unpaid.

The company has paid all outstanding amounts (including additional interests and penalties for the late payment) during the fourth quarter.

Management expects that the company will be able to meet all contractual obligations from borrowings on a timely basis going forward.

IFRS7p19 *Covenants*

Some of the company's credit contracts are subject to covenant clauses, whereby the company is required to meet certain key performance indicators. The company did not fulfil the debt/equity ratio as required in the contract for a credit line of C30,000, of which the company has currently drawn an amount of C15,000.

[1] These events or conditions may cast significant doubt about the entity's ability to continue as a going concern. When events or conditions have been identified that may cast significant doubt on an entity's ability to continue as a going concern, the auditor should: (1) Review management's plans for future actions based on its going concern assessment; (2) Gather sufficient appropriate audit evidence to confirm or dispel whether or not a material uncertainty exists through carrying out audit procedures considered necessary, including considering the effect of any plans of management and other mitigating factors; (3) Seek written representations from management regarding its plans for future action. If a material uncertainty related to events or conditions that may cast significant doubt on a company's ability to continue as a going concern exists, disclosure is required in the auditor's report. ISA 570, 'Going concern', establishes standards and provides guidance on the auditor's responsibility in the audit of financial statements with respect to the going concern assumption used in the preparation of the financial statements, including considering management's assessment of the entity's ability to continue as a going concern.

(All amounts in C thousands unless otherwise stated)

Due to this breach of the covenant clause, the bank is contractually entitled to request early repayment of the outstanding amount of C15,000. The outstanding balance was reclassified as a current liability[1]. Management started renegotiating the terms of the loan agreement when it became likely that the covenant clause may be breached.

The bank has not requested early repayment of the loan as of the date when these financial statements were approved by the board of directors. Management expects that a revised loan agreement will be in place during the first quarter of 2011.

[1] The reclassification of non-current debt to current liabilities would still be required if the terms of the loan were successfully renegotiated after the end of the reporting period.

(All amounts in C thousands unless otherwise stated)

Appendix IV – Critical accounting estimates and judgements not relevant to IFRS GAAP plc

Critical accounting estimates

1p125   The following critical accounting estimates may be applicable, among many other possible areas not presented in IFRS GAAP plc's consolidated financial statements.

(a) Useful lives of technology division's plant and equipment

The group's management determines the estimated useful lives and related depreciation charges for its plant and equipment. This estimate is based on projected product lifecycles for its high-tech segment. It could change significantly as a result of technical innovations and competitor actions in response to severe industry cycles. Management will increase the depreciation charge where useful lives are less than previously estimated lives, or it will write-off or write-down technically obsolete or non-strategic assets that have been abandoned or sold.

Were the actual useful lives of the technology division plant and equipment to differ by 10% from management's estimates, the carrying amount of the plant and equipment would be an estimated C1,000 higher or C970 lower.

(b) Warranty claims

The group generally offers three-year warranties for its personal computer products. Management estimates the related provision for future warranty claims based on historical warranty claim information, as well as recent trends that might suggest that past cost information may differ from future claims.

Factors that could impact the estimated claim information include the success of the group's productivity and quality initiatives, as well as parts and labour costs.

Were claims costs to differ by 10% from management's estimates, the warranty provisions would be an estimated C2,000 higher or C1,875 lower.

Critical accounting judgements

1p122   The following critical accounting judgements may be applicable, among many other possible areas not presented in IFRS GAAP plc's consolidated financial statements.

(a) Held-to-maturity investments

The group follows the IAS 39 guidance on classifying non-derivative financial assets with fixed or determinable payments and fixed maturity as held to maturity. This classification requires significant judgement. In making this judgement, the group evaluates its intention and ability to hold such investments to maturity.

If the group fails to keep these investments to maturity other than for specific circumstances explained in IAS 39, it will be required to reclassify the whole class as available-for-sale. The investments would, therefore, be measured at fair value not amortised cost.

If the class of held-to-maturity investments is tainted, the fair value would increase by C2,300, with a corresponding entry in the fair value reserve in shareholders' equity.

(All amounts in C thousands unless otherwise stated)

Appendix V – IFRS 9, Financial instruments

This appendix presents an illustrative example of the requirements of IFRS 9, 'Financial instruments', applicable to IFRS GAAP plc's financial statements. IFRS 9 allows for early adoption but is retrospectively applicable for annual periods beginning on or after 1 January 2013. If an entity adopts IFRS 9 for annual periods beginning before 1 January 2012, it does not need to restate prior periods (IFRS9p8.2.12) but can do so if it so chooses.

The main assumptions applied in this illustrative appendix are as follows:

1   IFRS GAAP plc decided to early adopt IFRS 9. It chose 31 December 2010 as the date of initial application.

2   The group decided to apply the limited exemption in IFRS9p8.2.12 and has not restated prior periods in its year of the initial application. Therefore:

    (a)   Where this exemption is applied, the entity should recognise any difference between the previous carrying amount and the carrying amount at the beginning of the annual reporting period that includes the date of initial application in the opening retained earnings (or other component of equity, as appropriate) of the reporting period that includes the date of initial application. In this appendix, IFRS plc does not have any such difference mainly because there were no changes in classification that could originate such a difference (that is, financial assets previously classified at amortised cost or cost and now classified as fair value through profit or loss or vice versa).

    (b)   The entity is not required to present a statement of financial position at the beginning of the earliest comparative period in accordance with IAS1p10(f), because comparative information is not restated as a result of early adoption.

    (c)   As the group is not restating prior periods, it discloses the applicable accounting policies for both periods, applying IAS 39 for the prior period and IFRS 9 for the current period. This appendix only includes the disclosures regarding IFRS 9.

    (d)   The previous point is also relevant for the notes regarding classification, measurement and disclosure of financial instruments previously applied, which are retained for the previous period. This illustrative appendix only includes the disclosures regarding IFRS 9 for the current period.

3   The group elected to present in other comprehensive income changes in the fair value of all its equity investments previously classified as available for sale, because its business model is not to hold these equity investments for trading. These investments do not meet the definition of held for trading of IAS39p1 and IAS39p9 (IFRS 9 App C26).

4   Debt securities and debentures were not considered to meet the criteria to be classified at amortised cost in accordance with IFRS 9, because the objective of the group's business model is not to hold these debt securities in order to collect their contractual cash flows. They were therefore reclassified from available for sale to financial assets at fair value through profit or loss.

5   The group did not have any financial assets designated as at fair value through profit or loss in the fair value option condition in accordance with IAS 39.

(All amounts in C thousands unless otherwise stated)

6   The group did not designate any financial asset as at fair value through profit or loss on initial application in accordance with IFRS9p4.5.

7   The group does not have unquoted equities or derivatives on unquoted equities.

Readers should refer to other PricewaterhouseCoopers publications where necessary.

(All amounts in C thousands unless otherwise stated)

Consolidated income statement

			As at 31 December	
1p81(b), 84, 1p10(b), 12, 1p113, 1p38		Note	2010	2009
	Continuing operations			
1p82(a)	Revenue	5	**211,034**	112,360
1p99, 103	Cost of sales		**(77,366)**	(46,682)
	Gross profit		**133,668**	65,678
1p99, 103	Distribution costs		**(52,140)**	(21,213)
1p99, 103	Administrative expenses		**(28,778)**	(10,426)
1p99, 103	Other income	27	**2,750**	1,259
1p85	Other (losses)/gains – net	26	**888**	63
1p82(aa)	Net gain/(loss) from derecognising financial assets measured at amortised cost		**–**	–
1p82(ca)	Net gain/ loss) on reclassification of financial assets from amortised cost to fair value through profit or loss		**–**	–
1p85	Loss on expropriated land	28	**(1,117)**	–
1p85	**Operating profit**		**55,271**	35,361
1p85	Finance income	31	**767**	1,609
1p82(b)	Finance costs	31	**(8,173)**	(12,197)
1p85	Finance costs – net	31	**(6,443)**	(10,588)
1p82(c)	Share of (loss)/profit of associates	8	**(174)**	145
1p85	**Profit before income tax**		**47,691**	24,918
1p82(d), 12p77	Income tax expense	32	**(14,616)**	(8,670)
1p85	**Profit for the year from continuing operations**		**32,075**	16,248
IFRS5p33(a)	**Discontinued operations**			
	Profit for the year from discontinued operations	16	**100**	120
1p82(f)	**Profit for the year**		**33,175**	16,368
	Profit attributable to:			
1p83(a)(ii)	– Owners of the parent		**30626**	15,512
1p83(a)(i)	– Minority interest		**2,549**	856
			33,175	16,368
	Earnings per share from continuing and operations attributable to the equity holders of the company during the year (expressed in C per share)			
	Basic earnings per share:			
33p66	– From continuing operations	34	**1.31**	0.75
33p68	– From discontinued operations		**0.01**	0.01
			1.32	0.76
	Diluted earnings per share:			
33p66	– From continuing operations	34	**1.19**	0.71
33p68	– From discontinued operations		**0.01**	0.01
			1.20	0.72

Note: IFRS plc has no 'Net gains/(losses) from derecognising financial assets measured at amortised cost' or 'Net gains/(losses) on reclassification of financial assets from amortised cost to fair value through profit or loss' amounts. However, these line items are shown for illustrative purposes, as they are required in IAS1p82(aa) and (ca) as IFRS 9 consequential amendments.

Appendix V – IFRS 9, Financial instruments

(All amounts in C thousands unless otherwise stated)

Consolidated statement of comprehensive income

		Note	Year ended 31 December 2010	2009
	Profit for the year		**33,175**	16,368
	Other comprehensive income:			
16p77(f)	Gains on revaluation of land and buildings	20	–	759
IFRS7 p20(a)(ii)	Available-for-sale financial assets	20	–	62
IFRS9 p5.4.1, IFRS7 p20(a)(viii)	Gain/(loss) arising on revaluation of financial assets at fair value through other comprehensive income	20	352	–
	Share of other comprehensive income of associates	20	(86)	91
19p93A	Actuarial loss on post employment benefit obligations	24	–	(494)
12p80(d)	Impact of change in Euravian tax rate on deferred tax	23	(10)	–
1Rp106(b), IFRS7p23(c)	Cash flow hedges	20	64	(3)
1p106(b)	Net investment hedge	20	(45)	40
1p106(b)	Currency translation differences	20	2,318	(261)
IFRS3p59	Increase in fair values of proportionate holding of ABC Group	20	850	–
	Other comprehensive income for the year, net of tax		**3,443**	194
	Total comprehensive income for the year		**36,618**	16,562
	Attributable to:			
1p83(b)(ii)	— Owners of the parent		**33,817**	15,746
1p83(b)(i)	— Minority interest		**2,801**	816
	Total comprehensive income for the year		**36,618**	16,562

Items in the statement above are disclosed net of tax. The income tax relating to each component of other comprehensive income is disclosed in note 32.

The notes on pages 43 to 115 are an integral part of these consolidated financial statements.

(All amounts in C thousands unless otherwise stated)

Consolidated balance sheet

	Note	As at 31 December 2010	2009
Assets			
Non-current assets			
Property, plant and equipment	6	**155,341**	100,233
Intangible assets	7	**26,272**	20,700
Investments in associates	8b	**13,373**	13,244
Deferred income tax assets	23	**3,520**	3,321
Available-for-sale financial assets	10, 14	**–**	14,910
Financial assets at fair value through other comprehensive income	14	**16,785**	–
Derivative financial instruments	11	**395**	245
Financial assets at fair value through profit or loss	14	**635**	–
Trade and other receivables	12	**2,322**	1,352
		218,643	154,005
Current assets			
Inventories	13	**24,700**	18,182
Trade and other receivables	12	**19,765**	18,330
Financial assets at fair value through other comprehensive income	14	**1,950**	–
Derivative financial instruments	11	**1,069**	951
Financial assets at fair value through profit or loss	14	**11,820**	7,972
Cash and cash equivalents	15	**17,928**	34,062
		77,232	79,497
Assets of disposal group classified as held for sale	16	**3,333**	–
		80,565	79,497
Total assets		**299,208**	233,502
Equity and liabilities			
Equity attributable to owners of the parent			
Ordinary shares	17	**25,300**	21,000
Share premium	17	**17,144**	10,494
Other reserves	20	**15,389**	7,005
Retained earnings	19	**67,601**	48,681
		125,434	87,180
Minority interests		**7,189**	1,766
Total equity		**132,623**	88,946

The reference codes in the left margin:

1p54, 1p113, 1p38, 1p60 — Assets / Non-current assets
1p54(a) — Property, plant and equipment
1p54(c) — Intangible assets
1p54(e) — Investments in associates
1p54(n), 1p54(d) — Deferred income tax assets
1p54(d), IFRS 7p8(d) — Available-for-sale financial assets
1p54(d), IFRS 7 p11A — Financial assets at fair value through other comprehensive income
1p54(d), IFRS 7p8(a) — Derivative financial instruments
1p54(d), IFRS 7p8(a) — Financial assets at fair value through profit or loss
1p54(h), IFRS7p8(c) — Trade and other receivables
1p60, 1p66 — Current assets
1p54(g) — Inventories
1p54(h), IFRS7p8(c) — Trade and other receivables
1p54(d), IFRS 7 p11A — Financial assets at fair value through other comprehensive income
1p54(d), IFRS 7p8(a) — Derivative financial instruments
1p54(d), IFRS 7p8(a) — Financial assets at fair value through profit or loss
1p54(i), IFRS7p8 — Cash and cash equivalents
IFRS5p38 — Assets of disposal group classified as held for sale
1p54(r) — Equity attributable to owners of the parent
1p78(e) — Ordinary shares
1p78(e) — Share premium
1p78(e) — Other reserves
1p78(e) — Retained earnings
1p54(q) — Minority interests

Appendix V – IFRS 9, Financial instruments

(All amounts in C thousands unless otherwise stated)

		Note	As at 31 December 2010	2009
1p60	**Liabilities**			
	Non-current liabilities			
1p54(m), IFRS7p8(f)	Borrowings	22	115,121	96,346
1p54(m), IFRS7p8(e)	Derivative financial instruments	11	135	129
1p54(o), 1p56	Deferred income tax liabilities	23	12,370	9,053
1p54(l), 1p78(d)	Retirement benefit obligations	24	4,635	2,233
1p54(l), 1p78(d)	Provisions for other liabilities and charges	25	1,320	274
			133,581	108,035
1p60, 1p69	**Current liabilities**			
1p54(k), IFRS7p8(f)	Trade and other payables	21	16,670	12,478
1p54(n)	**Current income tax liabilities**		2,566	2,771
1p54(m), IFRS7p8(f)	Borrowings	22	11,716	18,258
1p54(m), IFRS7p8(e)	Derivative financial instruments	11	460	618
1p54(l)	Provisions for other liabilities and charges	25	2,222	2,396
			33,634	36,521
IFRS5p38	Liabilities of disposal group classified as held for sale	16	220	–
			33,854	36,521
	Total liabilities		167,435	144,556
	Total equity and liabilities		300,058	233,502

10p17 The notes on pages 1 to 118 are an integral part of these consolidated financial statements.

CD Suede
Chief Executive

G Wallace
Finance Director

Commentary — Consolidated balance sheet

IFRS9 p8.2.12 An entity should apply IFRS 9 retrospectively in accordance to the transition provisions. However, these transition provisions have an exception that allow an entity that adopts IFRS 9 for reporting periods beginning before 1 January 2012 not to restate prior periods. Therefore, the requirement to present a statement of financial position as at the beginning of the earliest comparative period in accordance with IAS1p10(f) is not required in this example.

(All amounts in C thousands unless otherwise stated)

Consolidated statement of changes in equity

1p106, 108,109		Note	Share capital	Share premium	Other reserves	Retained earnings	Total	Minority interest	Total equity
				Attributable to owners of the parent					
	Balance at 1 January 2009		20,000	10,424	6,364	48,470	85,258	1,500	86,758
	Comprehensive income								
1p106(d)(i)	Profit or loss					15,512	15,512	856	16,368
1p106(d)(ii)	**Other comprehensive income**								
16p77(f), 1p82(g) 16p41	Gain on the revaluation of land and buildings	20	–	–	759	–	759	–	759
	Depreciation transfer on land and buildings, net of tax	19	–	–	(87)	87	–	–	–
1p82(g), IFRS7 p20(a)(ii)	– Available-for-sale financial assets	20	–	–	62	–	62	–	62
1p82(h)	Share of other comprehensive income/(loss) of associates	–	–	–	91	–		91	–	
19p93(b)	Actuarial loss on post employment benefit obligations		–	–	–	(494)	(494)	–	(494)
1p82(g), IFRS7p23(c)	Cash flow hedges, net of tax	20	–	–	(3)	–	(3)	–	(3)
1p82(g), 39p102(a)	Net investment hedge	20	–	–	40	–	40	–	40
1p82(g), 21p52(b)	Currency translation differences	20	–	–	(221)	–	(221)	(40)	(261)
	Total other comprehensive income		–	–	641	(407)	234	(40)	194
1p106(a)	**Total comprehensive income**		**–**	**–**	**641**	**15,105**	**15,746**	**816**	**16,562**
	Transactions with owners								
	Employees share option scheme:								
IFRS2p50	– Value of employee services	19	–	–	–	822	822	–	822
IFRS2p50	– Proceeds from shares issued	17	1,000	70	–	–	1,070	–	1,070
	– Tax credit relating to share option scheme	19	–	–	–	20	20	–	20
1p106(d)(iii)	Dividends relating to 2008	35	–	–	–	– 15,736	– 15,736	– 550	– 16,286
1p106(d)(iii)	**Total transactions with owners**		**1,000**	**70**	**–**	**– 14,894**	**– 13,824**	**– 550**	**– 14,374**
	Balance at 1 January 2010		**21,000**	**10,494**	**7,005**	**48,681**	**87,180**	**1,766**	**88,946**
IFRS9 p8.2.12	Effect of change in accounting policy for classification and measurement of financial assets (note 2.1)		–	–	(150)	150	–	–	–
	Adjusted balance at 1 January 2010		**21,000**	**10,494**	**6,855**	**48,831**	**87,180**	**1,766**	**88,946**

(All amounts in C thousands unless otherwise stated)

		Note							
	Comprehensive income								
1p106(d)(i)	Profit or loss		–	–	–		30,626	2,549	33,175
1p82(g)	Gain on the revaluation of land and buildings		–	–	–	–	–	–	–
16p41	Depreciation transfer on land and buildings, net of tax	19	–	–	(100)	100	–	–	–
IFRS9 p5.4.1, IFRS7 p20(a)(viii)	Gain/(loss) arising on revaluation of financial assets at fair value through other comprehensive income	20	–	–	352	–	352	–	352
	Share of other comprehensive income/(loss) of associates		–	–	(86)	–	(86)	–	(86)
1p82(g), IFRS7p23(c)	Cash flow hedges, net of tax	20	–	–	64	–	64	–	64
1p82(g), 39p102(a)	Net investment hedge	20	–	–	(45)	–	(45)	–	(45)
1p82(g), 21p52(b)	Currency translation differences	20	–	–	2,066	–	2,066	252	2,318
IFRS3p59	Increase in fair values of proportionate holding of ABC Group	20	–	–	850	–	850	–	850
12p80(d)	Impact of the change in the Euravian tax rate on deferred tax	23	–	–	–	(10)	(10)	–	(10)
	Total other comprehensive income		–	–	3,111	90	3,191	252	3,443
1p106(a)	**Total comprehensive income for the period**		**–**	**–**	**3,111**	**29,866**	**33,817**	**2,801**	**36,618**
	Transactions with owners								
	Employees share option scheme:								
IFRS2p50	– Value of employee services	19	–	–	–	690	690	–	690
IFRS2p50	– Proceeds from shares issued	17	750	200	–	–	950	–	950
	– Tax credit relating to share option scheme	19	–	–	–	30	30	–	30
1Rp106(d)(iii)	Issue of ordinary shares related to business combination	17	3,550	6,450	–	–	10,000	–	10,000
1Rp106(d)(iii)	Purchase of treasury shares	19	–	–	–	(2,564)	(2,564)	–	(2,564)
	Convertible bond — equity component, net of tax	20	–	–	5,433	–	5,433	–	5,433
1Rp106(d)(iii)	Dividends relating to 2009	35	–	–	–	(10,102)	(10,102)	(1,920)	(12,022)
1Rp106(d)(iii)	Total contributions by and distributions to owners		4,300	6,650	5,433	(11,946)	4,437	(1,920)	2,517
	Changes in ownership interests in subsidiaries that do not result in a loss of control								
1Rp106(d)(iii)	Minority interest arising on business combination	39	–	–	–	–	–	4,542	4,542
1Rp106(d)(iii)	**Total transactions with owners**		**4,300**	**6,650**	**5,433**	**(11,946)**	**4,437**	**2,622**	**7,059**
	Balance at 31 December 2010		**25,300**	**17,144**	**15,389**	**66,751**	**125,434**	**7,189**	**132,623**

The notes on pages 1 to 118 are an integral part of these consolidated financial statements.

(All amounts in C thousands unless otherwise stated)

2 Summary of significant accounting policies

2.1 Basis of preparation

2.1.1 Changes in accounting policy and disclosures

(a) New and amended standards adopted by the group

(Refer to the note 2.1.1 in the main section of this publication.)

8p28

IFRS 9, 'Financial instruments: Classification and measurement', effective 1 January 2013. IFRS 9 was issued in November 2009. It replaces the parts of IAS 39 that relate to the classification and measurement of financial assets. IFRS 9 requires financial assets to be classified into two measurement categories: those measured as at fair value and those measured at amortised cost. The determination is made at initial recognition. The classification depends on the entity's business model for managing its financial instruments and the contractual cash flow characteristics of the instrument. Adoption of IFRS 9 is mandatory from 1 January 2013; earlier adoption is permitted.

8p28,
IFRS9
p8.2.1,
p8.2.3,
p8.2.12

The group has adopted IFRS 9 from 31 December 2010, as well as the related consequential amendments to other IFRSs, because this new accounting policy provides reliable and more relevant information for users to assess the amounts, timing and uncertainty of future cash flows. In accordance with the transition provisions of the standard, comparative figures have not been restated.

IFRS9
p8.2.4

The group's management has assessed the financial assets held by the group at the date of initial application of IFRS 9 (31 December 2010). The main effects resulting from this assessment were:

- Investments in debt securities, and debentures previously classified as available for sale, do not meet the criteria to be classified as at amortised cost in accordance with IFRS 9. They are now therefore classified as financial assets at fair value through profit or loss. As a result, on 1 January 2010 assets with a fair value of C680 at 1 January 2010 were transferred to investments held at fair value through profit or loss; their related fair value gains of C150 were reclassified from the available-for-sale investments reserve to retained earnings. In 2010, fair value gains related to these investments amounting to C15 were recognised in profit or loss, along with the related deferred tax expense of C5.
- Equity investments not held for trading that were previously measured at fair value and classified as available for sale have been designated as at fair value through other comprehensive income. As a result, fair value gains of C1,088 were reclassified from the available-for-sale investments reserve to the investments revaluation reserve at 1 January 2010.
- There was no difference between the previous carrying amount (IAS 39) and the revised carrying amount (IFRS 9) of the financial assets at 1 January 2010 to be recognised in opening retained earnings.

8p28(f)

The effect of this change in accounting policy on earnings per share is shown in note 34.

1p119

2.4 Foreign currency translation

(Refer to the note 2.4 in the main section of this publication.)

Appendix V – IFRS 9, Financial instruments

(All amounts in C thousands unless otherwise stated)

1p119   *(b) Transactions and balances*

21p21, 28,
21p32,
39p95(a),
39p102(a)
Foreign currency transactions are translated into the functional currency using the exchange rates prevailing at the dates of the transactions or valuation where items are re-measured. Foreign exchange gains and losses resulting from the settlement of such transactions and from the translation at year-end exchange rates of monetary assets and liabilities denominated in foreign currencies are recognised in the income statement, except when deferred in equity as qualifying cash flow hedges and qualifying net investment hedges.

Foreign exchange gains and losses that relate to borrowings and cash and cash equivalents are presented in the income statement within 'finance income or cost'. All other foreign exchange gains and losses are presented in the income statement within 'other (losses)/gains — net'.

21p30   Translation differences on non-monetary financial assets and liabilities such as equities held at fair value through profit or loss are recognised in profit or loss as part of the fair value gain or loss. Translation differences on non-monetary financial assets such as equity investments whose changes in the fair value are presented in other comprehensive income are included in the related reserve in equity.

(Refer to the note 2.4(c) onwards in the main section of this publication.)

2.9 Financial assets

2.9.1 Classification prior to 1 January 2010

(Refer to the note 2.9.1 in the main section of this publication.)

2.9.2 Recognition and measurement prior to 1 January 2010

(Refer to the note 2.9.2 in the main section of this publication.)

2.9.3 Classification from 1 January 2010

IFRS9p4.1 As from 1 January 2010, the group classifies its financial assets in the following categories: those to be measured subsequently at fair value, and those to be measured at amortised cost. This classification depends on whether the financial asset is a debt or equity investment.

Debt investments

(a) Financial assets at amortised cost

IFRS9p4.2 A debt investment is classified as 'amortised cost' only if both of the following criteria are met: the objective of the group's business model is to hold the asset to collect the contractual cash flows; and the contractual terms give rise on specified dates to cash flows that are solely payments of principal and interest on the principal outstanding. The nature of any derivatives embedded in the debt investment are considered in determining whether the cash flows of the investment are solely payment of principal and interest on the principal outstanding and are not accounted for separately.

(All amounts in C thousands unless otherwise stated)

(b) Financial assets at fair value

IFRS9p4.4 If either of the two criteria above are not met, the debt instrument is classified as 'fair value through profit or loss'.

IFRS9p4.5 The group has not designated any debt investment as measured at fair value through profit or loss to eliminate or significantly reduce an accounting mismatch.

IFRS9 p5.4.4, p5.4.5 All equity investments are measured at fair value. Equity investments that are held for trading are measured at fair value through profit or loss. For all other equity investments, the group can make an irrevocable election at initial recognition to recognise changes in fair value through other comprehensive income rather than profit or loss.

2.9.4 Recognition and measurement from 1 January 2010

39p38, IFRS9 p3.1.2 Regular purchases and sales of financial assets are recognised on the trade-date — the date on which the group commits to purchase or sell the asset. Financial assets are derecognised when the rights to receive cash flows from the investments have expired or have been transferred and the group has transferred substantially all risks and rewards of ownership.

IFRS9 p5.1.1, IFRS 9 p5.2.1, 39p48, 48A, AG69-AG82 At initial recognition, the group measures a financial asset at its fair value plus, in the case of a financial asset not at fair value through profit or loss, transaction costs that are directly attributable to the acquisition of the financial asset. Transaction costs of financial assets carried at fair value though profit or loss are expensed in the income statement.

IFRS9 p5.4.1 A gain or loss on a debt investment that is subsequently measured at fair value and is not part of a hedging relationship is recognised in profit or loss and presented in the income statement within 'other (losses)/gains — net' in the period in which they arise.

IFRS9 p5.4.2 A gain or loss on a debt investment that is subsequently measured at amortised cost and is not part of a hedging relationship is recognised in profit or loss when the financial asset is derecognised or impaired and through the amortisation process using the effective interest rate method (note 2.11).

IFRS9 p5.4.4, p5.4.5 The group subsequently measures all equity investments at fair value. Where the group's management has elected to present unrealised and realised fair value gains and losses on equity investments in other comprehensive income, there is no subsequent recycling of fair value gains and losses to profit or loss. Dividends from such investments continue to be recognised in profit or loss as long as they represent a return on investment.

IFRS9p4.9 The group is required to reclassify all affected debt investments when and only when its business model for managing those assets changes.

2.11 Impairment of financial assets

(a) Assets carried at amortised cost

IFRS9 p5.2.2, 39p58, 39p59 The group assesses at the end of each reporting period whether there is objective evidence that a financial asset or group of financial assets measured at amortised cost is impaired. A financial asset or a group of financial assets is impaired and impairment losses are incurred only if there is objective evidence of impairment as a result of one or

(All amounts in C thousands unless otherwise stated)

more events that occurred after the initial recognition of the asset (a 'loss event') and that loss event (or events) has an impact on the estimated future cash flows of the financial asset or group of financial assets that can be reliably estimated.

(Refer to the note 2.11(a) in the main section of this publication.)

(b) Assets classified as available for sale (applicable until 31 December 2009)

(Refer to the note 2.11(b) in the main section of this publication.)

Commentary — Summary of significant accounting policies

(Refer to the 'Summary of significant accounting policies' commentary box in the main section of this publication.)

IFRS 9

IFRS9p4.1, p4.2, p4.4   IFRS 9 includes a single model that has only two classification categories: amortised cost and fair value. To qualify for amortised cost accounting, the instrument must meet two criteria: (1) the objective of the business model is to hold the financial asset for the collection of the cash flows; and (2) all contractual cash flows represent only principal and interest on that principal. All other instruments are mandatorily measured at fair value. Classification under IFRS 9 is determined at inception based on the two criteria previously described.

IFRS9p5.4.4, B5.12   IFRS 9 requires all equity investments to be measured at fair value. However an entity may make an irrevocable election at initial recognition to present all fair value changes for non-trading equity investments in other comprehensive income. There is no subsequent recycling of fair value gains and losses to profit or loss; there is therefore no impairment. The standard also requires recognition of dividends received from these investments in profit or loss.

IFRS9p4.9, p5.3.1, p5.3.2, B5.9-5.11   IFRS 9 prohibits reclassifications between fair value and amortised cost except in rare circumstances when the entity's business model changes. All reclassifications are accounted for prospectively. Any difference between the carrying amount and fair value on a reclassification is recognised in a separate line in profit or loss. To ensure full transparency, the standard requires additional disclosures for any reclassifications.

IFRS9p4.5   IFRS 9 continues to allow entities the option to designate assets at fair value through profit or loss at initial recognition where this significantly reduces an accounting mismatch. The designation at fair value through profit or loss is irrevocable.

IFRS9 p8.2.11, pB5.5-5.8   IFRS 9 removes the exemption allowing unquoted equities and derivatives on unquoted equities to be measured at cost. Such investments are required to be measured at fair value through profit or loss. IFRS 9 provides guidance on when cost may be an appropriate estimate of fair value. Any difference between the previous carrying amount in accordance with IAS 39 and fair value (IFRS 9) should be recognised in the opening retained earnings of the reporting period that includes the date of initial application.

(All amounts in C thousands unless otherwise stated)

IFRS 9 **p8.1.1-** **8.2.2,** **p8.2.12**	The effective date of IFRS 9 is 1 January 2013; early application is permitted. IFRS 9 should be applied retrospectively. However, if adopted before 1 January 2012, comparative periods do not need to be restated. In addition, entities adopting before 1 January 2011 are allowed to designate any date between then and the date of issuance of IFRS 9 as the date of initial application, which is the date upon which the classification of financial assets is determined.
IFRS9 **p8.2.3**	If the date of initial application of IFRS 9 is not at the beginning of a reporting period, the entity should disclose that fact and the reasons for using that date of initial application.
IFRS9 **p8.2.4**	At the date of initial application of IFRS 9, an entity should assess whether a financial asset meets the criteria in IFRS9p4.2(a) on the basis of the facts and circumstances that exist at the date of initial application.
IFRS9 **p8.2.7**	An entity may, at the date of initial application of IFRS 9, designate a financial asset at fair value through profit or loss (IFRS9p4.5) or an investment in an equity instrument at fair value through other comprehensive income (IFRS9p5.4.4). Such designations are made on the basis of the facts and circumstances that exist at the date of initial application.
IFRS9 **p8.2.12**	If an entity does not restate prior periods because it adopted IFRS 9 before 1 January 2012, it should recognise any difference between the previous carrying amount and the carrying amount at the beginning of the annual reporting period that includes the date of initial application in the opening retained earnings (or other component of equity, as appropriate) of the reporting period that includes the date of initial application.
IFRS9 **pB5.14**	IFRS 9p5.4.4 permits an entity to make an irrevocable election to present in other comprehensive income changes in the fair value of an investment in an equity instrument that is not held for trading. Such an investment is not a monetary item. The gain or loss that is presented in other comprehensive income in accordance with IFRS 9p5.4.4 therefore includes any related foreign exchange component.

3 Financial risk management

3.1 Financial risk factors

(Refer to the note 3.1 in the main section of this publication.)

(a) Market risk

(Refer to the note 3.1(a) in the main section of this publication.)

(ii) Price risk

IFRS7p33
(a)(b) The group is exposed to equity securities price risk because of investments held by the group and classified on the consolidated balance sheet at fair value. The group is not exposed to commodity price risk. To manage its price risk arising from investments in

(All amounts in C thousands unless otherwise stated)

equity securities, the group diversifies its portfolio. Diversification of the portfolio is done in accordance with the limits set by the group.

The group's investments in equity of other entities that are publicly traded are included in one of the following three equity indexes: DAX equity index, Dow Jones equity index and FTSE 100 UK equity index.

(iii) Cash flow and fair value interest rate risk

(Refer to the note 3.1(a)(iii) in the main section of this publication.)

IFRS7p40
IFRS7IG36 At 31 December 2010, if interest rates on Currency-denominated borrowings had been 0.1% higher/lower with all other variables held constant, post-tax profit for the year would have been C22 (2009: C21) lower/higher, mainly as a result of higher/lower interest expense on floating rate borrowings and C5 lower/higher as a result of a decrease/ increase in the fair value of fixed rate financial assets measured at fair value through profit or loss. Other components of equity in 2009 would have been C3 lower/higher for fixed rate financial assets classified as available for sale. At 31 December 2010, if interest rates on UK pound-denominated borrowings at that date had been 0.5% higher/lower with all other variables held constant, post-tax profit for the year would have been C57 (2009: C38) lower/higher, mainly as a result of higher/lower interest expense on floating rate borrowings; and C6 lower/higher mainly as a result of a decrease/increase in the fair value of fixed rate financial assets classified at fair value through profit or loss. Other components of equity in 2009 would have been C4 lower/higher mainly as a result of a decrease/increase in the fair value of fixed rate financial assets classified as available for sale.

(Refer to the note 3.1(a)(iii) in the main section of this publication.)

3.3 Fair value estimation

(Refer to the note 3.3 in the main section of this publication.)

IFRS7
p27B(a) The following table presents the group's assets and liabilities that are measured at fair value at 31 December 2010. (Refer to the analysis for the comparative year in the main section of this publication.)

	Level 1	Level 2	Level 3	Total
Assets				
Financial assets at fair value:				
– Trading derivatives	–	250	111	361
– Trading equity securities	11,820	–	–	11,820
– Investment equity securities	18,735	–	–	18,735
– Debt investments	288	347	–	635
Derivatives used for hedging	–	1,103	–	1,103
Total assets	**30,843**	**1,700**	**111**	**32,654**
Liabilities				
Financial liabilities at fair value through profit or loss:				
– Trading derivatives	–	268	–	268
Derivatives used for hedging	–	327	–	327
Total liabilities	**–**	**595**	**–**	**595**

(Refer to the note 3.3 in the main section of this publication.)

(All amounts in C thousands unless otherwise stated)

1p125   **4.1 Critical accounting estimates and assumptions**

(Refer to the note 4.1 in the main section of this publication.)

(c) Fair value of derivatives and other financial instruments

IFRS7p27(a) The fair value of financial instruments that are not traded in an active market (for example, over-the-counter derivatives) is determined by using valuation techniques. The group uses its judgement to select a variety of methods and make assumptions that are mainly based on market conditions existing at the end of each reporting period. The group has used discounted cash flow analysis for various debt investments that are not traded in active markets.

The carrying amount of such debt investments would be an estimated C12 lower or C15 higher were the discount rate used in the discount cash flow analysis to differ by 10% from management's estimates.

(Refer to the note 4.1(d) onwards in the main section of this publication.)

1p122   **4.2 Critical judgements in applying the entity's accounting policies**

(Refer to the note 4.2 in the main section of this publication.)

(b) Impairment of available-for-sale equity investments

(Refer to the note 4.2(b) in the main section of this publication.)

Appendix V – IFRS 9, Financial instruments

(All amounts in C thousands unless otherwise stated)

9a Financial instruments by category

IFRS7p6-8 Financial assets	2010
Financial assets measured at fair value through profit or loss	
IFRS9p.4.4,	
IFRS 7p8(a) Financial assets held for trading:	
– Investments in equity instruments held for trading (note 14)	11,820
– Derivatives used for hedging (note 11)	1,103
– Derivatives used for trading (note 11)	361
	13,284
Financial assets at fair value through profit or loss:	
IFRS9p4.5,	
IFRS7p8(a) – Investments in debt securities (note 14)	635
	635
Financial assets measured at fair value through other comprehensive income:	
IFRS9	
p5.4.4 – Investments in equity instruments (note 14)	18,735
	18,735
IFRS9 4.2 Financial assets measured at amortised cost:	
– Trade and other receivables excluding pre-payments (note 12)	20,787
– Cash and cash equivalents (note 15)	17,928
	38,715
Total	**71,369**

IFRS7p6-8 Financial assets	2009
Loans and receivables:	
– Trade and other receivables excluding pre-payments (note 12)	18,536
– Cash and cash equivalents (note 15)	34,062
Assets at fair value through profit and loss:	
– Derivative financial instruments (note 11)	321
– Financial assets at fair value through profit or loss (note 14)	7,972
Derivatives used for hedging (note 11)	875
Available for sale (note 10)	14,910
Total	**76,676**

Pre-payments are excluded from the trade and other receivables balance, as this analysis is required only for financial instruments (C1,300 and C1,146 as of 2010 and 2009, respectively).

The categories in this disclosure for financial assets are determined by IFRS 9 in 2010 and by IAS 39 in 2009 (note 2.9). There are no changes to the disclosure categories for financial liabilities.

(All amounts in C thousands unless otherwise stated)

IFRS7p6-8	**Financial liabilities**	**2010**	**2009**
	Liabilities at fair value through the profit and loss:		
	– Derivative financial instruments (note 11)	268	298
	Derivatives used for hedging (note 11)	327	449
	Other financial liabilities at amortised cost:		
	– Borrowings (excluding finance lease liabilities)	117,839	104,006
	– Finance lease liabilities	8,998	10,598
	– Trade and other payables excluding statutory liabilities	15,668	11,518
	Total	**143,100**	**126,869**

Statutory liabilities are excluded from the trade payables balance, as this analysis is required only for financial instruments.

9b Credit quality of financial assets

(Refer to the note 9b in the main section of this publication.)

		2010	**2000**
DV	**Investments in debt securities**		
	A (debt securities at fair value through profit or loss)	635	–
	A (debt securities classified as available for sale)	–	264
		635	**264**

(Refer to the note 9b in the main section of this publication.)

Appendix V – IFRS 9, Financial instruments

(All amounts in C thousands unless otherwise stated)

9c Classification of financial assets at the date of initial application

IFRS7p44I The classification and measurement category for each class of financial assets at the date of initial application were as follows:

Financial asset	Measurement category		Carrying amount		
	Original (IAS 39)	New (IFRS 9)	Original (IAS 39)	New (IFRS 9)	Diff-erence
Equity investments (note 10)	Available for sale	Financial assets at fair value through other comprehensive income	18,735	18,735	–
Debentures (note 10)	Available for sale	Financial asset at fair value through profit or loss	210	210	–
Cumulative redeemable preference shares (note 10)	Available for sale	Financial asset at fair value through profit or loss	78	78	–
Debt securities (note 10)	Available for sale	Financial asset at fair value through profit or loss	347	347	–
Interest rate swaps (note 11)	Derivatives used for hedging	Derivatives used for hedging	408	408	–
Forward foreign exchange contracts – cash flow hedges (note 11)	Derivatives used for hedging	Derivatives used for hedging	695	695	–
Forward foreign exchange contracts – trading (note 11)	Financial asset at fair value through profit or loss	Financial asset at fair value through profit or loss	361	361	–
Equity investments – held for trading (note 14)	Financial asset at fair value through profit or loss	Financial asset at fair value through profit or loss	11,820	11,820	–
Trade and other receivables (note 12)	Loans and receivables	Financial assets at amortised cost	18,065	18,065	–
Loans to related parties (note 12)	Loans and receivables	Financial assets at amortised cost	2,722	2,722	–
Cash and cash equivalents (note 15)	Loans and receivables	Financial assets at amortised cost	17,928	17,928	–
Total			**71,369**	**71,369**	**–**

IFRS7p44J Debt securities, debentures and preference shares that are not equity do not meet the criteria to be classified as at amortised cost in accordance with IFRS 9, because the objective of the group's business model is not to hold these debt securities in order to collect their contractual cash flows. Therefore, they were re-classified from available for sale to financial assets at fair value through profit or loss.

IFRS7 p11A(b), 39p1 The group elected to present in other comprehensive income changes in the fair value of all its equity investments previously classified as available for sale, because the business model is to hold these equity investments for long-term strategic investment and not for trading.

(All amounts in C thousands unless otherwise stated)

IFRS7 p44I(c) The group did not have any financial assets in the statement of financial position that were previously designated as fair value through profit or loss but are no longer so designated. Neither did it designate any financial asset at fair value through profit or loss on initial application of IFRS 9.

Commentary

IFRS9 pB8.1 At the date of initial application of IFRS 9, an entity must determine whether the objective of the its business model for managing any of its debt investments meets the condition in IFRS9.4.2(a) or if its equity investments are eligible for the election in IFRS9.5.4.4. For that purpose, an entity should determine whether financial assets meet the definition of held for trading based on the facts and circumstances that exist at the date of initial application.

39p1 In accordance with IAS39.1 (IFRS 9 consequential amendment), a financial asset is held for trading if:

(a) it is acquired or incurred principally for the purpose of selling or repurchasing it in the near term;
(b) on initial recognition it is part of a portfolio of identified financial instruments that are managed together and for which there is evidence of a recent actual pattern of short-term profit-taking; or
(c) it is a derivative.

For the purpose of this illustrative appendix, the equity investments previously classified as available for sale do not meet the definition of financial assets held for trading.

IFRS7p44I IFRS 7 requires an entity, when it first applies IFRS 9, to disclose for each class of financial assets at the date of initial application:

(a) the original measurement category and carrying amount determined in accordance with IAS 39;
(b) the new measurement category and carrying amount determined in accordance with IFRS 9; and
(c) the amount of any financial asset that were previously designated as measured at fair value through profit or loss but are no longer so designated.

IFRS9 p8.2.12 The original and new carrying amounts to be included in this disclosure should be at the beginning of the annual reporting period that includes the date of initial application.

IFRS7p44J An entity should disclose qualitative information to enable users to understand the following aspects, when it first applies IFRS 9:

(a) how it applied the classification requirements in IFRS 9 to those financial assets whose classification has changed as a result of applying IFRS 9.
(b) the reasons for any designation or de-designation of financial assets or financial liabilities as measured at fair value through profit or loss.

Appendix V – IFRS 9, Financial instruments

(All amounts in C thousands unless otherwise stated)

10 Available-for-sale financial assets and equity investments at fair value through OCI

		2009
	At 1 January	14,096
	Exchange differences	(435)
	Additions	1,126
	Disposals	–
	Net gains/(losses) transfer from equity (note 20)	(152)
1p79(b)	Net gains/(losses) transfer to equity (note 20)	275
	At 31 December	**14,910**
1p66	Less: non-current portion	(14,910)
1p66	**Current portion**	–

IFRS7 p20(a)(ii) — During 2009 the group removed profits of C187 and losses C35 from equity into the income statement. Losses in the amount of C20 were due to impairments.

IFRS7 p27(b), 31, 34 — Available-for-sale financial assets include the following:

	2009
Listed securities:	
– Equity securities – UK	8,300
– Equity securities – Europe	2,086
– Equity securities – US	4,260
– Debt securities with fixed interest ranging from 6.3% to 6.5% and maturity dates between July 2011 and May 2013	264
	14,910

IFRS7 p34(c) — Available-for-sale financial assets are denominated in the following currencies:

	2009
UK pound	8,121
Euros	2,086
US dollar	4,260
Other currencies	443
	14,910

IFRS7p27, 1p79(b) — The fair values of unlisted securities are based on cash flows discounted using a rate based on the market interest rate and the risk premium specific to the unlisted securities (2009: 5.8%).

IFRS7 p36(a) — The maximum exposure to credit risk at the reporting date is the carrying value of the debt securities.

IFRS7 p36(c) — None of these financial assets is either past due or impaired.

(All amounts in C thousands unless otherwise stated)

Investments at fair value through OCI

	2010
At 1 January	–
Balance transferred from AFS	14,910
Debt securities transferred from AFS to FVTPL	(680)
Exchange differences	646
Acquisition of sub (note 39)	473
Additions	3,967
Disposals	(1,256)
Net gains/(losses) transfer to equity (note 20)	675
At 31 December	**18,735**

1p79(b) appears against the "Net gains/(losses) transfer to equity (note 20)" row.

14 Financial assets at fair value

IFRS7p8(a), *(a) Financial assets held for trading*
31, 34(c)

	2010	2009
Listed securities – held-for-trading:		
– Equity securities – UK	5,850	3,560
– Equity securities – Europe	4,250	3,540
– Equity securities – US	1,720	872
	11,820	**7,972**

7p15 Financial assets at fair value through profit or loss are presented within 'operating activities' as part of changes in working capital in the statement of cash flows (note 36).

Changes in fair values of financial assets at fair value through profit or loss are recorded in 'other (losses)/gains — net' in the income statement (note 26).

IFRS7p27 The fair value of all equity securities is based on their current bid prices in an active market.

IFRS7p8(a), *(b) Financial assets at fair value through profit or loss*
31, 34(c)

	2010
Listed securities:	
– Debentures with fixed interest of 6.5% and maturity date of 27 August 2012	210
– Cumulative 9.0% redeemable preference shares	78
Unlisted securities:	
– Debt securities with fixed interest ranging from 6.3% to 6.5% and maturity dates between July 2011 and May 2013	347
	635
Less non-current portion	(635)
Current portion	**–**

IFRS7p27, The fair values of unlisted securities are based on cash flows discounted using a rate
1p79(b) based on the market interest rate and the risk premium specific to the unlisted securities (2009: 6%).

Appendix V – IFRS 9, Financial instruments

(All amounts in C thousands unless otherwise stated)

IFRS7
p36(a)

The maximum exposure to credit risk at the reporting date is the carrying value of the debt securities.

IFRS7
p11A

(c) Financial assets at fair value through other comprehensive income

	2010
Listed securities:	
– Equity securities – UK	8,335
– Equity securities – Europe	5,850
– Equity securities – US	4,550
	18,735
Less non-current portion	**(16,785)**
Current portion	**1,950**

IFRS7
p11A(b),
39p1

The group has designated the above equity investments at fair value through other comprehensive income, because they are held for long-term investment rather than for trading.

IFRS7
p11A(d)

Dividends recognised during 2010 related to these equity investments are shown in note 27.

IFRS7
p11A(d),
p11B

During 2010, the group disposed of investments with a cost of C1,256 from investments in equity instruments measured at fair value through other comprehensive income. The investments were sold to maintain the group's desired balance of investments between different industries. The fair value of these investments at the date of derecognition was C1,386. The cumulative gain on disposal was C130. There were no dividends recognised during the period relating to these derecognised equity investments. As these investments were disposed of prior to the date of application of IFRS 9, they are treated in accordance with IAS 39, and the gain on disposal was transferred to the profit or loss.

Commentary

If the investments disposed of had been accounted for in accordance with IFRS 9, the group would have been required to disclose the amount of any transfer from the investment reserve to any other reserve [IFRS9.11A(e)].

IFRS7
p34(c)

Financial assets in equity and debt investments measured at fair value are denominated in the following currencies:

	2010
UK pound	13,747
Euros	10,100
US dollar	6,270
Other currencies	1,073
	31,190

(All amounts in C thousands unless otherwise stated)

19 Retained earnings

1p106(d)	At 1 January 2009	48,470
	Profit for the year	15,512
1p106(d)	Dividends paid relating to 2008	(15,736)
IFRS2p50	Value of employee services	822
16p41	Depreciation transfer on land and buildings net of tax	87
12p68C	Tax credit relating to share option scheme	20
19p93A	Actuarial loss on post employment benefit obligations net of tax	(494)
	At 31 December 2009	**48,681**
IFRS9 p8.2.12	Effect of change in accounting policy for classification and measurement of financial assets (note 2.1)	150
	Profit for the year	30,262
1p106(d)	Dividends relating to 2009	10,102
IFRS2p50	Value of employee services	690
16p41	Depreciation transfer on land and buildings net of tax	100
12p68C	Tax credit relating to share option scheme	30
1p97(a)	Purchase of treasury shares	(2,564)
19p93A	Actuarial loss on post employment benefit obligations net of tax	–
12p80(d)	Impact of change in UK tax rate on deferred tax	(10)
	At 31 December 2010	**67,601**

(All amounts in C thousands unless otherwise stated)

20 Other reserves

	Convertible bond	Land and buildings revaluation	Hedging reserve	Available-for-sale invest-ments	Invest-ments revalu-ation reserve	Trans-lation	Total
At 1 January 2009	–	1,152	65	1,320	–	3,827	6,364
16p39, IFRS7 p20(a)(ii) Revaluation – gross (notes 6 and 10)	–	1,133	–	275	–	–	1,408
Revaluation transfer – gross				(152)	–		(152)
12p61, 81(a) Revaluation – tax (note 32)	–	(374)	–	(61)	–	–	(435)
28p39 Revaluation – associates (note 8)	–	0	–	(14)	–	–	(14)
Depreciation transfer –							
16p41 gross	–	(130)	–	0	–	–	(130)
16p41 Depreciation transfer – tax	–	43	–	0	–	–	43
1p96(b) Cash flow hedges:							
IFRS7p23(c) – Fair value gains in year	–	–	300	–	–	–	300
– Tax on fair value gains							
12p61, 81(a) (note 32)	–	–	(101)	–	–	–	(101)
IFRS7p23(d) – Transfers to sales	–	–	(236)	–	–	–	(236)
– Tax on transfers to sales							
12p61, 81(a) (note 32)	–	–	79	–	–	–	79
IFRS7p23(e) – Transfers to inventory	–	–	(67)	–	–	–	(67)
– Tax on transfers to							
12p61, 81(a) inventory (note 32)	–	–	22	–	–	–	22
Net investment hedge							
39p102(a) (note 11)	–	–	–	–	–	40	40
Currency translation							
1p106(d) differences:							
21p52(b) – Group	–	(50)	–	–	–	(171)	(221)
28p39 – Associates	–	–	–	–	–	105	105
At 31 December 2009	–	1,774	62	1,368	–	3,801	7,005

(All amounts in C thousands unless otherwise stated)

		Convertible bond	Land and buildings revaluation	Hedging reserve	Available-for-sale investments	Investments revaluation reserve	Translation	Total
IFRS9 p8.2.12	Effect of change in accounting policy for classification and measurement of financial assets (note 2.1)							
	– Reclassification to retained earnings, items now classified as FVTPL.	–	–	–	(150)	–	–	(150)
	– Reclassification to investments revaluation reserve	–	–	–	(1,088)	1,088	–	-
	– Cumulative gain/(loss) on disposal transferred to profit or loss	–	–	–	(130)	–	–	(130)
IFRS9 p5.4.1, IFRS7 p20(a)(viii)	Gain/(loss) arising on revaluation of financial assets at fair value through other comprehensive income	–	–	–	–	675	–	675
12p61, 81(a)	Revaluation – tax (note 32)	–	–	–	–	(193)	–	(193)
28p39	Revaluation – associates (note 8)	–	–	–	–	(12)	–	(12)
16p41	Depreciation transfer – gross	–	(149)	–	–	–	–	(149)
16p41	Depreciation transfer – tax	–	49	–	–	–	–	49
1p96(b) IFRS7p23(c)	Cash flow hedges: – Fair value gains in year	–	–	368	–	–	–	368
12p61, 81(a)	– Tax on fair value gains (note 32)	–	–	(123)	–	–	–	(123)
IFRS7p23(d)	– Transfers sales	–	–	(120)	–	–	–	(120)
12p61, 81(a)	– Tax on transfers to sales (note 32)	–	–	40	–	–	–	40
IFRS7p23(e)	– Transfers to inventory	–	–	(151)	–	–	–	(151)
12p61, 81(a)	– Tax on transfers to inventory (note 32)	–	–	50	–	–	–	50
39p102(a)	Net investment hedge (note 11)	–	–	–	–	–	(45)	(45)
1p106(d) 21p52(b)	Currency translation differences: – Group	–	15	–	–	–	2,051	2,066
28p39	– Associates	–	–	–	–	–	(74)	(74)
	Convertible bond – equity component (note 22)	7,761	–	–	–	–	–	7,761
12p61, 81(a)	Tax on equity component on convertible bond (note 32)	(2,328)	–	–	–	–	–	(2,328)
	At 31 December 2009	**5,433**	**1,689**	**126**	**0**	**1,558**	**5,733**	**14539**

(All amounts in C thousands unless otherwise stated)

26 Other (losses) / gains – net

		2010	2009
IFRS7 p20(a)(i) IFRS9 p5.4.1	Financial assets held for trading at fair value through profit or loss (note 14):		
	– Fair value losses	(508)	(238)
	– Fair value gains	1,571	–
IFRS7 p20(a)(i)	Foreign exchange forward contracts:		
	– Held for trading	86	88
21p52(a)	– Net foreign exchange gains/(losses) (note 33)	(277)	200
IFRS7p24(a)	Ineffectiveness on fair value hedges (note 11)	(1)	(1)
IFRS7p24(b)	Ineffectiveness on cash flow hedges (note 11)	17	14
		888	**63**

27 Other income

		2010	2009
	Gain on remeasuring existing interest in ABC group on acquisition (note 39)	850	–
18p35(b)(v)	Dividend income on available-for-sale financial assets	–	883
IFRS7 p11A(d)	Dividend income on financial assets at fair value through other comprehensive income	1,100	–
18p35(b)(v)	Dividend income on financial assets at fair value through profit or loss	800	310
	Investment income	800	1,193
	Insurance reimbursement	–	66
		2,750	**1,259**

The insurance reimbursement relates to the excess of insurance proceeds over the carrying values of goods damaged.

(All amounts in C thousands unless otherwise stated)

31 Finance income and costs

		2010	2009
IFRS7 p20(b)	Interest expense:		
	– Bank borrowings	**(5,317)**	(10,646)
	– Dividend on redeemable preference shares (note 22)	**(1,950)**	(1,950)
	– Convertible bond (note 22)	**(3,083)**	–
	– Finance lease liabilities	**(550)**	(648)
37p84(e)	– Provisions: unwinding of discount (note 25)	**(44)**	(37)
21p52(a)	Net foreign exchange gains on financing activities (note 33)	**2,594**	996
	Fair value gains on financial instruments:		
IFRS7p23(d)	– Interest rate swaps: cash flow hedges, transfer from equity	**102**	88
IFRS7 p24(a)(i)	– Interest rate swaps: fair value hedges	**16**	31
IFRS7 p24(a)(ii)	Fair value adjustment of bank borrowings attributable to interest rate risk	**(16)**	(31)
	Finance costs	**(8,248)**	(12,197)
	Less: amounts capitalised on qualifying assets	**75**	–
	Total finance cost	**(8,173)**	–
	Finance income:		
	– Interest income on short-term bank deposits	**550**	489
IFRS7p20(b)	– Interest income on available-for-sale financial assets	**–**	984
IFRS7p20(b)	– Interest income on loans to related parties (note 40)	**217**	136
	Finance income	**767**	1,609
	Net finance costs	**(7,406)**	(10,588)

32 Income tax expense

		2010	2009
	Current tax:		
12p80(a)	Current tax on profits for the year	14,082	6,035
12p80(b)	Adjustments in respect of prior years	150	–
	Total current tax	**14,232**	**6,035**
	Deferred tax (note 23):		
12p80(c)	Origination and reversal of temporary differences	481	2,635
12p80(d)	Impact of change in the Euravian tax rate	(97)	–
	Total deferred tax	**384**	**2,635**
	Income tax expense	**14,616**	**8,670**

Appendix V – IFRS 9, Financial instruments

(All amounts in C thousands unless otherwise stated)

12p81(c) The tax on the group's profit before tax differs from the theoretical amount that would arise using the weighted average tax rate applicable to profits of the consolidated entities as follows:

	2010	2009
Profit before tax	47,691	24,918
Tax calculated at domestic tax rates applicable to profits in the respective countries	15,458	7,475
Tax effects of:		
– Associates' results reported net of tax	5	(44)
– Income not subject to tax	(1,072)	(212)
– Expenses not deductible for tax purposes	1,592	1,104
– Utilisation of previously unrecognised tax losses	(1,450)	–
– Tax losses for which no deferred income tax asset was recognised	30	347
Re-measurement of deferred tax – change in the Euravian tax rate	(97)	–
Adjustment in respect of prior years	150	–
Tax charge	**14,616**	**8,670**

12p81(d) During the year, as a result of the change in the Euravian corporation tax rate from 30% to 28% that was substantively enacted on 26 June 2010 and that will be effective from 1 April 2011, the relevant deferred tax balances have been re-measured. Deferred tax expected to reverse in the year to 31 December 2011 has been measured using the effective rate that will apply in Euravia for the period (28.5%).

12p81(d) The weighted average applicable tax rate was 33% (2009: 30%). The increase is caused by a change in the profitability of the group's subsidiaries in the respective countries partially offset by the impact of the reduction in the Euravian tax rate.

12p81(ab) The tax (charge)/credit relating to components of other comprehensive income is as follows:

	2010			2009		
	Before tax	Tax (charge) credit	After tax	Before tax	Tax (charge) credit	After tax
Fair value gains:						
1p90 – Land and buildings	–	–	–	1,133	(374)	759
1p90 – Available-for-sale financial assets	–	–	–	123	(61)	62
1p90 – Financial assets at fair value through other comprehensive income	545	(193)	352	–	–	–
1p90 Share of other comprehensive income of associates	(12)	–	(12)	(14)	–	(14)
1p90 Actuarial loss on retirement benefit obligations	–	–	–	(705)	211	(494)
1p90 Impact of change in the Euravian tax rate on deferred tax	–	(10)	(10)	–	–	–
1p90 Cash flow hedges	97	(33)	64	(3)	–	(3)
1p90 Net investment hedge	(45)	–	(45)	40	–	40
1p90 Currency translation differences	2,244	–	2,244	(156)	–	(156)
IFRS3p59 Increase in fair values of proportionate holding of ABC Group (note 39)	850	–	850	–	–	–
Other comprehensive income	**3,694**	**(241)**	**3,453**	**418**	**(224)**	**194**
Current tax	–	–	–	–	–	–
Deferred tax (note 23)	–	(241)	–	–	(224)	–
	–	**(241)**	–	–	**(224)**	–

(Refer to the note 32 in the main section of this publication.)

34 Earnings per share

(Refer to the note 34 in the main section of this publication.)

(c) Effect of changes in accounting policies

8p28 (f)   The effects of changes in accounting policy described in note 2.1 on both basic and diluted earnings per share are summarised as follows:

	Effect on profit for the year (C thousands)		Effect on basic earnings per share (C per share)		Effect on diluted earnings per share (C per share)	
	2010	**2009**	**2010**	**2009**	**2010**	**2009**
Changes in accounting policies relating to:						
– Reclassification and measurement of financial assets – IFRS 9	10	–	–	–	–	–
– Other (specify as applicable)	–	–	–	–	–	–
	10	**–**	**–**	**–**	**–**	**–**

Appendix VI – First-time adoption of IFRS

In the case of IFRS 1, a number of implementation choices exist and only one possible combination is illustrated. The publication does not repeat all of the requirements of IFRS 1 and should be read in conjunction with the standard and related implementation guidance.

When preparing financial statements in accordance with IFRSs, an entity should have regard to its local legal and regulatory requirements. This appendix does not consider any requirements of a particular jurisdiction.

Transition to IFRS

These are the Group's first consolidated financial statements prepared in accordance with IFRSs.

The accounting policies set out in note 2 have been applied in preparing the financial statements for the year ended 31 December 2010, the comparative information presented in these financial statements for the year ended 31 December 2009 and in the preparation of an opening IFRS balance sheet at 1 January 2009 (the Group's date of transition).

In preparing its opening IFRS balance sheet, the Group has adjusted amounts reported previously in financial statements prepared with [country] GAAP. An explanation of how the transition from [country] GAAP to IFRSs has affected the Group's financial position, financial performance and cash flows is set out in the following tables and notes that accompany the tables.

1 Initial elections upon adoption

Set out below are the applicable IFRS 1 exemptions and exceptions applied in the conversion from [country] GAAP to IFRS.

1.1 IFRS exemption options

1.1.1. Exemption for business combinations

IFRS 1 provides the option to apply IFRS 3, 'Business combinations', prospectively from the transition date or from a specific date prior to the transition date. This provides relief from full retrospective application that would require restatement of all business combinations prior to the transition date. The group elected to apply IFRS 3 prospectively to business combinations occurring after its transition date. Business combinations occurring prior to the transition date have not been restated.

1.1.2. Exemption for fair value as deemed cost

The group elected to measure certain items of property, plant and equipment at fair value as at 1 January 2009.

1.1.3. Exemption for cumulative translation differences

IFRS 1 permits cumulative translation gains and losses to be reset to zero at the transition date. This provides relief from determining cumulative currency translation differences in accordance with IAS 21, 'The effects of changes in foreign exchange rates', from the date a subsidiary or equity method investee was formed or acquired. The group elected to reset all cumulative translation gains and losses to zero in opening retained earnings at its transition date.

1.1.4. Exemption for employee benefits

IFRS 1 provides retrospective relief from applying IAS 19, 'Employee benefits', for the recognition of actuarial gains and losses. In line with the exemption, the group elected to recongise all cumulative actuarial gains and losses that existed at its transition date in opening retained earnings for all its employee benefit plans.

The remaining voluntary exemptions do not apply to the group:

- Share-based payment (IFRS 2) and leases (IAS 17), as [country] accounting and the IFRSs were already aligned as regards these transactions;

- Insurance contracts (IFRS 4), as this is not relevant ot the company's operations.

- Assets and liabilities of subsidiaries, associates and joint ventures, as only the group's consolidated financial statements have been prepared in accordance with IFRSs;

- Compound financial instruments, because the group does not have these types of financial instrument as at the date of transition to IFRS;

- Decomimissioning liabilities included in the cost of land, buildings and equipment, as the group does not have liabilities of this type; and

- Financial assets or intangible assets accounted for under IFRIC 12, as the group has not entered into agreements within the scope of IFRIC 12.

1.2 IFRS mandatory exceptions

Set out below are the applicable mandatory exceptions in IFRS 1 applied in the conversion from [country] GAAP to IFRS.

1.2.1 Hedge accounting exception

Hedge accounting can only be applied prospectively from the transition date to transactions that satisfy the hedge accounting criteria in IAS 39, 'Financial instruments: Recognition and measurement', at that date. Hedging relationships cannot be designated retrospectively, and the supporting documentation cannot be created retrospectively. As a result, only hedging relationships that satisfied the hedge accounting criteria as of 1 January 2009 are reflected as hedges in the group's results under IFRS.

1.2.2 Exception for estimates

IFRS estimates as at 1 January 2009 are consistent with the estimates as at the same date made in conformity with [country] GAAP.

The other compulsory exceptions of IFRS 1 have not been applied as these are not relevant to the group:

- Derecognition of financial assets and financial liabilities; and

- Non-controlling interests.

2 Reconciliations of [country] GAAP to IFRS

IFRS 1 requires an entity to reconcile equity, comprehensive income and cash flows for prior periods. The group's first-time adoption did not have an impact on the total operating, investing or financing cash flows. The following tables represent the reconciliations from [country] GAAP to IFRS for the respective periods noted for equity, earnings and comprehensive income.

(All amounts in C thousands unless otherwise stated)

Reconciliation of shareholders' equity as at 1 January 2009

	Under previous [Country GAAP]	(a) Conso- lidation	(b) Appraisal report of property, plant and equipment	(c) Impair- ment of PP&E	(d) Goodwill and negative goodwill	(e) Pre- operating expenses
Assets						
Non-current assets						
Property, plant and equipment	82,214	–	75,000	(50,000)	–	–
Intangible assets	19,637	–	–	–	2,950	(1,125)
Investments in associates	13,208	(200)	–	–	–	–
Deferred income tax assets	3,567	–	–	–	–	–
Available-for-sale financial assets	14,096	–	–	–	–	–
Derivative financial instruments	–	–	–	–	–	–
Trade and other receivables	–	–	–	–	–	–
	132,722	**(200)**	**75,000**	**(50,000)**	**2,950**	**(1,125)**
Current assets						
Inventories	16,754	500	–	–	–	–
Trade and other receivables	17,007	2,000	–	–	–	–
Available-for-sale financial assets	–	–	–	–	–	–
Derivative financial instruments	–	–	–	–	–	–
Financial assets at fair value through profit or loss	5,432	–	–	–	–	–
Cash and cash equivalents (excluding bank overdrafts)	17,587	–	–	–	–	–
	56,780	**2,500**	**–**	**–**	**–**	**–**
Assets of disposal group classified as held for sale	–	–	–	–	–	–
	56,780	**2,500**	**–**	**–**	**–**	**–**
Total assets	**189,502**	**2,300**	**75,000**	**(50,000)**	**2,950**	**(1,125)**

(All amounts in C thousands unless otherwise stated)

(f)	(g)	(h)	(i)	(j)	(k)		
	Cumulative				Interest		
Tax and	trans-	Adjust-			on	Total	
social	lation	ment to	Hedge	Inventory	capital	impact of	
contri-	adjust-	pension	accounting	valuation	and	change	**Under**
bution	ment	obligations	exception	method	dividends	to IFRS	**IFRS**
–	–	–	–	–	–	25,000	107,214
–	–	–	–	–	–	1,825	21,462
–	–	–	–	–	–	(200)	13,008
–	–	–	–	–	–	–	3,567
–	–	–	–	–	–	–	14,096
–	–	–	–	–	–	–	–
–	–	–	–	–	–	–	–
–	–	–	–	–	–	26,625	159,347
–	–	–	–	400	–	900	17,654
–	–	–	–	–	–	2,000	19,007
–	–	–	–	–	–	–	–
–	–	–	–	–	–	–	–
–	–	–	–	–	–	–	5,432
–	–	–	–	–	–	–	17,587
–	–	–	–	400	–	2,900	59,680
–	–	–	–	–	–	–	–
–	–	–	–	400	–	2,900	59,680
–	–	–	–	400	–	29,525	219,027

Appendix VI – First-time adoption of IFRS

(All amounts in C thousands unless otherwise stated)

Reconciliation of shareholders' equity as at 1 January 2009 (continued)

	Under previous [Country GAAP]	(a) Conso- lidation	(b) Appraisal report of property, plant and equipment	(c) Impair- ment of PP&E	(d) Goodwill and negative goodwill	(e) Pre- operating expenses
Equity and liabilities						
Equity attributable to owners of the parent						
Ordinary shares	20,000	–	–	–	–	–
Share premium	10,424	–	–	–	–	–
Other reserves	(69,463)	–	75,000	–	–	–
Retained earnings	87,040	(200)	–	(50,000)	2,950	(1,125)
	48,001	(200)	75,000	(50,000)	2,950	(1,125)
	–	–	–	–	–	–
Non-controlling interests	(1,000)	2,500	–	–	–	–
Total equity	**47,001**	2,300	75,000	(50,000)	2,950	(1,125)
Liabilities						
Non-current liabilities						
Borrowings	93,478	–	–	–	–	–
Derivative financial instruments	–	–	–	–	–	–
Deferred income tax liabilities	2,110	–	–	–	–	–
Retirement benefit obligations	537	–	–	–	–	–
Provisions for other liabilities and charges	–	–	–	–	–	–
	96,125	–	–	–	–	–
Current liabilities						
Trade and other payables	25,422	–	–	–	–	–
Current income tax liabilities	2,019	–	–	–	–	–
Borrowings	17,012	–	–	–	–	–
Derivative financial instruments	–	–	–	–	–	–
Provisions for other liabilities and charges	1,923	–	–	–	–	–
	46,376	–	–	–	–	–
Liabilities of disposal group classified as held for sale	–	–	–	–	–	–
	46,376	–	–	–	–	–
Total liabilities	**142,501**	–	–	–	–	–
Total equity and liabilities	**189,502**	2,300	75,000	(50,000)	2,950	(1,125)

(All amounts in C thousands unless otherwise stated)

(f) Tax and social contribution	(g) Cumulative translation adjustment	(h) Adjustment to pension obligations	(i) Hedge accounting exception	(j) Inventory valuation method	(k) Interest on capital and dividends	Total impact of change to IFRS	Under IFRS
–	–	–	–	–	–	–	20,000
–	–	–	–	–	–	–	10,424
–	(3,000)	–	–	–	–	72,000	2,537
(4,504)	3,000	(1,000)	–	400	15,736	(34,743)	52,297
(4,504)	0	(1,000)	–	400	15,736	37,257	–
–	–	–	–	–	–	–	85,258
–	–	–	–	–	–	2,500	1,500
(4,504)	–	(1,000)	–	400	15,736	39,757	86,758
–	–	–	–	–	–	–	93,478
–	–	–	–	–	–	–	–
4,504	–	–	–	–	–	4,504	6,614
–	–	1,000	–	–	–	1,000	1,537
–	–	–	–	–	–	–	–
4,504	–	1,000	–	–	–	5,504	101,629
–	–	–	–	–	(15,736)	(15,736)	9,686
–	–	–	–	–	–	–	2,019
–	–	–	–	–	–	–	17,012
–	–	–	–	–	–	–	–
–	–	–	–	–	–	–	1,923
–	–	–	–	–	(15,736)	(15,736)	30,640
–	–	–	–	–	–	–	–
–	–	–	–	–	–	–	30,640
4,504	–	1,000	–	–	(15,736)	(10,232)	132,269
–	–	–	–	400	–	29,525	219,027

Appendix VI – First-time adoption of IFRS

(All amounts in C thousands unless otherwise stated)

Reconciliation of shareholders' equity as at 31 December 2009

	Under previous [Country GAAP]	(a) Conso-lidation	(b) Appraisal report of property, plant and equipment	(c) Impair-ment of PP&E	(d) Goodwill and negative goodwill	(e) Pre-operating expenses
Assets						
Non-current assets						
Property, plant and equipment	75,433	–	73,800	(49,000)	–	–
Intangible assets	18,350	–	–	–	3,100	(750)
Investments in associates	13,444	(200)	–	–	–	–
Deferred income tax assets	3,321	–	–	–	–	–
Available-for-sale financial assets	14,910	–	–	–	–	–
Derivative financial instruments	245	–	–	–	–	–
Trade and other receivables	1,352	–	–	–	–	–
	127,055	(200)	73,800	(49,000)	3,100	(750)
Current assets						
Inventories	17,312	500	–	–	–	–
Trade and other receivables	16,330	2,000	–	–	–	–
Available-for-sale financial assets	–	–	–	–	–	–
Derivative financial instruments	951	–	–	–	–	–
Financial assets at fair value through profit or loss	7,972	–	–	–	–	–
Cash and cash equivalents (excluding bank overdrafts)	34,062	–	–	–	–	–
	76,627	2,500	–	–	–	–
Assets of disposal group classified as held for sale	–	–	–	–	–	–
	76,627	–	–	–	–	–
Total assets	203,682	–	–	–	–	–

(All amounts in C thousands unless otherwise stated)

(f) Tax and social contri-bution	(g) Cumulative trans-lation adjust-ment	(h) Adjust-ment to pension obligations	(i) Hedge accounting exception	(j) Inventory valuation method	(k) Interest on capital and dividends	Total impact of change to IFRS	**Under IFRS**
–	–	–	–	–	–	24,800	100,233
–	–	–	–	–	–	2,350	20,700
–	–	–	–	–	–	(200)	13,244
–	–	–	–	–	–	–	3,321
–	–	–	–	–	–	–	14,910
–	–	–	–	–	–	–	245
–	–	–	–	–	–	–	1,352
–	–	–	–	–	–	**26,950**	**154,005**
–	–	–	–	370	–	870	18,182
–	–	–	–	–	–	2,000	18,330
–	–	–	–	–	–	–	–
–	–	–	–	–	–	–	951
–	–	–	–	–	–	–	7,972
–	–	–	–	–	–	–	34,062
–	–	–	–	370	–	2,870	79,497
–	–	–	–	–	–	–	
–	–	–	–	–	–	–	**79,497**
–	–	–	–	–	–	–	**233,502**

Appendix VI – First-time adoption of IFRS

(All amounts in C thousands unless otherwise stated)

Reconciliation of shareholders' equity as at 31 December 2009 (continued)

	Under previous [Country GAAP]	(a) Conso-lidation	(b) Appraisal report of property, plant and equipment	(c) Impair-ment of PP&E	(d) Goodwill and negative goodwill	(e) Pre-operating expenses
Equity and liabilities						
Equity attributable to owners of the parent						
Ordinary shares	21,000	–	–	–	–	–
Share premium	10,494	–	–	–	–	–
Other reserves	(63,795)	–	73,800	–	–	–
Retained earnings	91,945	(200)	–	(49,000)	3,100	(750)
	59,644	(200)	73,800	(49,000)	3,100	(750)
Non-controlling interests	(734)	2,500	–	–	–	–
Total equity	**58,910**	2,300	73,800	(49,000)	3,100	(750)
Liabilities						
Non-current liabilities						
Borrowings	96,171	–	–	–	–	–
Derivative financial instruments	129	–	–	–	–	–
Deferred income tax liabilities	342	–	–	–	–	–
Retirement benefit obligations	1,233	–	–	–	–	–
Provisions for other liabilities and charges	274	–	–	–	–	–
	98,149	–	–	–	–	–
Current liabilities						
Trade and other payables	22,580	–	–	–	–	–
Current income tax liabilities	2,771	–	–	–	–	–
Borrowings	18,258	–	–	–	–	–
Derivative financial instruments	618	–	–	–	–	–
Provisions for other liabilities and charges	2,396	–	–	–	–	–
	46,623	–	–	–	–	–
Liabilities of disposal group classified as held for sale	–	–	–	–	–	–
	46,623	–	–	–	–	–
Total liabilities	**144,772**	–	–	–	–	–
Total equity and liabilities	**203,682**	2,300	73,800	(49,000)	3,100	(750)

(All amounts in C thousands unless otherwise stated)

(f) Tax and social contri-bution	(g) Cumulative trans-lation adjust-ment	(h) Adjust-ment to pension obligations	(i) Hedge accounting exception	(j) Inventory valuation method	(k) Interest on capital and dividends	Total impact of change to IFRS	Under IFRS
–	–	–	–	–	–	–	21,000
–	–	–	–	–	–	–	10,494
–	(3,000)	–	–	–	–	70,800	7,005
(8,711)	3,000	(1,000)	(175)	370	10,102	(43,264)	48,681
(8,711)	0	(1,000)	(175)	370	10,102	27,536	**87,180**
–	–	–	–	–	–	2,500	1,766
(8,711)	0	(1,000)	(175)	370	10,102	**30,036**	**88,946**
–	–	–	175	–	–	175	96,346
–	–	–	–	–	–	–	129
8,711	–	–	–	–	–	8,711	9,053
–	–	1,000	–	–	–	1,000	2,233
–	–	–	–	–	–	–	274
8,711	–	**1,000**	**175**	–	–	**9,886**	**108,035**
–	–	–	–	–	(10,102)	(10,102)	12,478
–	–	–	–	–	–	–	2,771
–	–	–	–	–	–	–	18,258
–	–	–	–	–	–	–	618
–	–	–	–	–	–	–	2,396
–	–	–	–	–	–	–	**36,521**
–	–	–	–	–	–	–	–
–	–	–	–	–	–	(10,102)	36,521
8,711	–	**1,000**	**175**	–	**(10,102)**	**(216)**	**144,556**
–	–	0	–	370	–	29,820	233,502

(All amounts in C thousands unless otherwise stated)

Reconciliation of comprehensive income for the year ended 31 December 2009

	Under previous [Country GAAP]	(a) Consolidation	(b) Appraisal report of property, plant and equipment	(c) Impairment of PP&E	(d) Goodwill and negative goodwill
Continuing operations					
Revenue	112,360	–	–	–	–
Operating costs	(79,644)		(1,200)	1,000	2,500
Income from operations	32,716	–	(1,200)	1,000	2,500
Financial income	1,609	–	–	–	–
Financial expenses	(12,022)	–	–	–	–
Financial expenses, net	(10,413)	–	–	–	–
Equity in earnings (losses) of associates	145	–	–	–	–
Pre-tax profit	22,448	–	(1,200)	1,000	2,500
Income tax	(8,380)	–	408	(340)	–
Profit for the year from continuing operations	14,068	–	(792)	660	2,500
Discontinued operations					
Profit for the year from discontinued operations	120	–	–	–	–
Profit for the year	14,188	–	(792)	660	2,500
Profit attributable to:					
Owners of the company	–	–	(792)	660	2,500
Non-controlling interests	–	–	–	–	–

(All amounts in C thousands unless otherwise stated)

	(e)	(f)	(i)	(j)		
	Preoperating expenses	Tax	Hedge accounting exception	Inventory valuation method	Total impact of change to IFRS	**Under IFRS**
	–	–	–	–	–	112,360
	375			(30)	2,645	(76,999)
	375	–	–	(30)	2,645	35,361
	–	–	–	–	–	1,609
	–	–	(175)	–	(175)	(12,197)
	–	–	(175)	–	(175)	(10,588)
	–	–	–	–	–	145
	375	–	(175)	(30)	2,470	24,918
	(128)	(300)	60	10	(290)	(8,670)
	247	(300)	(115)	(20)	2,180	16,248
	–	–	–	–	–	120
	247	(300)	(115)	(20)	2,180	16,368
	247	(300)	(115)	(20)	2,180	15,512
	–	–	–	–	–	856

(All amounts in C thousands unless otherwise stated)

Reconciliation of comprehensive income as at 31 December 2009

	Note	Under previous [Country GAAP]	Total impact of change to IFRS	**Under IFRS**
Profit for the year				16,368
Other comprehensive income (net of tax):				
Gains on revaluation of land and buildings		759	–	759
Available-for-sale financial assets		62	–	62
Share of other comprehensive income (loss) of associates		91	–	91
Actuarial loss on post employment benefit obligations	(h)	–	(494)	(494)
Cash flow hedges		(3)	–	(3)
Net investment hedge		40	–	40
Currency translation differences		(261)	–	(261)
Other comprehensive income for the year		**688**	**(494)**	**194**
Total comprehensive income for the year				16,562
Attributable to:				
Owners of the company				15,746
Non–controlling interests				816
				16,562

Reconciliation of cash flow statement

The transition from [country] GAAP to IFRS has had no effect on the reported cash flows generated by the group. The reconciling items between the [country] GAAP presentation and the IFRS presentation have no net impact on the cash flows generated.

3 Notes to the reconciliation of [country] GAAP and IFRS

(a) Consolidation

Under [country] GAAP, a subsidiary was excluded from consolidation and included in the financial statements under the equity method. This entity was consolidated for IFRS purposes.

A special purpose entity (SPE) that was not previously consolidated under [country] GAAP is being consolidated to meet the requirement of IFRS. Trade accounts receivable related to this entity total C2,000 as at 1 January 2009 and 31 December 2009.

(b) Appraisal report of property, plant and equipment

Management applied the fair value as deemed cost exemption to certain machinery, buildings and land of its subsidiary [name]. The appraisal report of the property, prepared as at 1 January 2009 determined its fair value as C175,000, a C75,000 increase as compared to its carrying amount of C100,000 under [country] GAAP. The increase as at 31 December 2009 was C73,800.

(c) Impairment of property, plant and equipment

The impairment charge of C50,000 as at 1 January 2009 arose in the manufacturing unit '[Factory A]', which is the company's manufacturing plant in 'A' Land, following a decision

(All amounts in C thousands unless otherwise stated)

to reduce the manufacturing output allocated to the operation. Factory A is a cash generating unit (CGU) under IAS 36.

The impact on comprehensive income for the year ended 31 December 2009 was C1,000 due to the recognition of lower depreciation in the year.

The recoverable amount of this CGU was estimated based on value-in-use calculation as this was determined to be higher than fair value less costs to sell. These calculations use cash flow projections based on financial budgets approved by management for a five-year period. Cash flows beyond the five-year period are extrapolated using the estimated growth rates stated below. The growth rate does not exceed the long-term average growth rate for the manufacturing business in which the CGU operates. The following are key assumptions used in the value-in-use calculation:

- Gross margin[1] 30.0%
- Growth rate[2] 1.8%
- Discount rate[3] 10.5%

Management determined the budgeted gross margin based on past performance and their expectations for market development. The weighted average growth rates used are consistent with forecasts included in industry reports. The discount rates used are pre-tax and reflect specific risks in relation to the relevant CGU.

A change in management's gross margin estimate by 10% increase the impairment by C500. If management reduces the growth rate by 10% , impairment would increase by C30. An increase in the discount rate by 10% would increase impairment by C50.

(d) Goodwill and negative goodwill

Under [country] GAAP, goodwill was being amortised over a period corresponding to its estimated economic recovery. In accordance with IFRS, goodwill is not amortised; it is, instead, tested for impairment annually. The amortisation for the year ended 31 December 2009 was C2,500.

Under [country] GAAP, when the amount paid in an acquisition is lower than the carrying amount of the acquired net assets and liabilities, an entity is required to recognise such amount as negative goodwill in the balance sheet (in liabilities) and amortise it over the period considered to justify negative goodwill. In accordance with IFRS, the difference between the amount paid and the fair value of the acquired net assets and liabilities is recognised in profit or loss immediately. Negative goodwill was C2,950 as at 1 January 2009 and C600 as at 31 December 2009.

(e) Pre-operating expenses

Under [country] GAAP, up to 31 December 2009 it was the group's accounting practice to capitalise pre-operating expenses in 'Deferred charges'. IFRS prescribes that pre-operating expenses cannot be attributed to the cost of property, plant and equipment or the formation of intangible assets and are immediately recognised as expenses. Accordingly, the balances of C1,125 and C750, as at 1 January and 31 December 2009, respectively, and the C375 amortisation recognised in 2009 were adjusted against retained earnings.

[1] Budgeted gross margin.

[2] Weighted average growth rate used to extrapolate cash flows after the budget period.

[3] Pre-tax discount rate applied to cash flow projections.

Appendix VI – First-time adoption of IFRS

(All amounts in C thousands unless otherwise stated)

(f) Tax

Changes in deferred tax represent the impact of deferred taxes on the adjustments necessary for the transition to IFRS and total C4,504 as at 1 January 2009 and C8,711 as at 31 December 2009, and C300 in the 2009 income statement.

(g) Cumulative translation adjustment

The group has elected to reset the cumulative translation adjustment account to zero as at 1 January 2009. Under [country] GAAP, as at this date there was a translation reserve of C3,000 eliminates against retained earnings. Total equity was not changed as a result of this reclassification.

(h) Adjustment to pension obligations

The group elected to apply IFRS 1 employee benefits exemption. Accordingly, cumulative net actuarial losses totaling C1,000 were recognised in retained earnings as at 1 January 2009.

Under IFRSs the group accounting policy is to recognise all actuarial gains and losses in other comprehensive income. Under [country] GAAP the company recognised gains and losses in the profit or loss over the employees' remaining service period.

(i) Hedge accounting exception

The group held interest rate swaps at the transition date as hedges of cash flow risk related to the company's variable rate debt instruments. Under [country] GAAP, the swaps were accounted for as hedges. Changes in their fair value were initially recognised in other comprehensive income and transferred to the statement of income as the variable interest expense was recongised on the debt instrument. The method of assessing hedge effectiveness used under [country] GAAP did not qualify these instruments for hedge accounting under IFRS and the group has discontinued hedge accounting on transition to IFRS. As a result, changes in the fair value of the swap occurring after 1 January 2009 under IFRS are recognised directly in profit or loss. An additional amount of C175 corresponding to unrealised losses, was recorded in the IFRS financial statements for the year ended 31 December 2009.

(j) Inventory valuation method

Under [country] GAAP, the group applied the average cost method to measure inventories. Under IFRS, the group restated its opening balance sheet by retrospectively applying the first in, first out (FIFO) method. The impact of this change on inventory valuation was a C400 increase as at 1 January 2009 and C370 as at 31 December 2009.

(k) Interest on capital and dividends

Under [country] GAAP, interest on capital and dividends are recognised at year-end, even if dividends have not been officially declared. Under IFRS, a liability for dividends is recognised when they are declared. The amount of C15,736 refers to dividends that were declared after 1 January 2009. The amount of C10,102 as at 31 December 2009 was adjusted for recognition in the following year.

(All amounts in C thousands unless otherwise stated)

(l) Retained earnings

Except for the reclassification items, all the adjustments above were recognised against opening retained earnings and other reserves as at 1 January 2009.

(All amounts in C thousands unless otherwise stated)

Appendix VII – Forthcoming requirements

Below is a list of standards/interpretations that have been issued and are effective for periods after 1 January 2010.

Topic	Key requirements	Effective date
Amendment to IAS 32, 'Financial instruments: Presentation – Classification of rights issues'	The IASB amended IAS 32 to allow rights, options or warrants to acquire a fixed number of the entity's own equity instruments for a fixed amount of any currency to be classified as equity instruments provided the entity offers the rights, options or warrants pro rata to all of its existing owners of the same class of its own non-derivative equity instruments.	1 February 2010
IFRIC 19, 'Extinguishing financial liabilities with equity instruments'	Clarifies the requirements of IFRSs when an entity renegotiates the terms of a financial liability with its creditor and the creditor agrees to accept the entity's shares or other equity instruments to settle the financial liability fully or partially.	1 July 2010
Amendment to IFRS 1, 'First-time adoption of International Financial Reporting Standards – Limited exemption from comparative IFRS 7 disclosures for first-time adopters'	Provides the same relief to first-time adopters as was given to current users of IFRSs upon adoption of the amendments to IFRS 7. Also clarifies the transition provisions of the amendments to IFRS 7.	1 July 2010
IAS 24, 'Related party disclosures' (revised 2009)	Amends the definition of a related party and modifies certain related party disclosure requirements for government-related entities.	1 January 2011.
Amendment to IFRIC 14, 'IAS 19 – The limit on a defined benefit assets, minimum funding requirements and their interaction'	Removes unintended consequences arising from the treatment of prepayments where there is a minimum funding requirement. Results in prepayments of contributions in certain circumstances being recognised as an asset rather than an expense.	1 January 2011
IFRS 9, 'Financial instruments'	IFRS 9 is the first standard issued as part of a wider	1 January 2013

(All amounts in C thousands unless otherwise stated)

Topic	Key requirements	Effective date
	project to replace IAS 39. IFRS 9 retains but simplifies the mixed measurement model and establishes two primary measurement categories for financial assets: amortised cost and fair value. The basis of classification depends on the entity's business model and the contractual cash flow characteristics of the financial asset. The guidance in IAS 39 on impairment of financial assets and hedge accounting continues to apply. Prior periods need not be restated if an entity adopts the standard for reporting periods beginning before 1 January 2012.	
Improvements to IFRSs 2010		
The amendments are generally applicable for annual periods beginning after 1 January 2011 unless otherwise stated. Early application is permitted.		
IFRS 1, 'First-time adoption of International Financial Reporting Standards'	*(a) Accounting policy changes in the year of adoption* Clarifies that, if a first-time adopter changes its accounting policies or its use of the exemptions in IFRS 1 after it has published an interim financial report in accordance with IAS 34, 'Interim financial reporting', it should explain those changes and update the reconciliations between previous GAAP and IFRS.	Applied prospectively.
	(b) Revaluation basis as deemed cost Allows first-time adopters to use an event-driven fair value as deemed cost, even if the event occurs after the date of transition, but before the first IFRS financial statements are issued. When such remeasurement occurs after the date of transition to IFRSs, but during the period covered by its first IFRS	Entities that adopted IFRSs in previous periods are permitted to apply the amendment retrospectively in the first annual period after the amendment is effective, provided the measurement date is within the period covered by the first IFRS financial statements.

Appendix VII – Forthcoming requirements

(All amounts in C thousands unless otherwise stated)

Topic	Key requirements	Effective date
	financial statements, any subsequent adjustment to that event-driven fair value is recognised in equity.	
	(c) Use of deemed cost for operations subject to rate regulation	Applied prospectively.
	Entities subject to rate regulation are allowed to use previous GAAP carrying amounts of property, plant and equipment or intangible assets as deemed cost on an item-by-item basis. Entities that use this exemption are required to test each item for impairment under IAS 36 at the date of transition.	
IFRS 3, 'Business combinations'	*(a) Transition requirements for contingent consideration from a business combination that occurred before the effective date of the revised IFRS*	Applicable to annual periods beginning on or after 1 July 2010. Applied retrospectively.
	Clarifies that the amendments to IFRS 7, 'Financial instruments: Disclosures', IAS 32, 'Financial instruments: Presentation', and IAS 39, 'Financial instruments: Recognition and measurement', that eliminate the exemption for contingent consideration, do not apply to contingent consideration that arose from business combinations whose acquisition dates precede the application of IFRS 3 (as revised in 2008).	
	(b) Measurement of non-controlling interests	Applicable to annual periods beginning on or after 1 July 2010.
	The choice of measuring non-controlling interests at fair value or at the proportionate share of the acquiree's net assets applies only to instruments that represent present ownership interests and entitle their holders to a proportionate share of the net assets in the event of	Applied prospectively from the date the entity applies IFRS 3.

(All amounts in C thousands unless otherwise stated)

Topic	Key requirements	Effective date
	liquidation. All other components of non-controlling interest are measured at fair value unless another measurement basis is required by IFRS.	
	(c) Un-replaced and voluntarily replaced share-based payment awards	Applicable to annual periods beginning on or after 1 July 2010. Applied prospectively.
	The application guidance in IFRS 3 applies to all share-based payment transactions that are part of a business combination, including un-replaced and voluntarily replaced share-based payment awards.	
IFRS 7, 'Financial instruments'	Emphasises the interaction between quantitative and qualitative disclosures about the nature and extent of risks associated with financial instruments.	1 January 2011. Applied retrospectively.
IAS 1, 'Presentation of financial statements'	Clarifies that an entity will present an analysis of other comprehensive income for each component of equity, either in the statement of changes in equity or in the notes to the financial statements.	1 January 2011. Applied retrospectively.
IAS 27, 'Consolidated and separate financial statements'	Clarifies that the consequential amendments from IAS 27 made to IAS 21, 'The effect of changes in foreign exchange rates', IAS 28, 'Investments in associates', and IAS 31, 'Interests in joint ventures', apply prospectively for annual periods beginning on or after 1 July 2009, or earlier when IAS 27 is applied earlier.	Applicable to annual periods beginning on or after 1 July 2010. Applied retrospectively.
IAS 34, 'Interim financial reporting'	Provide guidance to illustrate how to apply disclosure principles in IAS 34 and add disclosure requirements around: ■ The circumstances likely to affect fair values of financial instruments and their classification;	1 January 2011 Applied retrospectively.

Appendix VII – Forthcoming requirements

(All amounts in C thousands unless otherwise stated)

Topic	Key requirements	Effective date
	■ Transfers of financial instruments between different levels of the fair value hierarchy; ■ Changes in classification of financial assets; and ■ Changes in contingent liabilities and assets	
IFRIC 13, 'Customer loyalty programmes'	The meaning of 'fair value' is clarified in the context of measuring award credits under customer loyalty programmes.	1 January 2011